Beginning Android ADK with Arduino

Mario Böhmer

Apress®

Beginning Android ADK with Arduino

ISBN-13 (pbk): 978-1-4302-4197-3

ISBN-13 (electronic): 978-1-4302-4198-0

President and Publisher: Paul Manning
Lead Editor: Kate Blackham
Technical Reviewer: Friedger Müffke
Editorial Board: Steve Anglin, Ewan Buckingham, Gary Cornell, Louise Corrigan, Morgan Ertel, Jonathan Gennick, Jonathan Hassell, Robert Hutchin son, Michelle Lowman, James Markham, Matthew Moodie, Jeff Olson, Jeffrey Pepper, Douglas Pundick, Ben Renow-Clarke, Dominic Shakeshaft, Gwenan Spearing, Matt Wade, Tom Welsh
Coordinating Editor: Tracy Brown
Copy Editor: Elizabeth Berry
Compositor: Bytheway Publishing Services
Indexer: SPI Global
Artist: SPI Global
Cover Designer: Anna Ishchenko

Distributed to the book trade worldwide by Springer Scie nce+Business Media New York, 233 Spring Street, 6th Floor, New York, NY 10 013. Phone 1-800-SPRINGER, fax (201) 348-4505, e-mail orders-ny@springer-sbm.com, or vi sit www.springeronline.com.

For information on translations, please e-mail rights@apress.com, or visit www.apress.com.

Apress and friends of ED book s may be purchased in bulk f or academic, corporate, or promo tional use. eBoo k versions and licenses are also available for most ti tles. For more information, reference our Special Bulk Sales–eBook Licensing web page at www.apress.com/bulk-sales.

Any source code or other supplementary materials referenced by the author i n this text is av ailable to re aders at www.apress.com. For detailed inf ormation about how to lo cate your book's source code, go to www.apress.com/source-code/.

This book is dedicated to the most important person in my life, the wonderful Anja Friedrich.

I could never have done it without your love and support.

I love you!

Contents at a Glance

Contents

About the Author

Mario Böhmer is a mobile software developer from the greater area of Berlin, Germany. He has been working in the mobile industry since 2007. He graduated as an associate engineer for data technology at the Siemens Technik Akademie in Berlin and worked for three years for Germany's biggest mobile content provider. Currently he works for Germany's biggest real estate Internet platform, Immobilienscout24. He was one of the finalists of the Google ADK Challenge for Google Developer Day 2011 in Berlin. In addition to being a mobile enthusiast, he is also a DIY maker, an electronics tinkerer, a makerbot operator, and an infrequent guitar player.

About the Technical Reviewer

Friedger Müffke is the founder and president of OpenIntents, which is designed to implement open intents and interfaces to make Android mobile applications work more closely together. Friedger is the founder and organizer of the Android conference and barcamp Droidcon, first held in 2009 in Berlin. He also worked with the ADK for Google Developer Day 2011 in Berlin and created a directory of open Android accessories at `www.open-accessories.com`.

Acknowledgments

Writing this book on such a tight schedule was really hard work. Luckily I had a lot of people who supported me and helped through this process. I would like to thank Michelle Lowman for making the contact and for giving me the opportunity to write this book. Thanks to Friedger Müffke, who agreed to be my tech reviewer and who provided valuable technical hints and improvements. I'd also like to thank Tracy Brown, Kate Blackham, Elizabeth Berry, and the whole Apress crew. Thanks to Google and especially the Android Developer Team for creating a great mobile platform. Thanks also to the Android Developer Relations Team, especially to Sparky Rhode, Richard Hyndman, and Nick Butcher for supporting the Android developer community here in Europe. Thanks to Massimo Banzi and the whole Arduino Team for creating such a great electronics platform. I'd also like to thank the whole Fritzing Team for providing such a powerful tool and helping the maker community share their projects more easily. Without such a vibrant maker, hacker, and developer community, books like this would not be possible. So additional thanks to the c-base spacestation hackerspace in Berlin, the GTUG Berlin, Adafruit Industries, Sparkfun Electronics, the Arduino community, and the Android community. I would like to thank my employer, Immobilienscout24, for giving me the opportunity to write this book and for supporting me when deadlines needed to be held. I'm glad to work with such talented, motivating, and fun colleagues.

Last, but most important, I would like to thank my friends and family for lifting up my spirits and for giving me the necessary motivation to do all this. Anja, thanks for all your love and support.

Preface

This book explains how to set up projects for Android devices communicating with external hardware with the help of the Android Open Accessory Development Kit (ADK). You will learn how to configure your development environment, how to select hardware and set up circuits accordingly, and how to program Android applications and the hardware counterparts. The book will teach you the basics you need to let your own ideas come to life. Through several projects, you will get to know the features of the ADK-compatible hardware boards, sensors, and actuators, and how you can interact with them through an Android application.

Who Should Read This Book

Generally, anyone who is interested in mobile programming and hardware tinkering will enjoy the numerous possibilities the ADK provides. Having experience in Android programming is a plus but not completely necessary. You should, however, have a basic understanding of the Java programming language and general programming fundamentals and algorithms. It will also be helpful if you have experimented with electrical circuits before. But don't be afraid if you haven't—I will guide you through the circuit setup so you won't accidentally blow up your hardware. The projects are designed to build upon each other so that you can apply the things you already learned along the way. All in all you should have fun experimenting and innovating.

Additional Resources Needed

In addition to your computer, which you'll need for programming purposes, and an ADK-compatible hardware board, you will need a set of software and hardware components to be able to follow the projects explained in this book.

The hardware components are mostly basic parts such as LEDs, wires, and other passive and active components. I tried to keep the hardware costs to a minimum by choosing projects where only basic, affordable, and easily-accessible parts are needed. The hardware parts are described in detail where needed within the specific project. I compiled a list of all the necessary hardware parts you will need throughout the book up front, so that you can get all the parts together first. Nothing is more annoying than starting a project and having to wait a week for some parts to arrive.

- 1 × ADK-compatible development board (refer to Chapter 1 for board specifics)

- 1 × breadboard

- Breadboard wires or ordinary electronics wires

- 1 × LED with operating voltage of 5V

- 1 × IR emitter or IR LED

- 1 × IR detector or IR phototransistor

- 1 × button or switch

- 1 × potentiometer

- 1 × piezo buzzer

- 1 × photoresistor

- 1 × 4.7kΩ thermistor

- 1 × NPN transistor (BC547B)

- 1 × servo with operating voltage of 3V or 5V

- 1 × DC motor with operating voltage of 3V or 5V (external battery needed if > 5V)

- 1 × roll of household aluminum foil

- 1 × adhesive tape

- Resistors (220Ω, 10kΩ, and 1MΩ, or a complete set)

All of the software components are free and some of them are even open source. The necessary software is listed in Chapter 1 and I provided a step-by-step installation guide to properly set up your working environment. When you are working with the project code later on, you can type the source code examples on your own while following the book, or you can simply download the source code from the Apress web site to use the code snippets in the book as a reference. You can find the code at www.apress.com.

The Outline at a Glance

The book is divided into ten chapters. After an introduction, which explains the setup of your development environment and the ADK-compatible boards, you will immediately dive right into your first project to get familiar with the process of setting up an ADK experiment. For the most part the following chapters build upon each other and will teach you everything from making a simple LED blink to designing an advanced alarm system utilizing different sensors, as well as using the capabilities of an Android device. Here is a quick summary of the chapters:

- *Chapter 1: Introduction*: The introduction gives you an overview of what the ADK is all about and presents some of the ADK-enabled hardware boards out in the wild. It should also help you set up your development environment so that you can follow the projects in each chapter.

- *Chapter 2: Android and Arduino: Getting to Know Each Other*: This chapter will guide you through the process of writing the necessary software to establish a connection between your ADK board and your Android device. You will also learn the fundamentals of enabling the communication between both devices.

- *Chapter 3: Outputs*: ADK development boards provide different means for output purposes. The projects in this chapter will show you how to utilize those output features in a digital and analog context by controlling the state of an LED. You will use your Android device to switch the LED on and off and you will be able to control its intensity.

- *Chapter 4: Inputs*: The input capabilities of an ADK board enable you to read data from sensors or measure changes in the voltage applied to its input pins. This chapter's projects will show you how to read and process received input values in a digital and analog context by changing the pin state of a digital input pin with a button and by changing analog input readings with a potentiometer. On the push of a button, your Android device will vibrate to give user feedback and you will visualize changes in the analog input readings with a progress bar.

- *Chapter 5: Sounds*: This chapter will show you how to use the piezo buzzer as a multi-purpose component to not only generate sound but also to sense sound in the proximity. You will use your Android device to choose the frequency of the sound generated and you will build a knock sensor that changes the background of your application on each knock.

- *Chapter 6: Light Intensity Sensing*: To recognize changes in the surrounding ambient light can be useful for numerous applications. This chapter's project will show you how to use a photoresistor to sense these lighting changes. Your Android device will evaluate those changes to light up or dim its screen to adjust to the current lighting level.

- Chapter 7: *Temperature Sensing*: Electronic devices often have to work under extreme conditions. So keeping track of the current temperature can be essential at times. This chapter will show you how to sense and calculate the current temperature with the help of a thermistor. The current temperature value will be drawn onto your Android device's screen using the 2D graphics capabilities of the Android system.

- *Chapter 8: A Sense of Touch*: Touch interfaces have become part of everyday life. Every project feels fancier when you have a touch interface to control it . This chapter will show you how you can build your own low-budget touch sensor. You will use your Android device in conjunction with the touch sensor to build a simple game-show buzzer that plays a buzzing sound and vibrates when activated.

- *Chapter 9: Making Things Move*: Robots are probably the most exciting thing to experiment with in hobby electronics. Since robots require some means of movement, you will need to understand the actuators available to help you with that. This chapter will show you how to control servos and DC motors to make your future projects move in any way. You will use your Android device's accelerometer sensor to control your actuators by tilting your device along the x-axis and the y-axis.

- *Chapter 10: Alarm System*: In the final chapter, you will utilize a lot of your previously gained knowledge to build your very own alarm system. In two projects you will get to know two different ways of triggering an alarm, through a tilt-switch and a self-built IR light barrier, and you will learn how your Android device can enhance the alarm system. You will also learn how to send text messages via SMS and you will use the device's camera to take a picture of a possible intruder.

CHAPTER 1

Introduction

In May 2011, Google held its annual developer conference, the Google IO, to present its newest technologies to approximately 5,000 attendees. In addition to improvements in its already well-known technologies such as the Google APIs or the core search technology, Google placed the focus on two major themes: Chrome and Android. As always, the newest advances in the Android Platform were presented and discussed, but what Google announced a bit later in the Android keynote was a bit of a surprise: Google's first standard for Android devices to communicate with external hardware. The Android Open Accessory Standard and the Accessory Development Kit (ADK) will be the key for communicating with hardware and building external accessories for Android devices. To encourage development, Google handed out ADK hardware packages to interested attendees and showed some examples of ADK projects, such as a treadmill which transmitted data to a connected Android device and a huge tilt labyrinth, which could be controlled with an Android device. Shortly after the event, the first DIY projects surfaced which already showed the great potential of the ADK.

Since I couldn't attend the event, I had no chance to get my hands on one of those kits; at the time, there was only one distributor for the Google ADK boards and this distributor wasn't prepared for such a big demand. That didn't stop me from building an alternative myself and from experiencing the joy of this new field in Android development. Over time, many more distributors have produced derivatives of the original Google ADK boards, which are, for the most part, cheaper and only provide the basics to get you started hacking your project together.

You probably just want to dive right in, but first you should learn about the specifics of the ADK and set up your development environment. You wouldn't build a house before you knew how to do it or without having the proper tools, would you?

What Is the ADK?

The Accessory Development Kit (ADK) is basically a micro-controller development board that adheres to the simple Open Accessory Standard Protocol created by Google as a reference implementation. Although that could be any board fulfilling the specification to be ADK compatible, most boards are based on the Arduino design, which is an open hardware platform created in 2005. Those boards are USB-enabled micro-controller boards based on the Arduino Mega2560 and the implementation of the Circuits@Home USB Host Shield. However, there are other board designs known to be ADK compatible, such as PIC-based boards or even plain USB host chip boards such as the VNCII by FTDI. Google decided to build its reference kit upon the Arduino Mega2560 design and provided the software and hardware resources as open source. This was a clever move because the Arduino community has grown tremendously over the last years, enabling designers, hobbyists, and average Joes to easily make their ideas come to life. With the ever-growing communities of both factions of Android and Arduino enthusiasts, the ADK had a pretty good start.

To communicate with the hardware boards, an Android-enabled device needs to fulfill certain criteria. With Android Honeycomb version 3.1 and backported version 2.3.4, the necessary software APIs were introduced. However, the devices also have to ship with a suitable USB driver. This driver enables general USB functionality but, in particular, it enables the so-called accessory mode. The accessory mode allows an Android device that has no USB host capabilities to communicate with external hardware, which in turn acts as the USB host part.

The specification of the Open Accessory Standard stipulates that the USB host has to provide power for the USB bus and can enumerate connected devices. The external device has to provide 500mA at 5V for charging purposes of the Android device according to the USB 2.0 specification.

The ADK also provides firmware for the development board which comes in the form of a set of source code files, libraries, and a *demokit sketch*, which is the Arduino term for a project or source code file. The firmware cares about the enumeration of the USB bus and finding a connected device that is accessory mode–compatible.

Google also provides an example app for the Android device that easily accesses and demonstrates the capabilities of the reference board and its sensors and actuators. If you are working with a derivative board that doesn't have the same variety of sensors, you still can work with the example app, but you might want to strip the code down to only the basic part of the communication.

When you set up an ADK hardware project you are building a so-called *Android accessory*. Your hardware project is an accessory for the Android device such as, for example, a keyboard would be for a PC, with the difference being that your accessory provides the power for the whole system. Accessories need to support the already mentioned power supply for the device and they must adhere to the Android accessory protocol. The protocol dictates that the accessory follows four basic steps to establish a communication to the Android device:

1. The accessory is in wait state and tries to detect any connected devices.

2. The accessory checks for accessory mode support of the device.

3. The accessory tries to set the device in accessory mode if it is necessary.

4. If the device supports the Android accessory protocol, the accessory establishes the communication.

If you want to learn more about the ADK and the Open Accessory Standard have a look at the Android developer pages at `http://developer.android.com/guide/topics/usb/adk.html`.

Hardware Development Boards

This section will give you an overview of the variety of ADK-compatible development boards that are currently on the market. Note that I can't guarantee the completeness of this list because the community advances at such a pace that new boards could pop up at any time. I will concentrate on the most popular boards out there as of this writing.

The Google ADK

The Google ADK is the reference kit presented at the Google IO in May 2011 and it was the first board adhering to the Open Accessory Standard. The kit comes with the ADK base board and a demo shield, as shown in Figure 1-1.

Figure 1-1. Google ADK board and Demo Shield

The base board (Figure 1-2) contains the DC power connector, the USB connector (A-type receptacle) to connect your phone or tablet to, and the micro USB connector (micro B-type receptacle) to connect to your computer for programming and debugging purposes. It has an ATmega2560 AVR chip from Atmel mounted on top, optimized for C-compiled code, which makes it pretty fast and easily programmable instead of comparable microcontrollers that have to be programmed in the assembler language. The ATmega2560 has an internal flash memory of 256 Kbytes and an 8-bit CPU and it operates at 16MHz. It provides 8KB of SRAM and 4KB of EEPROM. The IO ports of the ATmega chip control 16 analog pins that provide 10 bits of input resolution enabling analog-to-digital conversion of 1,024 different values. They measure from ground to 5V by default. The chip has 54 digital pins with 14 of them being PWM (pulse width modulation) enabled to allow, for example, dimming of LEDs or controlling servos. In the middle of the board is a reset button to reset the program execution on the board. The board's operating voltage is 5V. Although you can power the board via a USB cable, you should consider using a power adapter if you intend to control servos or drive motors.

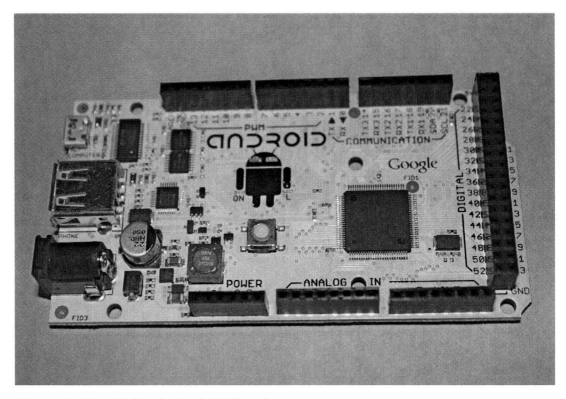

Figure 1-2. *A closer look at the Google ADK board*

The *Demo Shield* is an additional board containing a broad variety of different sensors and actuators. *Shield* is an Arduino term for an extension board that can be put on top of an Arduino base board. The connection is made via stackable pin headers. The IO pins of the base board are mostly delegated to the pins of the shield so they can be reused. However, certain shields might occupy pins to operate their sensors. The demo shield itself is presoldered with male pin headers so no additional shields can be stacked on top. This doesn't come as a surprise, since the shield uses most of the pins to let the base board communicate with all of its sensors. Since the shield hides the reset button of the base board, it contains one itself so that you can still make use of the reset functionality. The most important parts, however, are the sensors and actuators and there are a lot of them.

- One analog joystick
- Three buttons
- Three RGB LEDs
- A transistor functioning as a temperature sensor
- An IC with an integrated photo diode for light sensing

- A capacitive touch area in the form of the Android logo

- Two relays with screw terminals which can switch external circuits with 24V up to 1A

- Three servo connectors

The Google ADK was originally produced by a Japanese company for the Google IO. It can be ordered at `www.rt-net.jp/shop/index.php?main_page=product_info&cPath=3_4&products_id=1`. At a price of approximately $400 (not including sales tax), it is one of the priciest boards out there.

The Arduino ADK

The Arduino ADK (Figure 1-3) is an ADK-compatible base board from the makers of the Arduino series themselves. It is also based on the ATmega2560 and only differs slightly from the Google reference board.

Figure 1-3. Arduino ADK board

The Arduino ADK board also has a DC power connector and a USB connector (A-type receptacle) mounted to connect to an Android device. The programming and debugging connector, however, differs in being a standard USB connector (B-type receptacle). The reset button is situated at the far end of the board and the ATmega chip sits in the middle of the board. The IO pin layout is exactly the same as in the Google board and it has the same analog and digital pin characteristics. The Arduino ADK, however, has two ICSP 6-pin headers for In-Circuit Serial Programming (ICSP) of microchips. Sharing the same pin layout and form factor, the Arduino ADK and the Google ADK are compatible with the Demo Shield and other Arduino based shields.

The Arduino ADK is made in Italy and can be ordered directly from the Arduino site at `http://store.arduino.cc/ww/index.php?main_page=product_info&cPath=11_12&products_id=144` or from one of its numerous distributors worldwide found at `http://arduino.cc/en/Main/Buy`.

At a price of about $90 (not including possible shipping costs and taxes), it is way more affordable than the Google ADK for the average hobbyist and hardware hacker.

The IOIO

The IOIO (pronounced yo-yo) board (Figure 1-4) is a PIC micro-controller–based development board developed by Sparkfun Electronics before the announcement of the Open Accessory Standard.

Figure 1-4. Sparkfun IOIO board

The IOIO board was designed to work with all Android devices with version 1.5 and above. The original firmware design was targeted to work with the Android Debug Bridge (ADB), which is normally used within the development process of an Android application for debugging processes and for file system operations. After the announcement of the Open Accessory Standard the IOIO was updated with a new firmware to support both the Open Accessory Protocol and, as a fallback, the ADB protocol to still support older devices. The firmware is still in beta as of the time of writing this book. Since you need to update the firmware of the board through a PIC programmer in order to make the board ADK compatible, it might not be the perfect choice for an inexperienced tinkerer.

The hardware specifics of the board are as follows. The IOIO has a form factor of about a quarter of the size of a regular ADK-compatible board, which makes it one of the smallest boards available. Nevertheless, it nearly keeps up with the numerous IO pins of its big brothers. Many of the overall 48 IO pins have several operating modes, which can make the pin assignments a bit confusing.

From the 48 IO pins, all pins can be used as general purpose input output ports. Additionally, 16 of those pins can be used as analog inputs, 3 pairs of pins can be used for I²C communication, 1 pin can be used as a peripheral input, and 28 pins can be used for peripheral inputs and outputs. Normally, the pins are 3.3V tolerant only, but 22 pins are capable of tolerating 5V inputs and outputs. The I²C pins provide a fast and simple two-wire interface to communicate with external integrated circuits such as sensor boards.

Apart from the IO pins the board provides 3 Vin pins for power supply of the board. On the bottom side of the board you can solder an additional JST connector to connect a LiPo battery as the power supply. An operating voltage of 5V to 15V should be supplied. Additionally, it has 3 pins for 3.3V output, 3 pins for 5V output, and a 9 pin-area for ground.

The only connector on this board is the required USB (A-type receptacle) connector. That is because programming the hardware is not necessary, unlike for the other ADK-compatible boards, which need C-compiled code for the hardware part. The IOIO provides a firmware that implements all necessities. You only need to write the Android part by using a high-level API for easy pin access.

One interesting component of the board is a small trimmer potentiometer that can limit the charging current of the Android device so that it won't draw too much power when the board is in battery mode. The IOIO has a PIC micro-controller chip instead of the AVR chip most of the other boards use. The PIC24FJ256-DA206 chip operates at 32MHz, has 256KB of programmable memory and 96KB of RAM.

The IOIO was developed by Sparkfun Electronics and can be ordered via the Sparkfun web site at `www.sparkfun.com/products/10748` or through one of its distributors.

With a price of about $50 before shipping and taxes, it is one of the cheapest boards out there but not one of the friendliest to beginners.

The Seeeduino ADK Main Board

The Seeeduino ADK board (Figure 1-5), also derived from the ATmega board, looks quite similar to the standard Arduino ADK board but, at second glance, it has some nice extra features.

Figure 1-5. Seeeduino ADK board (image courtesy of Seeedstudio)

It has 56 digital IO pins with 14 of them being PWM capable, 16 analog input pins, and 1 ICSP header. The connectors on the board are of the same type as in the original Google design. It has a DC power connector, a USB connector (A-type receptacle), and a micro USB connector (micro B-type receptacle).

The biggest difference with most other Atmega-like boards is that the Seeeduino ADK board already ships with the MicroBridge firmware so that it works in ADK mode with Android devices with OS version 2.3.4 and above and in ADB mode with devices that have OS versions previous to version 2.3.4, much like the IOIO does.

The Seeeduino ADK board was developed by Seeedstudio and can be ordered at the company's web site at `www.seeedstudio.com/depot/seeeduino-adk-main-board-p-846.html` or from one of their distributors.

It is priced at $79 (before shipping and taxes), which makes it a very affordable but powerful board.

More ADK Possibilities

After you have seen the most common boards with ADK support out there, you'll probably wonder if that's all there is. Although the Open Accessory Standard is only about a year old, the number of boards already available is incredible, with many still to come in this young but rapidly evolving field of open source hardware. There are still plenty of other possibilities for developing with the Open Accessory Standard. Some represent pure DIY (do-it-yourself) approaches, while others are extensions for boards that have been in use since before the ADK came out.

One early approach was to port the ADK to the common Arduino Uno or Duemilanove. The only thing you needed was an additional USB host shield to connect the Android device to. I was one of those early DIY hackers who went in that direction. At the time, it was the only affordable alternative to the original Google reference board. Nowadays, I wouldn't recommend it; there are already perfect all-in-one boards that don't need additional shields, hacking, or stripping of code. If you still want to use your regular Arduino there are a lot of shops carrying USB host shields you can use:

- www.circuitsathome.com/products-page/arduino-shields/usb-host-shield-2-0-for-arduino/

- www.sparkfun.com/products/9947

- www.dfrobot.com/index.php?route=product/product&filter_name=usb%20host&product_id=498

- http://emartee.com/product/42089/Arduino%20ADK%20Shield%20For%20Android

You may have read about the possibility of enabling communication with Android devices running an OS version lower than 2.3.4, which some boards provide. If also you want to support that in your projects you should have a look at the microbridge project that uses the ADB to establish the communication. Check the project page for further details, at http://code.google.com/p/microbridge/.

Some of the all-in-one boards also come bundled as a kit to let you tinker away with a bunch of sensors. Those kits usually provide some of the same sensors that the Google Demo Shield features.

The Arduino store sells an ADK Sensor Kit that consists of an Arduino ADK Mega board with a Mega Sensor Shield. The sensor shield has 22 3-pin connectors to easily connect sensor modules without having to worry about wiring and setup. For more information go to http://store.arduino.cc/eu/index.php?main_page=product_info&cPath=2&products_id=140.

Seeedstudio also has a kit called Grove ADK Dash Kit. Like the Arduino kit, it also provides an easy plug-and-play mechanism to start right away and it features a broad set of sensors for all kinds of purposes. It is available at http://www.seeedstudio.com/depot/grove-adk-dash-kit-p-929.html.

If you still want a kit based on the original Google design but importing the Japanese original is not an option, you can also consider the following German clone, which is nearly an exact clone with the minor improvement of providing a gold-plated touch area that has better conductivity and hinders oxidation. It is also a bit more affordable than the original and, depending on where you live, the shipping costs may be lower. Check out www.troido.de/de/shoplsmallgbuy-android-stufflsmallg/product/view/1/1 for more information.

Which Board Should You Use?

Now that you have read about the variety of boards supporting the Open Accessory Standard that are already out there you might wonder which board is the right one for your own project. This is always a hard question, for which there is no single answer. You should plan your project thoroughly ahead of time to analyze which board fits best.

If you are a beginner in the world of hardware development and ADK, you should stick to the boards that are most commonly used out in the wild. As of this writing, that would be the Google ADK board, which was given out to hundreds of developers attending the Google IO 2011. If you are not one of the lucky ones to have received one of these boards and your budget is pretty tight—which is usually the case—consider the standard Arduino ADK board. Both of these boards are used in most hacker and maker projects I have seen so far and they have a huge community built around them to help you if you are in need.

Table 1-1 gives you an overview of the boards under discussion.

Table 1-1. Comparison of the Most Common ADK-Enabled Boards

ADK Boards	Google ADK	Arduino ADK	Seeeduino ADK	Sparkfun IOIO
Processor	ATmega2560	ATmega2560	ATmega2560	PIC24FJ256
CPU clock speed	16 MHz	16 MHz	16 MHz	32 MHz
Flash memory	256 Kbytes	256 Kbytes	256 Kbytes	256 Kbytes
RAM	8 Kbytes	8 Kbytes	8 Kbytes	96 Kbytes
Digital IO pins	54 (14 PWM)	54 (14 PWM)	56 (14 PWM)	48 (28 PWM)
Analog input pins	16	16	16	16
Input voltage	5.5V - 16V	5.5V - 16V	6V - 18V	5V - 15V
Connectors	DC power	DC power	DC power	USB A-type
	USB A-type	USB A-type	USB A-type	
	USB micro B-type	USB B-type	USB micro B-type	

Supported Android Devices

The Open Accessory Standard was introduced as part of the Android API in Android Honeycomb version 3.1 with the rollout of more and more Android-enabled tablets. To not only support Honeycomb devices, Google decided to backport the necessary classes to version 2.3.4 making them available for phones also. The newer functionality was backported as a Google API add-on library. This library is basically a JAR file that has to be included in the build path of your Android project.

The first candidates to have received the necessary version updates and which supported the Open Accessory mode were the Motorola Xoom and the Google Nexus S. Other devices were soon to follow, which quickly led to the well-known problem of fragmentation. Normally, fragmentation is mostly a problem when it comes to different versions of the operating system, but now the problem was that even though a device had the necessary OS version of 2.3.4 or 3.1, it was still possible that the Open Accessory mode wouldn't work on the device. How could that happen? Well, the problem was that it is not sufficient to update only the system software. The USB drivers of the device must be compatible with the Open Accessory mode. Many developers updated their device or even rooted it to install a homebrew mod like Cyanogen Mod to finally run version 2.3.4, only to find that the USB drivers of the device manufacturer weren't compatible.

However, there are a lot of devices that have been tested and are said to work perfectly with the Open Accessory mode, some of them officially, others driven by DIY mods. Here is a list of some devices that have been verified by the community to work with the ADK:

- Google Nexus S
- Google Nexus One

- Motorola Xoom

- Acer Iconia A100

- Acer Iconia A500

- LG Optimus Pad

- ASUS Eee Pad Transfomer TF101

- Samsung Galaxy Tab 10.1

- Samsung Galaxy S

- Samsung Galaxy Ace

Personally, I would recommend using a Google developer device like the Nexus S, as those devices have the best support for the newest APIs and functionalities.

Setting Up the Development Environment

You know a lot about the history of the ADK and the technical specifics, but before your ideas can come to life you need to set up your working environment. You will need to program software for your Android device as well as for your hardware board to let both parties communicate with each other and to control actuators or read sensor values. The programming is done with the help of two Integrated Development Environments (IDEs). To program Android applications, Google recommends using the Eclipse IDE. The Eclipse IDE is the most common IDE for Java development with one of the biggest communities, a variety of plugins, and excellent support. Since the hardware boards are based on the Arduino design, you will program them with the Arduino IDE to write so-called *sketches* that will be uploaded to the board. In order for those IDEs to work properly you also need the Java Development Kit (JDK), which has more functionality than the normal Java Runtime Environment (JRE) and which your system probably has already installed. You will also need the Android SDK to write your Android applications.

This step-by-step guide will help you to set up the necessary development environment. Please follow the steps for your operating system of choice exactly. If you run into any problems you can also refer to the official installation guides on the software sites.

The Java Development Kit

The first thing you will need is the JDK. Go to `www.oracle.com/technetwork/java/javase/downloads/index.html` and click the JDK download button (Figure 1-6).

Figure 1-6. JDK download page

Accept the license agreement and choose the file for your operating system (Figure 1-7). The x86 files are suitable for 32-bit operating systems and the x64 files have to be installed on 64-bit systems, so make sure to select the correct one.

Java SE Development Kit 7

You must accept the Oracle Binary Code License Agreement for Java SE to download this software.

○ Accept License Agreement   ⊙ Decline License Agreement

Product / File Description	File Size	Download
Linux x86 - RPM Installer	77.28 MB	jdk-7-linux-i586.rpm
Linux x86 - Compressed Binary	92.17 MB	jdk-7-linux-i586.tar.gz
Linux x64 - RPM Installer	77.91 MB	jdk-7-linux-x64.rpm
Linux x64 - Compressed Binary	90.57 MB	jdk-7-linux-x64.tar.gz
Solaris x86 - Compressed Packages	154.74 MB	jdk-7-solaris-i586.tar.Z
Solaris x86 - Compressed Binary	94.75 MB	jdk-7-solaris-i586.tar.gz
Solaris SPARC - Compressed Packages	157.81 MB	jdk-7-solaris-sparc.tar.Z
Solaris SPARC - Compressed Binary	99.48 MB	jdk-7-solaris-sparc.tar.gz
Solaris SPARC 64-bit - Compressed Packages	16.28 MB	jdk-7-solaris-sparcv9.tar.Z
Solaris SPARC 64-bit - Compressed Binary	12.38 MB	jdk-7-solaris-sparcv9.tar.gz
Solaris x64 - Compressed Packages	14.66 MB	jdk-7-solaris-x64.tar.Z
Solaris x64 - Compressed Binary	9.39 MB	jdk-7-solaris-x64.tar.gz
Windows x86	79.48 MB	jdk-7-windows-i586.exe
Windows x64	80.25 MB	jdk-7-windows-x64.exe

Figure 1-7. JDK platform downloads

You may notice that there are no JDK files for Mac OS. Those are not distributed over the Oracle site because Apple provides its own version of the JDK. The JDK should come preinstalled on your Mac OS X system. You can verify that by typing `java -version` into a terminal window. You should see your currently installed Java version listed in the terminal window.

Installing on Windows

After you have downloaded the executable, open it and follow the instructions that will guide you through the installation process. Afterward, you should set the JDK path to your Windows `PATH` variable. The path variable is used to conveniently run executables from anywhere in your system. Otherwise, you would always have to type the complete path in order to execute something from the command line such as `C:\Program Files\Java\jdk1.7.0\bin\java`.

Eclipse also depends on the `JAVA_HOME` variable to be set. To set system environment variables you will have to do the following.

1. Right-click `My Computer` and select Properties as shown in Figure 1-8.

Figure 1-8. Open System Properties dialog

2. On the system Properties dialog select the **Advanced** tab. Near the bottom you should see the **Environment Variables** button (Figure 1-9), which opens the variables dialog to set User and System variables.

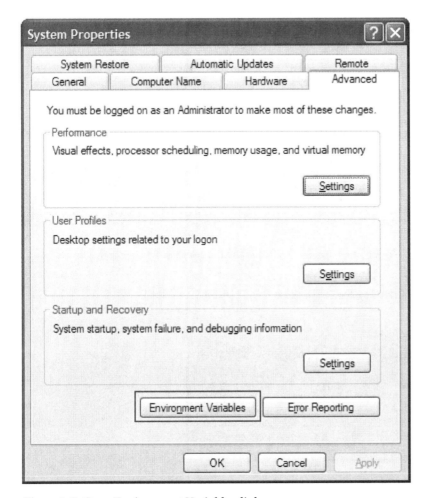

Figure 1-9. *Open Environment Variables dialog*

3.   Click New in the System Variables area and insert the following:

Variable Name: `JAVA_HOME`
Variable Value: `C:\Program Files\Java\jdk1.7.0`

4.   Click `OK`.

5.   Additionally edit the `PATH` variable by selecting it (Figure 1-10) and click `Edit`.
     Insert `%JAVA_HOME%/bin;` in front of the other values.

6.   Click `OK`.

7.   Now your JDK is set up and ready for work.

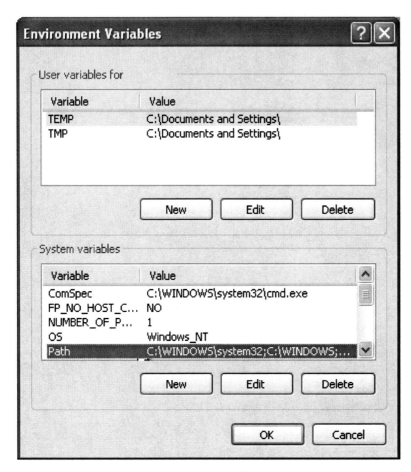

Figure 1-10. Setting up Environment Variables

Installing on Linux

Download the `tar.gz` file for your system (32-bit / 64-bit) and move the file to the location where you want the JDK to be installed. Usually the JDK is installed into `/usr/java/` but keep in mind that you need root permissions to install into that directory.

Unpack and install the JDK with:

```
# tar zxvf jdk-7-linux-i586.tar.gz
```

The JDK is installed in the `/jdk1.7.0` directory within your current directory.

To let your system know where you have installed the JDK and to be able to run it from anywhere in your system, you have to set the necessary environment variables. For that purpose, it is a good idea to create a short shell script which is placed in the `/etc/profile.d` directory.

Create a script called `java_env.sh` in that directory and add the following content to the script:

```
#!/bin/bash

JAVA_HOME=/usr/java/jdk1.7.0

PATH=$JAVA_HOME/bin:$PATH

export PATH JAVA_HOME
export CLASSPATH=.
```

The last thing to do is to set the permission on the newly created script so that the system will execute it at user login.

```
# chmod 755 java_env.sh
```

After a fresh login the environment variables will be set.

Installing on Mac OS X

As mentioned before, the JDK for Mac is not distributed via the Oracle download site. The JDK is preinstalled on Mac OS X but can also be downloaded through the Apple Store. If your environment variable for `JAVA_HOME` and `PATH` is not already set you can refer to the according steps used in the Linux installation, as Mac OS X is also Unix-based. You can check if the variables are set using the following command in a terminal window:

```
# echo $JAVA_HOME
```

And similar for the `PATH` variable:

```
# echo $PATH
```

The Android SDK

To be able to write Android applications you need the Android Software Development Kit, which provides all libraries and tools for all Android versions that are supported by Google right now.

You can download the SDK from the Android developer pages (Figure 1-11) at http://developer.android.com/sdk/index.html.

Download the Android SDK

Welcome Developers! If you are new to the Android SDK, please read the steps below, for an overview of how to set up the SDK.

If you're already using the Android SDK, you should update to the latest tools or platform using the *Android SDK and AVD Manager*, rather than downloading a new SDK starter package. See Adding SDK Components.

Platform	Package	Size	MD5 Checksum
Windows	android-sdk_r12-windows.zip	36486190 bytes	8d6c104a34cd2577c5506c55d981aebf
	installer_r12-windows.exe (Recommended)	36531492 bytes	367f0ed4ecd70aefc290d1f7dcb578ab
Mac OS X (intel)	android-sdk_r12-mac_x86.zip	30231118 bytes	341544e4572b4b1afab123ab817086e7
Linux (i386)	android-sdk_r12-linux_x86.tgz	30034243 bytes	f8485275a8dee3d1929936ed538ee99a

Figure 1-11. *Android SDK download page*

The site provides zipped archives of the SDK for Windows, Linux, and Mac. There is also another version for Windows, which is an executable and should guide you through the installation process. Since the initial setup is the same for all platforms, there will be no OS-specific steps.

After you have downloaded the SDK archive move it to a location of your choice and unzip it. You will see that both the add-ons and platforms directories are empty. Only the tools directory contains several binaries. The important file within that directory right now is the android script. It launches the SDK and AVD Manager (Figure 1-12).

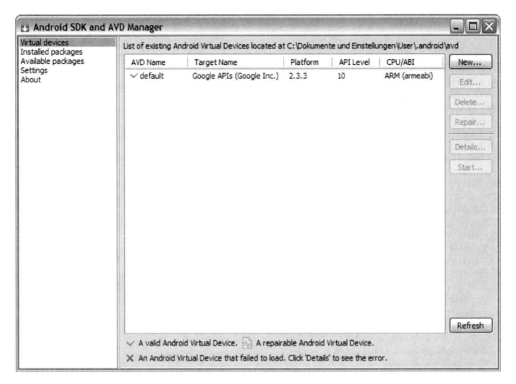

Figure 1-12. SDK Manager

The SDK Manager is the central core of the SDK. It manages the installed Android versions and it updates new versions and additional packages. With the SDK and AVD manager you can also set up emulators for testing Android applications.

At first startup it will connect to the Google servers to check for version updates and it will prompt you afterwards to install SDK packages (Figure 1-13). It is a good idea to just click Accept All and Install to install all SDK versions and additional packages. This can take a really long time depending on your Internet connection. If you want to only install the packages that are absolutely necessary, just accept the following packages and reject all others:

- Android SDK Platform-tools

- Documentation for Android SDK

- SDK Platform for Android 2.3.3, API 10 and all newer ones

- Samples for SDK API 10 and all newer ones

- Google APIs by Google Inc., Android API 10 and all newer ones

- Google USB Driver package

- Android Compatibility package

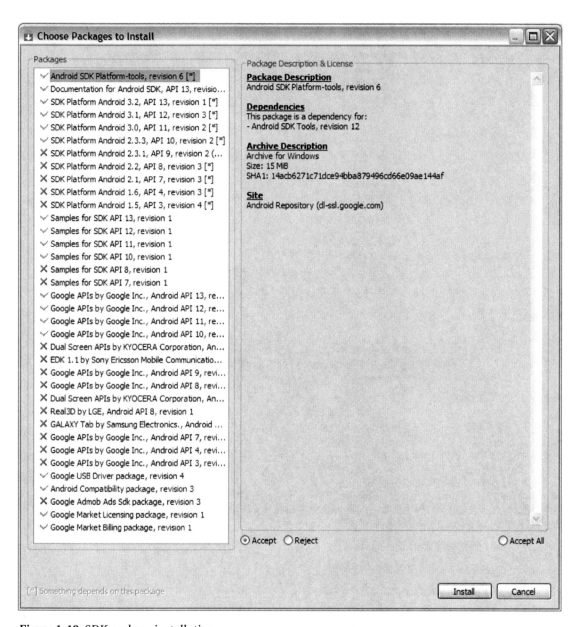

Figure 1-13. SDK package installation

You can uninstall and install the packages at any time by clicking installed and available packages to manage your SDK installation. When the SDK Manager is finished downloading all the necessary packages you will see that your SDK directory has grown and has some new folders in it. I will talk about some of them later, so there is no need to understand them now. The SDK is now ready for development.

The Eclipse IDE

The Eclipse Integrated Development Environment is one of the most commonly-used IDEs among software developers. It has a huge supportive community and some the most powerful plugins for all kinds of development scenarios. You will need Eclipse for developing your Android applications. The programming language for writing Android applications is Java. Though you are writing Java code, ultimately it will be compiled into Android-specific dex code and packaged into an archive file with the file ending .apk. This archive file will be put onto your Android device for installation.

To download Eclipse, go to www.eclipse.org/downloads/. Select your operating system in the upper-right corner of the distribution list (Figure 1-14).

Figure 1-14. Eclipse download site

You should choose the Eclipse Classic edition as it is not preconfigured for other purposes. Click the download button for your system type (32-bit/64-bit). Now select the default mirror page for the download or select a mirror nearest to you (Figure 1-15).

Eclipse downloads - mirror selection

All downloads are provided under the terms and conditions of the Eclipse Foundation Software User Agreement unless otherwise specified.

Download eclipse-SDK-3.7-win32.zip **from:**

[Germany] Artfiles New Media GmbH (http)

Checksums: [MD5] [SHA1] BitTorrent

...or pick a mirror site below.

Figure 1-15. Download mirror selection

The downloaded file will be either a `zip` or a `tar.gz` archive file depending on your operating system. You don't need to install Eclipse as it is packaged ready to run. Move the archive to the directory where you want Eclipse to be placed and extract it. The Eclipse IDE is now ready for normal Java development. However, you need to install an additional plugin and make some configurations in order to prepare Eclipse for the Android development.

The first thing you need is the Android Development Tools (ADT) plugin from Google. The ADT plugin enhances Eclipse with a mighty set of tools for Android development. Besides being able to set up Android-specific projects, you will also benefit from dedicated editors for user interface (UI) development, resource management, debug and monitoring views, and build and analytic tools. Details about the ADT plugin can be found at `http://developer.android.com/sdk/eclipse-adt.html`. The ADT plugin is installed from within Eclipse via its update mechanism.

Open Eclipse and click `Help`. Select `Install New Software` (Figure 1-16).

Figure 1-16. Eclipse plugin installation

Click **Add** in the upper-right corner. In the repository dialog you have to enter the update site URL and a name for identification (Figure 1-17). The name can be anything but it is recommended to use something descriptive like ADT Plugin. In the URL field enter `https://dl-ssl.google.com/android/eclipse/`. If you have trouble establishing SSL connections you can also use http as the protocol, but it is less secure.

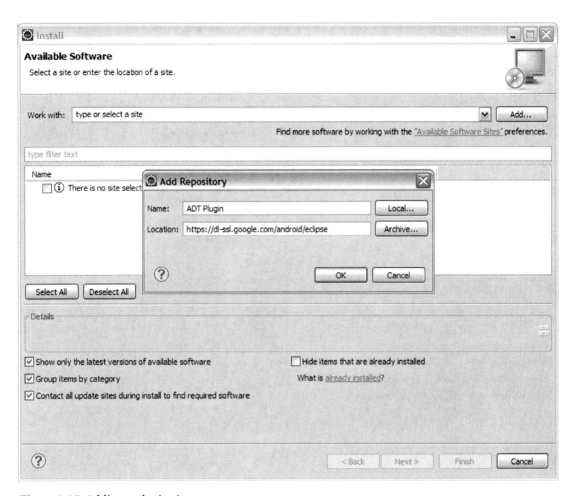

Figure 1-17. Adding a plugin site

The available software for that update site will be listed. Select the checkbox at Developer Tools and click Next (Figure 1-18).

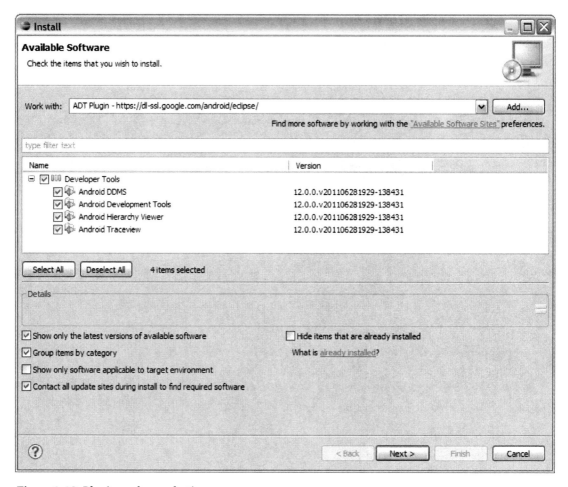

Figure 1-18. Plugin package selection

An installation summary will be presented to you where you can click **Next**. The last step is to accept the license agreements and click **Finish** (Figure 1-19).

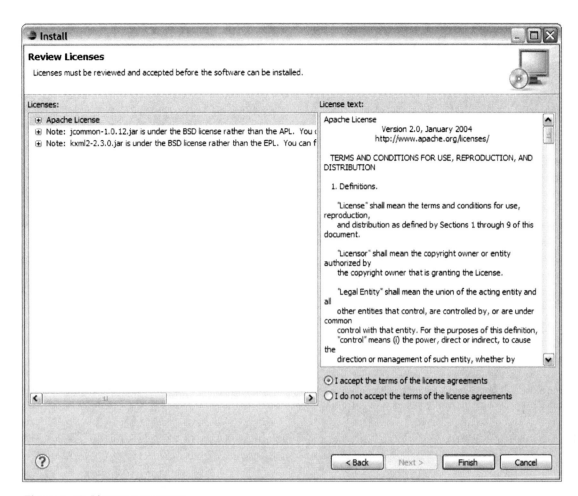

Figure 1-19. License agreement

If a dialog pops up saying that the authenticity or validity is not guaranteed, click OK. The plugin is now installed and Eclipse will prompt you to either restart Eclipse or just apply the changes. It is always a good idea to restart Eclipse so no side effects can occur while loading the plugin. Before you will be able to set up Android projects, you'll need to set up some preferences within Eclipse. Select Window and Preferences in the top bar (Figure 1-20).

Figure 1-20. Configuring the Preferences

In the left list select **Android**. If you click it the first time a modal dialog will pop up asking you to send usage statistics to the Google servers. You are not required to allow that, but you have to make a choice and click **Proceed** to close the dialog. Now you have to configure your Android SDK location. Click **Browse…** and select the directory where you placed your SDK installation as shown in Figure 1-21.

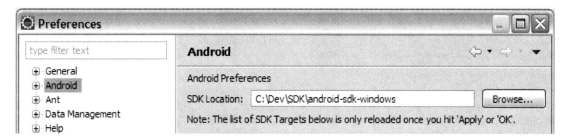

Figure 1-21. Setting up the Android SDK path

Apply the changes and click **OK**. You have completed the setup and are now ready to develop Android applications.

The Arduino IDE

The Arduino Integrated Development Environment is a pretty slim IDE compared to Eclipse. You will use it to write code for your Arduino-based micro-controller board. The Arduino IDE itself is based on Java but you will write your code in C. The IDE compiles the code using avr-gcc. The written software for the Arduino is a so-called sketch. The IDE (Figure 1-22) itself consists of a code editor with syntax highlighting, a console for debugging and messaging purposes, and it is connected to your hardware board by a serial connection (USB). The IDE comes with a lot of convenience libraries for all kinds of IO operations. The Arduino community has a huge ever-growing community of designers, hobbyists, and developers who also produce a diversity of libraries and sketches.

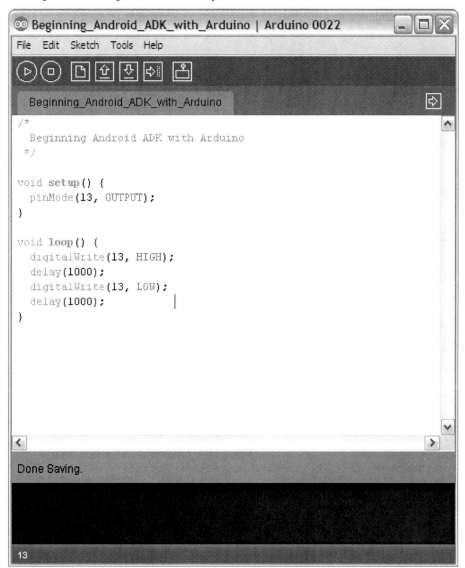

Figure 1-22. The Arduino IDE

You can download the IDE as an archive file or disk image, depending on your operating system, from the Arduino site (Figure 1-23) at `http://arduino.cc/en/Main/Software`.

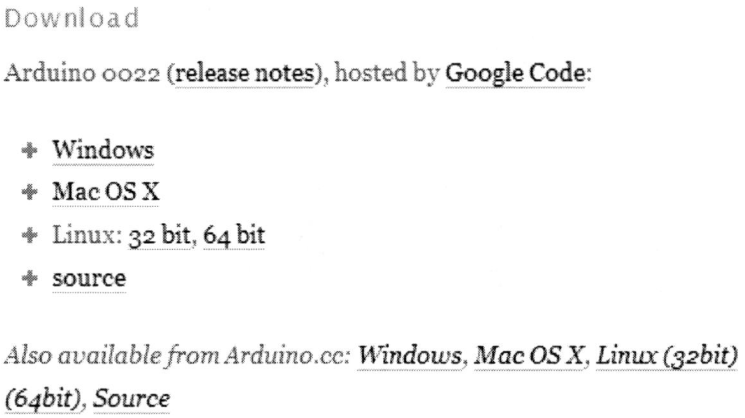

Download

Arduino 0022 (**release notes**), hosted by **Google Code**:

+ Windows
+ Mac OS X
+ Linux: 32 bit, 64 bit
+ source

Also available from Arduino.cc: *Windows*, *Mac OS X*, *Linux (32bit)*

(64bit), Source

Figure 1-23. *Arduino download site*

Installing the Arduino IDE on Windows and Linux

If you are using either Windows or Linux you will have to download an archive file that you can place in whatever directory you like. After that, unpack the archive. No installation is needed and the IDE is already ready to go.

Installing the Arduino IDE on Mac OS X

If you are using a Mac OS X system you will have to download a `.dmg` file, which is a disk-image. If the system does not mount it automatically, double-click the file. After it is mounted you will see a file called `Arduino.app`. Move this file into your Applications folder in your home directory. The IDE is now installed and ready for coding.

Installing Hardware Drivers

External hardware almost always needs so-called drivers. *A driver* is a piece of software that makes the hardware known to your operating system. The driver enables the OS to communicate with the external device. Since you have two hardware devices with which you want to communicate during the programming phase (the ADK board and the Android device), you will have to provide drivers for those devices also.

Installing the Hardware Drivers on Windows

Although the ADK boards are based on the ATmega 2560 for which the drivers are already deployed with the Arduino IDE, Windows users should download an archive file that contains driver definitions for the ADK type boards. To do that, go to the Arduino ADK detail page at `http://arduino.cc/en/Main/ArduinoBoardADK`.

You will find the archive file at the bottom of the page or at this URL:
`http://arduino.cc/en/uploads/Main/Arduino_ADK.zip`.

The archive contains only an `.inf` file. Connect your ADK board to your PC and you will be prompted to provide a driver or let the system search for one. Choose to manually install one and point to the mentioned `.inf` file. The system will install the driver and your ADK board is known to the system.

The Android device also needs a driver so that you will be able to deploy and debug your written applications. In most cases, the generic drivers provided by your Android SDK installation are sufficient. When you installed the additional SDK packages in the SDK Manager, you selected a package called `Google USB Driver Package, revision x`. When you connect your Android device for the first time you will be prompted to select a driver manually or let the system search for one. Again select to manually assign a driver and select the generic driver in your SDK installation directory at `%SDK_HOME%\extras\google\usb_driver`.

▪ **Note** In some cases you might need the specific manufacturer's USB drivers. You will find them on the manufacturer homepage. Samsung, for example, packages its drivers with its synchronization tool Kies.

Installing the Hardware Drivers on Linux

Linux systems should detect your hardware board and your Android device automatically. When you upload your code to the ADK board later on you can choose the ATmega2560 settings within the Arduino IDE. If you have any trouble setting up your board on a Linux machine refer to the installation guide at `www.arduino.cc/playground/Learning/Linux`.

Installing the Hardware Drivers on Mac OS X

On a Mac the same situation applies as on a Linux machine. The devices should be detected automatically. However, if you are having trouble with the ADK board it might help to install the FTDI drivers that came with the disk-image file you downloaded before. Just double-click the file called `FTDIUSBSerialDriver_xx_xx_xx_xx_xx_xx.mpkg`. Follow the installation instructions and restart your system. If you are still having trouble, you can refer to the installation guide at `http://arduino.cc/en/Guide/MacOSX`.

The ADK Reference Package

To give you a starting point for your ideas, Google provides an ADK reference package. This package contains the original designs of the board for manufacturing, firmware, a demo sketch for the ADK boards, and an example Android application that communicates with the ADK board. It can be downloaded at `https://dl-ssl.google.com/android/adk/adk_release_0512.zip`. You should download the reference package as it will be the basis for your first project and the examples throughout the book.

> ▪ **Note** The version of the ADK reference package may be updated from time to time. You will find the current link in the developer pages at `http://developer.android.com/guide/topics/usb/adk.html` in the ADK Components section.

Fritzing (Optional Software)

Though Fritzing is a completely optional open-source software component and not necessarily needed, I want to give you a short overview about how it can help you in your own projects later on. Fritzing is a powerful prototyping tool that lets you visualize your circuits and hardware designs in different forms. It aims to support hobbyists, designers, and makers in their project documentation, visualization, and manufacturing.

With Fritzing, you can create breadboard schematics such as that shown in Figure 1-24.

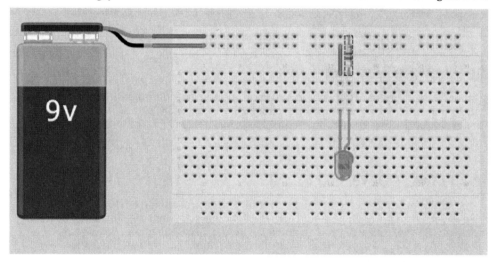

Figure 1-24. Fritzing breadboard schematic

You can abstract your design as a circuit schematic as shown in Figure 1-25.

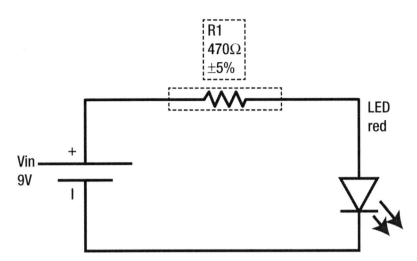

Figure 1-25. Fritzing circuit schematic

You can even translate your design into a PCB design (Figure 1-26) that can be manufactured later on.

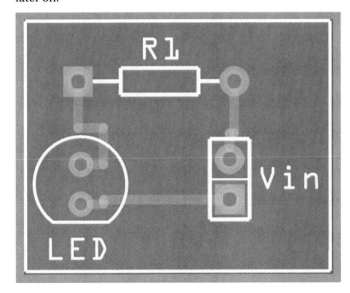

Figure 1-26. Fritzing PCB schematic

The tool has a variety of parts ranging from the most common, such as resistors and common ICs (integrated circuits), to several parts from the Sparkfun catalog up to individual user-generated parts. The community is growing among Arduino users and it is becoming more and more a pseudo standard. Though it might not be as powerful as CadSoft's EAGLE, which is the industry standard tool for electrical engineering, it still has everything a hobbyist or maker needs and its absolutely free. You will see Fritzing schematics used in all the projects in this book to help visualize the project setup. If you want to have a deeper look into it you can read more about Fritzing here at `http://fritzing.org`.

Ready, Set, Go

Congratulations! You have gone through the tedious task of setting up the development environment for the Android Open Accessory Development Kit. You have also learned a little bit about the history of the still-young ADK and which hardware exists out in the wild. The following chapters will take you by the hand and guide you through the process of creating an ADK project. Next, I will describe the basics you'll need to know about your ADK board and possible external components by setting up different kinds of experiments and projects. Each project teaches you a specific detail that you might need in a subsequent project. The examples build mostly upon each other; in the end, you will set up more sophisticated projects utilizing what you have learned so far. The projects will be based on the most common ADK-compatible board, the Arduino ADK board.

Now that you are ready for the fun, let's get you started with your first project.

CHAPTER 2

Android and Arduino: Getting to Know Each Other

Now that you have learned about the basics of both the Android and Arduino platforms, it is time to let them get to know each other. This chapter will guide you through your first Android Open Accessory Development Kit (ADK) project. You will learn the specifics of the Open Accessory Protocol and how it is implemented on both sides. You will write the code foundation you will use throughout the book for all further examples. To learn about the lifecycle and the anatomy of the code examples, you will begin by coding the all-time favorite "Hello World" for both platforms.

You will start by creating two very basic projects for Arduino and Android to learn how to set up a project on both platforms. Step by step you will implement the necessary functionality to let the Android device and the ADK board recognize each other when they are connected. Finally, you will implement the actual communication to send text messages from the Android device to the ADK board and vice versa.

Hello Arduino

First, open your installed Arduino IDE. Don't be afraid if you haven't worked with the Arduino IDE before. It has a very clear and basic structure and it provides just enough functionality for you to develop properly for the Arduino platform.

You'll see a big text-editable area in which you'll write your code (Figure 2-1). The code editor provides syntax highlighting but, unfortunately, no code completion, which can make developing against external libraries a little bit harder because you have to look up function definitions in the library code directly.

```
chapter02_helloworld

//includes would be placed here

//constant definition
#define ARRAY_SIZE 12

//global variable definition
char hello[ARRAY_SIZE] = {'h','e','l','l','o',' ',
'w','o','r','l','d','!'};

void setup() {
  //set baud rate for serial communication
  Serial.begin(115200);
}

void loop() {
  //print characters from array to serial monitor
  for(int x = 0; x < ARRAY_SIZE; x++) {
    Serial.print(hello[x]);
    delay(250);
  }
  Serial.println();
  delay(250);
}
```

Figure 2-1. Arduino IDE code editor

At the top of the editor is the action bar. The action bar gives you quick access to functionalities like compiling, file operations such as New, Open, Save, and Upload, and it starts the Serial Monitor for debugging purposes or sending commands directly to a connected board. In the system bar on top (shown in Figure 2-2), you can select more finely-grained operations, such as selecting the proper board, the communication port, importing external libraries, and many others.

Figure 2-2. Arduino IDE system bar and action bar

The status field at the bottom of the editor shows your compilation and upload progress as well as warnings or compile errors (see Figure 2-3). For a more detailed explanation of the Arduino IDE you can refer to the original documentation on the Arduino site at http://arduino.cc/en/Guide/Environment.

Done compiling.

Binary sketch size: 2968 bytes (of a 258048 byte maximum)

1

Figure 2-3. Arduino IDE status field

An Arduino sketch has two important methods. The first one is the setup method, which only runs once at the beginning of the code execution. This is the place where you would do your initializing routines. The second is the loop method. This method runs in an endless loop until the board is reset. This is the place where you would implement your program logic. As you can see in Figure 2-4, the lifecycle of an Arduino sketch is fairly simple.

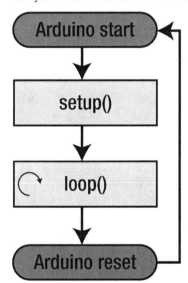

Figure 2-4. Sketch lifecycle

You can also define your own methods inside the same sketch, or link other source files or libraries. To link a piece of code, you use the #include directive known from C development. Includes are placed at the very top of the sketch. Global variables must also be defined at the top of the sketch below your include directives. Due to the fact that the Arduino ADK and most other ADK boards have a memory limit of 256Kbyte, you'll have to remember to write clean code, which means no code duplication and you must stick to the smallest possible data types in order to not run out of memory. Luckily, the compiler always shows you the exact size of your compiled code and warns you if it gets over the limit.

Now it's time to write your "Hello World" program for Arduino. In your Arduino IDE select New in the action bar. In the newly opened editor window, type in the code shown in Listing 2-1.

Listing 2-1. Arduino Hello World Sketch

```
//includes would be placed here

//constant definition
#define ARRAY_SIZE 12

//global variable definition
char hello[ARRAY_SIZE] = {'h','e','l','l','o',' ','w','o','r','l','d','!'};

void setup() {
  //set baud rate for serial communication
  Serial.begin(115200);
}

void loop() {
  //print characters from array to serial monitor
  for(int x = 0; x < ARRAY_SIZE; x++) {
    Serial.print(hello[x]);
    delay(250);
  }
  Serial.println();
  delay(250);
}
```

Let's talk about what the code does. At first, you defined a constant for the size of an array. Then you defined a char array with the size of that constant, which is 12. Since you have space for 12 characters in your char array you can put the characters for "hello world!" into it.

In the setup method you prepare your board for serial communication. The Serial object provides methods that simplify the serial communication. To start the communication, you call the begin method with the parameter 115200. This is the so-called *baud rate*, which defines how many bits per second can be transmitted. The receiving partner in the serial communication has to be configured for the same baud rate to read the transmitted data correctly.

As mentioned before, the loop method runs endlessly until the board is reset. In the loop method you print each character of the char array with the help of a for-loop, which iterates over all elements. To print out the elements to the Serial Monitor you use the print method of the Serial class. You also see a delay method being called between each character printout to slow down the output for better readability. The delay parameter is given in milliseconds.

When you have typed in everything, click Verify in the action bar to see if your code can be compiled without errors. If everything is okay, you can connect your ADK board to your computer. You need to tell the IDE to which port you connected your ADK board and which type of board it actually is so that the IDE can transmit the program code to the board in the correct way.

Click Tools ➤ Board and select Arduino Mega 2560 (see Figure 2-5).

Figure 2-5. Arduino IDE board selection

Now go to Tools ➤ Serial Port and select the port your board is connected to (Figure 2-6).

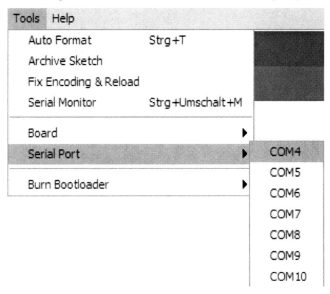

Figure 2-6. Arduino IDE serial port selection

When you have configured everything, click Upload in the action bar. Your code will be compiled and transferred to the ADK board. Once it has finished, the status field will display "Done Uploading". The code is now processed by your ADK board and begins to execute. Click Serial Monitor in the action bar of the IDE to open up the Serial Monitor and to see the printouts. To see the transmitted data correctly, make sure that you set the baud rate correctly to 115200 as in the code. This is done in the lower-right corner of the Serial Monitor. You should see now that "hello world!" is printed over and over again in the Serial Monitor window, as shown in Figure 2-7.

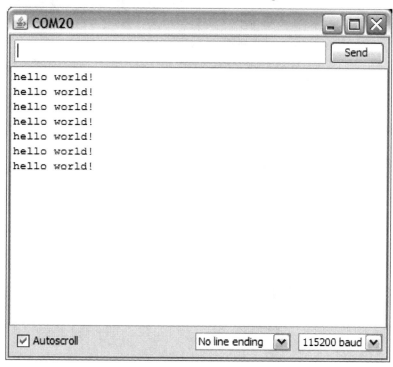

Figure 2-7. Arduino IDE Serial Monitor

Congratulations! You have written your first Arduino sketch and already set up everything to begin with the real ADK-specific part.

■ **Note** At the time of this writing, a new version of the Arduino IDE is being released. Version 1.0 introduces a lot of changes in the internal libraries and the IDE user interface. Some of the ADK-relevant libraries may not be fully compatible yet. If you have any trouble compiling the examples you may want to make sure to use an older version of the IDE. The examples in this book are written and compiled with the Arduino IDE revision 0022.

Hello Android

If you haven't worked with Android before, it is a good idea to familiarize yourself with the fundamentals of the platform first and learn a bit about its key components. As this could fill another book on its own, I highly recommend that you have a look at the Android Developer Pages and read your way through the basics and fundamentals so that you know what I'm talking about when I mention things like *Activities* or *BroadcastReceivers*. The following is a brief introduction to the fundamental components I just mentioned. For further details please refer to the Android Dev Guide.

- *Activity*: An Activity is a component that handles user interaction. Its main purpose is to provide a user interface in the form of content view elements—for example, for text display or text input. Activities are used to visualize the program flow. They can interact with each other and the system maintains them in a stack structure. This stack structure helps especially when the system needs to navigate from one to another.

- *Service*: Services are long running processes that don't need user interaction. They are not to be mistaken for threads as they are bound to the same application process. A Service can also be used to expose functionality to other applications.

- *BroadcastReceiver*: A BroadcastReceiver is a component that receives and handles broadcasts which can be sent by the system or other applications. When implemented, it can react on certain situations such as a low battery or it can even be used to start an application.

- *ContentProvider*: A ContentProvider is used to share data between multiple applications. It provides the means to access data in databases, for example. A popular ContentProvider in the Android system is the ContentProvider for your contacts, which can be used by a lot of applications.

You can find the Android Dev Guide and several other articles at http://developer.android.com/guide/index.html.

To write the Android "Hello World" equivalent, you'll have to open the Eclipse IDE. Once started, select File ➤ New ➤ Other (see Figure 2-8).

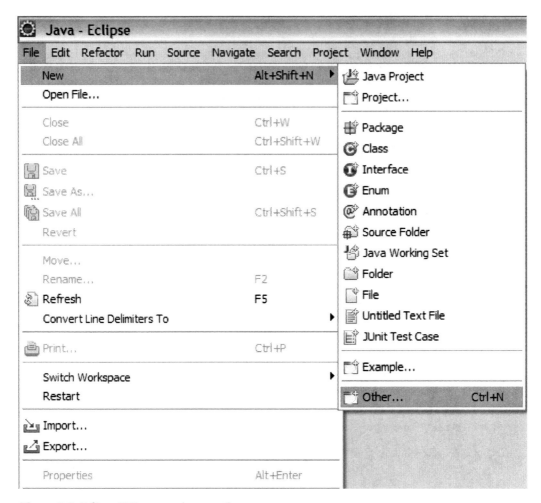

Figure 2-8. Eclipse IDE new project creation

A new dialog will pop up with a broad selection of project types. You need to select the Android Project and click Next as shown in Figure 2-9.

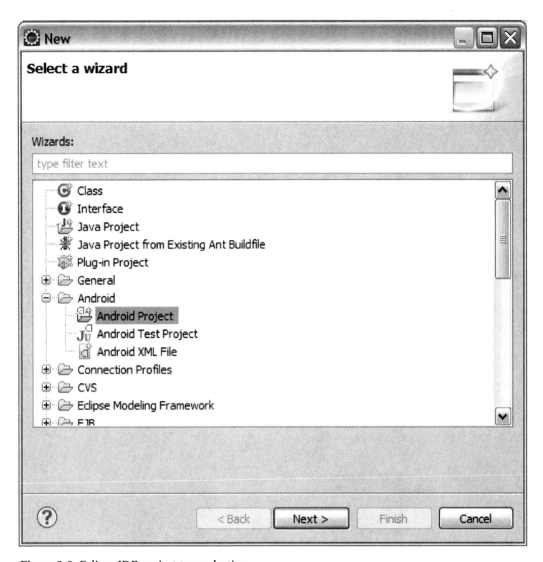

Figure 2-9. Eclipse IDE project type selection

In the next dialog you configure the project settings. Enter a name for the project, such as HelloWorld. Then select a build target. The target depends on what device you are using. If you use a device with Android Version 2.3.4 or higher then select the Google APIs platform 2.3.3 API level 10. If you are using a device with Android version 3.1 or higher, select Google APIs platform 3.1 API level 12. (See Figure 2-10.)

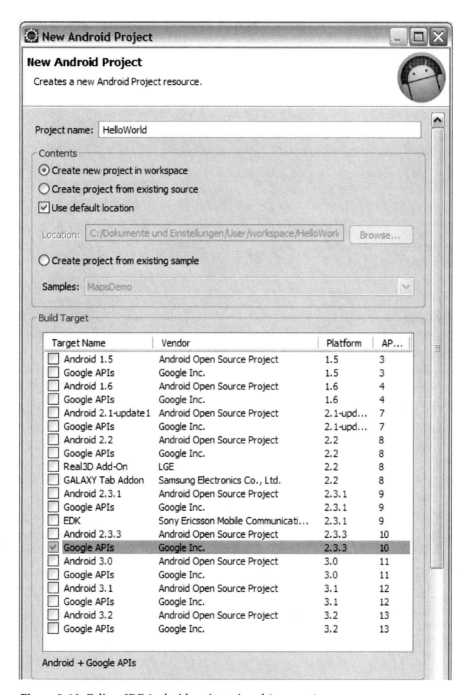

Figure 2-10. *Eclipse IDE Android project wizard (top part)*

Next, define your application name. You can also type HelloWorld. Now choose your package name. The package name will be the unique identifier in the Android Market and usually reflects your company or organization's domain name. For this example you can type helloworld.adk. Check the checkmark where it says Create Activity and type HelloWorldActivity. The Min SDK Version field describes which API levels your application is compatible with. Since you'll need the USB API features, you should choose 10 for API level 10 if you are using a 2.3.4 device or 12 for API level 12, otherwise. The rest of the settings can stay as they are. (See Figure 2-11.)

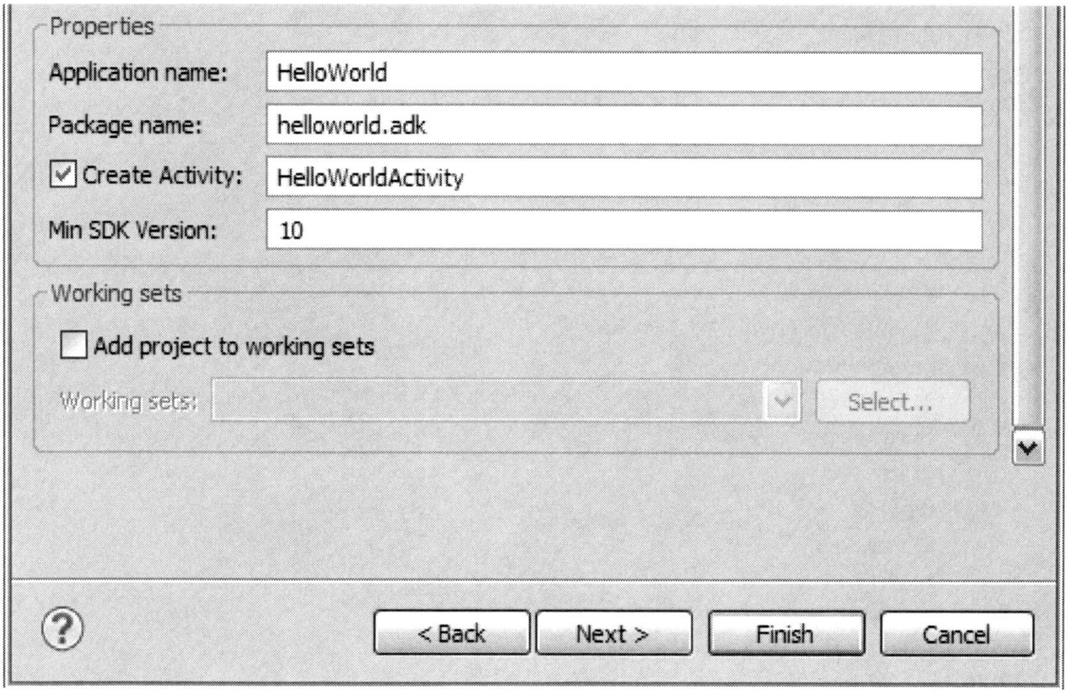

Figure 2-11. Eclipse IDE Android project wizard (bottom part)

Click Finish and wait for Eclipse to set up your first Android ADK project. Your newly created project should look like Figure 2-12.

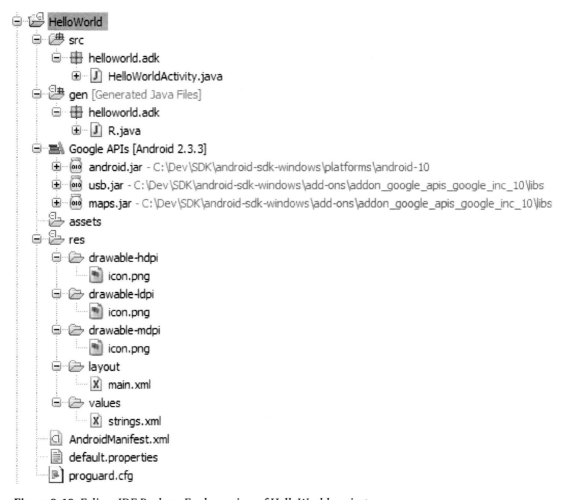

Figure 2-12. Eclipse IDE Package Explorer view of HelloWorld project

If you have a look at the Package Explorer area on the left you see that Eclipse created a new project with several folders and files. Let's see what they all mean.

The first thing you'll see is the src folder, which contains all the Java source code, you will write. You can already see that Eclipse has built your configured package structure and placed the given HelloWorldActivity.java file in it. Before taking a look at that one, you will explore the generated project some more.

Besides the src folder, there is also a folder called gen. This folder together with its content is generated automatically with each build of your project if there were changes in the resources within. Inside that folder is a file called R.java. This is a file where all your resources are indexed and mapped to integer numbers. These static numbers are used to access your resources in an easy way within your code. You should never touch the gen folder because the Android build process manages the R.java file directly and each change you do manually would be overwritten anyway in the next build.

The next things you see are the referenced libraries that will be used in your build path. You should see Google APIs with your configured target version next to it. If you expand the node you see that the project references an android.jar, which contains the system class files of your selected Android version, a usb.jar, which contains the USB specific classes you'll need for the USB communication with your ADK device, and a maps.jar, which is used for Google Maps integration.

The next folder is called assets and it usually contains additional resources that you must manage yourself. You'll have to reference them by their relative path within your application, as no references are put into the R.java file by the build system.

The second resource folder is a managed folder called res. Each resource put into that folder gets an auto-generated id within the R.java file for easy access. You can already see several subfolders inside the res folder. The drawable folders have a suffix with a screen density identifier. If you provide different images for different screen densities within those folders, the system will choose the correct files when your application is executed. There is also a folder called layout. This folder contains xml layout files that define the UI of your application. One layout file can have several view elements, which make up your user interface. The last folder you see is the values folder. In the values folder you can define xml files for static resources such as strings, dimensions, arrays, and many others.

In addition to all these folders, you will also see some standalone files: the AndroidManifest.xml, the default.properties, and the proguard.cfg. The only interesting file for you will be the AndroidManifest.xml which is the central registry for your application. Details about activities, services, permissions, mandatory device features, and many others have to be defined inside this file.

The generated project is more than just a skeleton. It is already a full-fledged application, although very rudimentary. All it does is display "Hello World, HelloWorldActivity". Let's have a look into the anatomy and the lifecycle of this application. The starting point of each Android application is the AndroidManifest.xml. Open it and have a look at its structure (Listing 2-2).

Listing 2-2. AndroidManifest.xml

```xml
<?xml version="1.0" encoding="utf-8"?>
<manifest xmlns:android="http://schemas.android.com/apk/res/android"
    package="helloworld.adk"
    android:versionCode="1"
    android:versionName="1.0">
    <uses-sdk android:minSdkVersion="10" />

    <application android:icon="@drawable/icon" android:label="@string/app_name">
        <activity android:name=".HelloWorldActivity" android:label="@string/app_name"
            android:screenOrientation="portrait">
            <intent-filter>
                <action android:name="android.intent.action.MAIN" />
                <category android:name="android.intent.category.LAUNCHER" />
            </intent-filter>
        </activity>
    </application>
</manifest>
```

You can see one application tag, the attributes of which define the icon and the label of your application. Both of these resources are referenced with the xml resource syntax @resource-type/id. The application name, which is referenced with @string/app_name, will be taken from the string defined in the strings.xml file in the res/values folder. The same resource lookup syntax applies to the drawables and all other resources you will see in any xml file.

Inside the application node you define all of your activities, services, content providers, and broadcast receivers. You have only one activity so far declared in the manifest. Take a look at that one. The name attribute has to be the class name of the activity. Since the class is within the application default package it is preceded by a dot. If you move the class to another package, make sure to update the name with the correct package structure or the system can't find it anymore.

The important thing in the activity node is the intent-filter. The intent-filter defines how the activity can be launched by the system and how it can be triggered.

In the action tag you can see that the activity is marked as the main activity of your application and will be launched first when the user starts the application.

The category tag specifies the launcher category which means that the application link, which will be put into the apps overview menu on the device, will start your activity.

On the same hierarchy level as the application tag you see the uses-sdk tag, which defines the Android API level version and is required. In this hierarchy level you would also define permissions which the user must grant in the installation process, such as, for example, accessing an accessory.

You already know where the starting point of your application is. Now let's have a look what your main activity actually does. Open the HelloWorldActivity.java file and look at its contents (Listing 2-3).

Listing 2-3. HelloWorldActivity.java

```
package helloworld.adk;

import android.app.Activity;
import android.os.Bundle;

public class HelloWorldActivity extends Activity {
    /** Called when the activity is first created. */
    @Override
    public void onCreate(Bundle savedInstanceState) {
        super.onCreate(savedInstanceState);
        setContentView(R.layout.main);
    }
}
```

As you can see, the file is really slim. The class has to extend the Activity class, which is part of the Android system. Since activities are responsible for providing a user interface, you have to provide some views to be shown to the user. Views are usually loaded at the creation time of an activity. The Android platform provides hooks into the lifecycle of an activity so that you can create resources, run your application logic, and clean up afterward in the corresponding phases of your activity. The lifecycle of an Android activity is a bit more complex than that of a simple Arduino sketch, as shown in Figure 2-13.

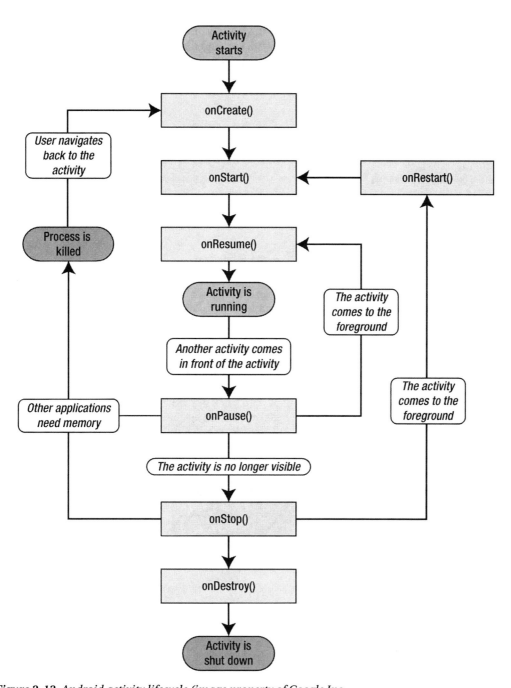

Figure 2-13. *Android activity lifecycle (image property of Google Inc.*
source: http://developer.android.com/guide/topics/fundamentals/activities.html)

You can see that the setContentView method is called with a layout resource as the parameter. This method takes the layout definition made in layout/main.xml and renders all its views onto the screen of the device. If you open this main.xml file you can see that it defines only two view elements (see Listing 2-4).

Listing 2-4. *Layout file main.xml*

```xml
<?xml version="1.0" encoding="utf-8"?>
<LinearLayout xmlns:android="http://schemas.android.com/apk/res/android"
    android:orientation="vertical"
    android:layout_width="fill_parent"
    android:layout_height="fill_parent"
    >
<TextView
    android:layout_width="fill_parent"
    android:layout_height="wrap_content"
    android:text="@string/hello"
    />
</LinearLayout>
```

The LinearLayout is a container view that can hold other Views or containers. The layout_width and layout_height attributes are set to stretch over the whole screen of the device. The orientation attribute specifies that the contained elements should be aligned vertically. The only element included in the LinearLayout right now is a TextView element. You can see from its attributes that it should fill the width of the screen but should only be as high as its own content. The text for the TextView is resolved by the @string/hello reference from the strings.xml file. If you switch from the xml editor to the graphical layout editor in Eclipse you should already see the text "Hello World, HelloWorldActivity!" on the virtual device screen. That's enough for now. Let's see the application on a real device.

Connect your Android device to your computer, right-click the project, select Run As, and choose Android Application. Your application should be packaged as an apk file and be pushed to the device for installation. If everything works correctly, you should see the application starting on your device. If the system couldn't recognize your device, due to missing drivers, for example, it will start an emulator with a default Android Virtual Device (AVD). When the application has been started, you should see something like Figure 2-14.

Figure 2-14. *HelloWorld application running on an Android device*

Getting To Know Each Other

Congratulations! You have written your first Arduino application and your first Android application. Now that you are a little bit more familiar with setting up a project and writing the code for both platforms, let's have a look at how both devices recognize each other with the help of the Open Accessory Protocol.

Extending Hello World for Arduino

The ADK reference package you downloaded earlier contains two libraries, which you will need to establish the USB communication. One is a modified version of the USB_Host_Shield library, originally created by Oleg Mazurov for Circuits@Home. The library was originally designed to work with an Arduino USB Host Shield. Only some minor modifications were made on the library since the USB chip on the ADK-compatible boards is equivalent to the USB host shield. The second library is the AndroidAccessory library, which is responsible for implementing the Open Accessory Protocol. Copy both library folders found at ADK_release_xxxx\firmware\arduino_libs\ to the libraries folder of your Arduino IDE installation at arduino-xxxx\libraries. Modify your Arduino HelloWorld sketch as shown in Listing 2-5.

Listing 2-5. Hello World Sketch Extended to Recognize Android Device

```
#include <Max3421e.h>
#include <Usb.h>
#include <AndroidAccessory.h>

#define ARRAY_SIZE 12

AndroidAccessory acc("Manufacturer", "Model", "Description",
                     "Version", "URI", "Serial");

char hello[ARRAY_SIZE] = {'h','e','l','l','o',' ',
'w','o','r','l','d','!'};

void setup() {
  Serial.begin(115200);
  acc.powerOn();
}

void loop() {
  if (acc.isConnected()) {
    for(int x = 0; x < ARRAY_SIZE; x++) {
      Serial.print(hello[x]);
      delay(250);
    }
    Serial.println();
    delay(250);
  }
}
```

As you can see, only three changes were necessary to prepare your sketch for the Open Accessory communication. The first thing you have to do here is to initialize an AndroidAccessory object, which implements the Open Accessory protocol so that you don't have to worry about it. You initialize it with some descriptive strings which define your created accessory. The fields are self-explanatory. The most important parameters are Manufacturer, Model, and Version. They will be used in the Android application to verify that you are communicating with the correct ADK board. Additionally, the URI parameter is used by the Android system to look for an appropriate Android application if none is installed. This can be a link to the Android Market or a product page.

In the setup routine you set the object into an active state with the powerOn method. The loop routine checks in each loop if something is connected to the accessory and only then executes the code within. Within this convenience method the actual connection protocol is implemented.

Three lines were all it took to enable the ADK board to recognize connected Android devices which support the accessory mode. It's as easy as that. If you upload the code to your ADK board, you will see that "hello world!" is only printed to the Serial Monitor if you connect your Android device to the ADK board. You will see something like the following printed to the Serial Monitor:

```
Device addressed... Requesting device descriptor.
found possible device. switching to serial mode
device supports protcol 1

Device addressed... Requesting device descriptor.
found android accessory device
config desc
interface desc
interface desc
5
7
```

The first paragraph tells you that, in general, a device has been recognized and that the device supports the Open Android Accessory Protocol. In the second paragraph, the device descriptor is read again to see if the Android device identifies itself as a device in accessory mode. Every USB device has such a descriptor to identify itself to the connecting system. You can see that the device was identified correctly as being accessory mode–compatible. Now the config and interface descriptor is being read and the last two numbers you will see are the input and output endpoints for the communication to be used. If everything worked out you will see that "hello world!" is printed character by character. If you want to know more about the internals of the AndroidAccessory library and how it implements the Open Accessory Protocol, you can have a look at the "Implementing the Android Accessory Protocol" section at http://developer.android.com/guide/topics/usb/adk.html.

Extending Hello World for Android

To prepare the Android application for the Open Accessory Protocol you won't have to write any code yet. The first thing you have to do is make some changes in the AndroidManifest.xml. You have to declare that you are using the USB feature. Since you want to communicate via USB, you need to declare the use of the USB library in the manifest for devices with an Android version lower than 3.1. Add the following lines to the AndroidManifest.xml:

```
<uses-feature android:name="android.hardware.usb.accessory" />

<application android:icon="@drawable/icon" android:label="@string/app_name">
    <uses-library android:name="com.android.future.usb.accessory" />
    …
</application>
```

This USB library was backported to Android version 2.3.4 and named `com.android.future.usb`. The classes for Android version 3.1 were put in the package named `android.hardware.usb`. If you want to support a broad range of devices you should use the `com.android.future.usb` package as it is compatible for both versions. On a Honeycomb device the classes in the `com.android.future.usb` package are solely wrapper classes which delegate to the classes in the `android.hardware.usb` package.

The next thing you need to declare is another intent-filter which starts the application when the Android device is connected to the accessory. Add the following lines inside the `activity` node for the `HelloWorldActivity`:

```
<activity android:name=".HelloWorldActivity" android:label="@string/app_name"
    android:screenOrientation="portrait">
    <intent-filter>
        <action android:name="android.intent.action.MAIN" />
        <category android:name="android.intent.category.LAUNCHER" />
    </intent-filter>
    <intent-filter>
        <action android:name="android.hardware.usb.action.USB_ACCESSORY_ATTACHED" />
    </intent-filter>
    <meta-data android:name="android.hardware.usb.action.USB_ACCESSORY_ATTACHED"
        android:resource="@xml/accessory_filter" />
</activity>
```

As you can see, a second intent-filter was added here which reacts on the `USB_ACCESSORY_ATTACHED` action. This triggers the `HelloWorldActivity` to be started when you attach your Android device to the ADK-compatible board. A new element has been added as well. The `meta-data` tag references additional resources, which can be provided for the intent-filters to further refine the filtering mechanism. The `accessory_filter.xml` referenced here defines a more finely grained filter criteria that will match only your accessory and no other. Create a folder named `xml` in the `/res` folder. Add a new file called `accessory_filter.xml` within that created folder. Now add the content shown in Listing 2-6 to the xml file.

Listing 2-6. *Defining a Meta File for Accessory Filtering*

```
<?xml version="1.0" encoding="utf-8"?>
<resources>
    <usb-accessory manufacturer="Manufacturer" model="Model" version="Version" />
</resources>
```

Note that the values you specify here have to be the same as in your Arduino sketch when you initialized the `AndroidAccessory` object. If those values match with the values transmitted by the board, the filter will trigger the Activity to start. Connect your Android device to your PC and upload the changed application. Now connect your device to the ADK board. You may see that a dialog pops up asking you if you want to always associate your application with the recognized intent. You can confirm that and, afterward, you will see that the application has been started. If you are experiencing that nothing happens after you connected your device, check if your filter matches the values you defined in the Arduino sketch. Another error source is that your board can't deliver enough power to power the Android device properly. As this is a requirement for the Open Accessory standard, make sure to power the board with an external power source, if necessary.

Let's Talk

So now you have ensured that both devices recognize each other but you want them to actually talk to each other. The communication is done in a rather simple self-defined protocol. Messages are sent and received via byte-streams. In an Android application this is done by reading from and writing to the input- and outputstream of a special file. On the Arduino side, the AndroidAccessory class provides methods to read and write messages. There are no constraints to what the communication protocol should look like. In the example demokit application, Google defines messages as 3-byte long byte-arrays. (See Figure 2-15). The first byte is the command type. It defines what kind of message is transmitted. The commands used in the demokit application are command types for servos, LEDs, the temperature sensor, and many others. The second byte is the actual target for that command. The Google Demo Shield has multiple LEDs and servo connectors and, to address the proper ones, the target byte is used. The third byte is the value that should be transmitted to or from that target. Generally, you can choose whatever message structure you want as you implement those messages yourself, but I would recommend sticking to the example, since you might find tutorials and examples throughout the Web that are built on the same message structure. Just keep in mind that you can only transmit bytes, so you would have to convert larger data-types accordingly. In most examples you will also follow this convention.

1-Byte	2-Byte	3-Byte
Command 0xF	Target 0xF	Value 0xF

Figure 2-15. Default message protocol defined by Google in the demokit application

For this first example, however, you will have to bend the rules a bit and define a custom protocol to transmit text messages (see Figure 2-16). The transmitted data is also a byte array, but in a slightly different form. The first byte will define the command type, the second byte will define the target, the third byte defines the length of the text message (not longer than 252 bytes), and the last remaining bytes define the actual text message.

1-Byte	2-Byte	3-Byte	n-Bytes
Command 0xF	Target 0xF	Checksum n	Message ...

Figure 2-16. Custom message protocol for sending and receiving text messages

Processing Commands for Arduino

The communication implementation in the Arduino sketch is straightforward. Extend the sketch as shown in Listing 2-7.

Listing 2-7. Communication Implementation in HelloWorld Sketch

```
#include <Max3421e.h>
#include <Usb.h>
#include <AndroidAccessory.h>

#define ARRAY_SIZE 25
#define COMMAND_TEXT 0xF
#define TARGET_DEFAULT 0xF

AndroidAccessory acc("Manufacturer", "Model", "Description",
                     "Version", "URI", "Serial");

char hello[ARRAY_SIZE] = {'H','e','l','l','o',' ',
'W','o','r','l','d',' ', 'f', 'r', 'o', 'm', ' ',
'A', 'r', 'd', 'u', 'i', 'n', 'o', '!'};

byte rcvmsg[255];
byte sntmsg[3 + ARRAY_SIZE];

void setup() {
  Serial.begin(115200);
  acc.powerOn();
}

void loop() {
  if (acc.isConnected()) {
    //read the sent text message into the byte array
    int len = acc.read(rcvmsg, sizeof(rcvmsg), 1);
    if (len > 0) {
      if (rcvmsg[0] == COMMAND_TEXT) {
        if (rcvmsg[1] == TARGET_DEFAULT){
          //get the textLength from the checksum byte
          byte textLength = rcvmsg[2];
          int textEndIndex = 3 + textLength;
          //print each character to the serial output
          for(int x = 3; x < textEndIndex; x++) {
            Serial.print((char)rcvmsg[x]);
            delay(250);
          }
          Serial.println();
          delay(250);
        }
      }
    }

    sntmsg[0] = COMMAND_TEXT;
    sntmsg[1] = TARGET_DEFAULT;
    sntmsg[2] = ARRAY_SIZE;
    for(int x = 0; x < ARRAY_SIZE; x++) {
```

```
      sntmsg[3 + x] = hello[x];
    }
    acc.write(sntmsg, 3 + ARRAY_SIZE);
    delay(250);
  }
}
```

Let's see what's new here. Since you want to send a more specific text to the Android device, you'll need to change the text message and its size constant.

```
#define ARRAY_SIZE 25
char hello[ARRAY_SIZE] = {'H','e','l','l','o',' ',
'W','o','r','l','d',' ', 'f', 'r', 'o', 'm', ' ',
'A', 'r', 'd', 'u', 'i', 'n', 'o', '!'};
```

The next thing you need to do is declare a byte array for the received message and one for the message to be sent.

```
byte rcvmsg[255];
byte sntmsg[3 + ARRAY_SIZE];
```

Note that the size of the byte array to be sent is as large as the message itself plus the additional bytes for the command type, the target, and the checksum. The command type byte and the target byte can be defined as constants as well.

```
#define COMMAND_TEXT 0xF
#define TARGET_DEFAULT 0xF
```

In the loop method you will handle the receiving and the sending of a message. First have a look at how a message is received:

```
if (acc.isConnected()) {
  //read the sent text message into the byte array
  int len = acc.read(rcvmsg, sizeof(rcvmsg), 1);
  if (len > 0) {
    if (rcvmsg[0] == COMMAND_TEXT) {
      if (rcvmsg[1] == TARGET_DEFAULT){
        //get the textLength from the checksum byte
        byte textLength = rcvmsg[2];
        int textEndIndex = 3 + textLength;
        //print each character to the serial output
        for(int x = 3; x < textEndIndex; x++) {
          Serial.print((char)rcvmsg[x]);
          delay(250);
        }
        Serial.println();
        delay(250);
      }
    }
  }
  ...
}
```

The read method of the AndroidAccessory object reads the inputstream and copies its content into the provided byte array. As parameters, the read method takes the byte array which should be filled, the length of that byte array, and a threshold value in case the transmission is not acknowledged. Afterward, a check is performed to see if the correct command and target type were transmitted; only then is the length of the transmitted message determined. The actual text message is read from the byte array within the for-loop and printed character by character to the serial output. After a message was received, another message is sent to the Android device, as shown here:

```
if (acc.isConnected()) {
  …
  sntmsg[0] = COMMAND_TEXT;
  sntmsg[1] = TARGET_DEFAULT;
  sntmsg[2] = ARRAY_SIZE;
  for(int x = 0; x < ARRAY_SIZE; x++) {
    sntmsg[3 + x] = hello[x];
  }
  acc.write(sntmsg, 3 + ARRAY_SIZE);
  delay(250);
}
```

Again, the byte array to be sent is built according to the self-defined protocol. The first byte is set with the command type constant, the second byte is set with the target constant and the third byte is set with the size of the actual text message as a checksum. Now the program loops through the hello char array to fill the byte array with the text message. When the byte array is all set, the write method of the AndroidAccessory object is called to transmit the data over the outputstream to the Android device. The write method has two parameters: the byte array to be transmitted and the size of the transmission in bytes.

As you can see, the Arduino sketch is very simple and the AndroidAccessory object does all the dirty work for you. Now let's have a look into the Android communication part.

Processing Commands for Android

Implementing the communication part in Android requires a bit more work than on the Arduino side. Extend the HelloWorldActivity class as shown in Listing 2-8. You will learn what each code snippet does after that.

Listing 2-8. HelloWorldActivity.java (Imports and Variables)

```
package helloworld.adk;

import java.io.FileDescriptor;
import java.io.FileInputStream;
import java.io.FileOutputStream;
import java.io.IOException;

import android.app.Activity;
import android.app.PendingIntent;
import android.content.BroadcastReceiver;
import android.content.Context;
import android.content.Intent;
import android.content.IntentFilter;
import android.os.Bundle;
import android.os.ParcelFileDescriptor;
import android.util.Log;
```

```
import android.widget.TextView;

import com.android.future.usb.UsbAccessory;
import com.android.future.usb.UsbManager;

public class HelloWorldActivity extends Activity {

    private static final String TAG = HelloWorldActivity.class.getSimpleName();

    private PendingIntent mPermissionIntent;
    private static final String ACTION_USB_PERMISSION = "com.android.example.USB_PERMISSION";
    private boolean mPermissionRequestPending;

    private UsbManager mUsbManager;
    private UsbAccessory mAccessory;
    private ParcelFileDescriptor mFileDescriptor;
    private FileInputStream mInputStream;
    private FileOutputStream mOutputStream;

    private static final byte COMMAND_TEXT = 0xF;
    private static final byte TARGET_DEFAULT = 0xF;

    private TextView textView;

    ...
```

First let's have a look at the variable declarations you need to make.

```
private static final String TAG = HelloWorldActivity.class.getSimpleName();
```

The constant TAG is an identifier for the current class and is used only for logging purposes in Android. If you have a look at the logcat view in Eclipse while a device or an emulator is running, you will see that logged messages are associated to a TAG, which simplifies reading the log output. (See Figure 2-17.) You can define any string for that purpose, but it is a good idea to use the application name or even the class name for debugging purposes.

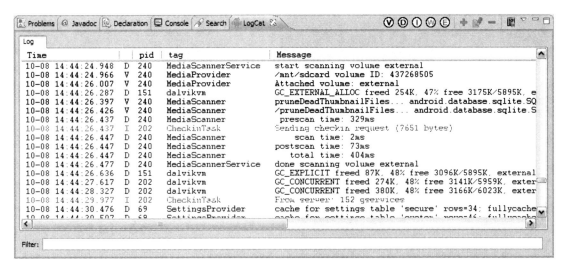

Figure 2-17. *Eclipse logcat view*

```
private static final byte COMMAND_TEXT = 0xF;
private static final byte TARGET_DEFAULT = 0xF;
```

COMMAND_TEXT and TARGET_DEFAULT are the same constants as the ones used in the Arduino sketch. They make up the first two bytes of the data protocol.

```
private PendingIntent mPermissionIntent;
private static final String ACTION_USB_PERMISSION = "com.android.example.USB_PERMISSION";
private boolean mPermissionRequestPending;
```

Establishing a connection to an external device has to be permitted by the user. When the user is granting the rights to connect to your ADK board, the PendingIntent will broadcast the ACTION_USB_PERMISSION with a flag reflecting whether the user confirmed or denied the access. The Boolean variable mPermissionRequestPending is only used to not show the permission dialog again if the user interaction is still pending.

```
private UsbManager mUsbManager;
private UsbAccessory mAccessory;
private ParcelFileDescriptor mFileDescriptor;
private FileInputStream mInputStream;
private FileOutputStream mOutputStream;
```

The UsbManager is a system service that manages all interaction with the USB port of the device. It is used to enumerate the connected devices and to request and check the permission to connect to an accessory. The UsbManager is also responsible for opening the connection to the external device. The UsbAccessory is a reference to the connected accessory. The ParcelFileDescriptor is obtained when the connection to the accessory is established. It is used to get access to the input- and outputstream of the accessory.

```
private TextView textView;
```

The only user-visible UI element is the textView, which should display the transmitted message from the ADK board.

That's all about the variables you'll need to declare. Now we will have a look at the lifecycle methods of the activity (Listing 2-9).

Listing 2-9. HelloWorldActivity.java (Lifecycle Methods)

```java
/** Called when the activity is first created. */
@Override
public void onCreate(Bundle savedInstanceState) {
    super.onCreate(savedInstanceState);

    mUsbManager = UsbManager.getInstance(this);
    mPermissionIntent = PendingIntent.getBroadcast(this, 0, new Intent(
        ACTION_USB_PERMISSION), 0);
    IntentFilter filter = new IntentFilter(ACTION_USB_PERMISSION);
    filter.addAction(UsbManager.ACTION_USB_ACCESSORY_DETACHED);
    registerReceiver(mUsbReceiver, filter);

    setContentView(R.layout.main);
    textView = (TextView) findViewById(R.id.textView);
}

/** Called when the activity is resumed from its paused state and
immediately after onCreate(). */
@Override
public void onResume() {
    super.onResume();

    if (mInputStream != null && mOutputStream != null) {
        return;
    }

    UsbAccessory[] accessories = mUsbManager.getAccessoryList();
    UsbAccessory accessory = (accessories == null ? null : accessories[0]);
    if (accessory != null) {
        if (mUsbManager.hasPermission(accessory)) {
            openAccessory(accessory);
        } else {
            synchronized (mUsbReceiver) {
                if (!mPermissionRequestPending) {
                    mUsbManager.requestPermission(accessory, mPermissionIntent);
                    mPermissionRequestPending = true;
                }
            }
        }
    } else {
        Log.d(TAG, "mAccessory is null");
    }
}

/** Called when the activity is paused by the system. */
@Override
public void onPause() {
```

```
        super.onPause();
        closeAccessory();
    }

    /** Called when the activity is no longer needed prior to being
    removed from the activity stack. */
    @Override
    public void onDestroy() {
        super.onDestroy();
        unregisterReceiver(mUsbReceiver);
    }
```

The first lifecycle callback method of each activity class is the onCreate method. This method is usually the place where you make your basic initializations. Be careful, though. The onCreate method is only called once when the activity is created by the system. The activity will live on until the system needs to free up memory and kills it or if you explicitly call the finish method on that activity to tell the system that the activity is no longer needed.

```
    /** Called when the activity is first created. */
    @Override
    public void onCreate(Bundle savedInstanceState) {
        super.onCreate(savedInstanceState);

        mUsbManager = UsbManager.getInstance(this);
        mPermissionIntent = PendingIntent.getBroadcast(this, 0, new Intent(
                        ACTION_USB_PERMISSION), 0);
        IntentFilter filter = new IntentFilter(ACTION_USB_PERMISSION);
        filter.addAction(UsbManager.ACTION_USB_ACCESSORY_DETACHED);
        registerReceiver(mUsbReceiver, filter);

        setContentView(R.layout.main);
        textView = (TextView) findViewById(R.id.textView);
    }
```

The most important thing that needs to be done in lifecycle callback methods is to delegate the call to the parent class that is extended; otherwise, an exception will occur. The delegating call super.onCreate(savedInstanceState) allows the parent activity class to do all its initialization logic and then the HelloWorldActivity can continue with its own initialization. Next, a reference to the USB system service is obtained so that you can call its methods later on. Now a PendingIntent with the ACTION_USB_PERMISSION parameter is defined. You will need it when you request the user's permission to connect to a USB device. The intent filter you see here is used in conjunction with a broadcast receiver to make sure that the application only listens to certain broadcasts. The filter defines that it reacts on the ACTION_USB_PERMISSION action you defined as a constant in the beginning and on the ACTION_USB_ACCESSORY_DETACHED action, for when the ADK accessory is disconnected. The registerReceiver method registers the broadcast receiver with the described intent filter at the system. So when a broadcast is sent by the system, the broadcast receiver will be notified and can take the relevant action.

The last thing you need to do in the onCreate method is set up your UI elements so that the user can actually see something happening. You already learned that UI layouts in Android are mostly defined in xml files. Again you use the setContentView method to load your layout. The last line in the code is used to get a reference to a view element from that layout, so that it can be managed in the code. The findViewById method takes a view identifier and returns the generic view element for that reference. That's the reason why you need to make a cast to the proper implementation of that view element. To be able to reference Views from a layout xml file those views need to have an identifier defined. Open the main.xml file at res/layout/ and add the id attribute to the TextView.

```
<TextView
    android:id="@+id/textView"
    android:layout_width="fill_parent"
    android:layout_height="wrap_content"
    android:text="@string/hello"
/>
```

A new syntax for dynamic resource generation can be seen here. The syntax @+id/textView means that this view element should have the id textView assigned to it. The plus sign in front of id means, that if this id doesn't exist already in the R.java file, it should be created as a new reference there.

You have completed the creation phase of the Activity. Now you get to the next important lifecycle phase, the onResume lifecycle hook. The onResume method is called each time your activity returns from its paused state. When you leave your activity to start a new one or to return to your device's home screen, your activity will be set into a pause state rather than to be killed. This is done by the system to preserve time and memory allocation in case the activity is shown again shortly. In the paused state the activity is no longer visible to the user. If the activity should be shown again it is only returned from its paused state and set into a resumed state rather than fully initialized again. When this happens, the onResume lifecycle method is called. The onResume method should not be responsible for doing major initializations. In this case it should rather check if you are still able to communicate with the accessory. That's exactly what you are doing here.

```
@Override
public void onResume() {
    super.onResume();

    if (mInputStream != null && mOutputStream != null) {
        return;
    }

    UsbAccessory[] accessories = mUsbManager.getAccessoryList();
    UsbAccessory accessory = (accessories == null ? null : accessories[0]);
    if (accessory != null) {
        if (mUsbManager.hasPermission(accessory)) {
            openAccessory(accessory);
        } else {
            synchronized (mUsbReceiver) {
                if (!mPermissionRequestPending) {
                    mUsbManager.requestPermission(accessory, mPermissionIntent);
                    mPermissionRequestPending = true;
                }
            }
        }
    } else {
        Log.d(TAG, "mAccessory is null");
    }
}
```

If the input- and outputstream is still active you are good to go for communication and can return prematurely from the onResume method. Otherwise, you have to get a reference of the accessory from the UsbManager. If you already have the user's permission to communicate with the device you can open and reassign the input- and outputstreams. This part is implemented in an own method called openAccessory, but more on that later. The last two lifecycle methods I want to talk about here are the onPause method and the onDestroy method.

```
@Override
public void onPause() {
    super.onPause();
    closeAccessory();
}

@Override
public void onDestroy() {
    super.onDestroy();
    unregisterReceiver(mUsbReceiver);
}
```

The opposite of the onResume method is the onPause method. You already learned about the paused state of an activity and, since you open the connection to your accessory in the onResume method, you should care about closing the connection to free up memory in the onPause method.

If the lifecycle method onDestroy is called, your Activity will be killed and is no longer present on the applications activity stack. This lifecycle phase can be described as the opposite of the onCreate method. Whereas you did all your initializations in the onCreate phase, you would do deinitializations and clean ups in the onDestroy phase. Since the application has only this single activity, the application will be killed as well by the system when onDestroy is called on the activity. You registered a broadcast receiver at creation time to listen to your accessory-specific events. As the application ceases to exist you should unregister this broadcast receiver in here. For that purpose the unregisterReceiver method is called with the broadcast receiver as the parameter.

That concludes the lifecycle methods. So far it has been fairly easy. The implementation of the communication part looks a bit tricky at first, but don't worry. I'll guide you through it (see Listing 2-10).

Listing 2-10. HelloWorldActivity.java (Establishing the Accessory Connection)

```
private final BroadcastReceiver mUsbReceiver = new BroadcastReceiver() {
    @Override
    public void onReceive(Context context, Intent intent) {
        String action = intent.getAction();
        if (ACTION_USB_PERMISSION.equals(action)) {
            synchronized (this) {
                UsbAccessory accessory = UsbManager.getAccessory(intent);
                if (intent.getBooleanExtra(UsbManager.EXTRA_PERMISSION_GRANTED, false)) {
                    openAccessory(accessory);
                } else {
                    Log.d(TAG, "permission denied for accessory " + accessory);
                }
                mPermissionRequestPending = false;
            }
        } else if (UsbManager.ACTION_USB_ACCESSORY_DETACHED.equals(action)) {
            UsbAccessory accessory = UsbManager.getAccessory(intent);
            if (accessory != null && accessory.equals(mAccessory)) {
```

```
                    closeAccessory();
                }
            }
        }
    };

    private void openAccessory(UsbAccessory accessory) {
        mFileDescriptor = mUsbManager.openAccessory(accessory);
        if (mFileDescriptor != null) {
            mAccessory = accessory;
            FileDescriptor fd = mFileDescriptor.getFileDescriptor();
            mInputStream = new FileInputStream(fd);
            mOutputStream = new FileOutputStream(fd);
            Thread thread = new Thread(null, commRunnable, TAG);
            thread.start();
            Log.d(TAG, "accessory opened");
        } else {
            Log.d(TAG, "accessory open fail");
        }
    }

    private void closeAccessory() {
        try {
            if (mFileDescriptor != null) {
                mFileDescriptor.close();
            }
        } catch (IOException e) {
        } finally {
            mFileDescriptor = null;
            mAccessory = null;
        }
    }
```

The first thing you see here is the implementation of a BroadcastReceiver. You know now that you need to register and unregister a broadcast receiver in the respective lifecycle methods, but now let's see how the broadcast receiver should be implemented.

```
private final BroadcastReceiver mUsbReceiver = new BroadcastReceiver() {

    @Override
    public void onReceive(Context context, Intent intent) {
        String action = intent.getAction();
        if (ACTION_USB_PERMISSION.equals(action)) {
            synchronized (this) {
                UsbAccessory accessory = UsbManager.getAccessory(intent);
                if (intent.getBooleanExtra(UsbManager.EXTRA_PERMISSION_GRANTED, false)) {
                    openAccessory(accessory);
                } else {
                    Log.d(TAG, "permission denied for accessory " + accessory);
                }
                mPermissionRequestPending = false;
            }
        } else if (UsbManager.ACTION_USB_ACCESSORY_DETACHED.equals(action)) {
```

```
            UsbAccessory accessory = UsbManager.getAccessory(intent);
            if (accessory != null && accessory.equals(mAccessory)) {
                closeAccessory();
            }
        }
    }
};
```

The broadcast receiver is implemented as an anonymous inner class for the type BroadcastReceiver. The only method you'll have to overwrite is the onReceive method which is called by the system if this broadcast receiver is registered and matches the provided intent-filter. Remember that two actions are defined in the intent-filter. You will have to check which action occurred when the broadcast receiver is called. If you receive the action describing that a permission request has been answered you'll have to check if the user granted permission to communicate with your accessory. If so, you can open the communication channels of the accessory. The second action which could have triggered the broadcast receiver is the notification that the accessory has been detached from the Android device. In that case, you need to clean up and close your communication channels. As you can see, the BroadcastReceiver calls the openAccessory method and the closeAccessory method to open and close the communication channels to the accessory. Let's have a look at those methods next.

```
private void openAccessory(UsbAccessory accessory) {
    mFileDescriptor = mUsbManager.openAccessory(accessory);
    if (mFileDescriptor != null) {
        mAccessory = accessory;
        FileDescriptor fd = mFileDescriptor.getFileDescriptor();
        mInputStream = new FileInputStream(fd);
        mOutputStream = new FileOutputStream(fd);
        Thread thread = new Thread(null, commRunnable, TAG);
        thread.start();
        Log.d(TAG, "accessory opened");
    } else {
        Log.d(TAG, "accessory open fail");
    }
}
```

In the openAccessory method you delegate to the USB service method, which is also called openAccessory, to obtain a FileDescriptor for your accessory. The FileDescriptor manages the input- and outputstream which you will use to communicate with your device. Once the streams have been assigned you will also start a separate thread which will do the actual receiving and sending of messages, but more on that later.

If you don't have the permission to connect to your accessory yet and you are not in a pending state for the user's permission, you must request permission for your accessory by calling the requestPermission method on the USB service. The requestPermission method has two parameters, the accessory for which you request the permission and a pending intent. This pending intent is the mPermissionIntent you defined in the onCreate method and it's responsible for sending a broadcast with the ACTION_USB_PERMISSION as soon as the user grants or denies permission to communicate with the accessory. As you may remember, you registered a broadcast receiver in the onCreate method as well, which has an intent-filter for that exact same action. Once the broadcast is sent, the broadcast receiver will react on it.

The closeAccessory method is responsible for closing all remaining open connections to the accessory.

```
private void closeAccessory() {
    try {
        if (mFileDescriptor != null) {
            mFileDescriptor.close();
        }
    } catch (IOException e) {
    } finally {
        mFileDescriptor = null;
        mAccessory = null;
    }
}
```

All it does is close the accessory's FileDescriptor. The system will handle all underlying OS resources associated with its streams.

When you finally open a connection to the accessory, you can send and receive data back and forth. Listing 2-11 shows the actual communication implementation.

Listing 2-11. HelloWorldActivity.java (Communication Implementation)

```
Runnable commRunnable = new Runnable() {

    @Override
    public void run() {
        int ret = 0;
        byte[] buffer = new byte[255];

        while (ret >= 0) {
            try {
                ret = mInputStream.read(buffer);
            } catch (IOException e) {
                break;
            }

            switch (buffer[0]) {
                case COMMAND_TEXT:

                    final StringBuilder textBuilder = new StringBuilder();
                    int textLength = buffer[2];
                    int textEndIndex = 3 + textLength;
                    for (int x = 3; x < textEndIndex; x++) {
                        textBuilder.append((char) buffer[x]);
                    }

                    runOnUiThread(new Runnable() {

                        @Override
                        public void run() {
                            textView.setText(textBuilder.toString());
                        }
                    });
```

```
                    sendText(COMMAND_TEXT, TARGET_DEFAULT, "Hello World from Android!");
                    break;

                default:
                    Log.d(TAG, "unknown msg: " + buffer[0]);
                    break;
            }

        }
    }
};

public void sendText(byte command, byte target, String text) {
    int textLength = text.length();
    byte[] buffer = new byte[3 + textLength];
    if (textLength <= 252) {
        buffer[0] = command;
        buffer[1] = target;
        buffer[2] = (byte) textLength;
        byte[] textInBytes = text.getBytes();
        for (int x = 0; x < textLength; x++) {
            buffer[3 + x] = textInBytes[x];
        }
        if (mOutputStream != null) {
            try {
                mOutputStream.write(buffer);
            } catch (IOException e) {
                Log.e(TAG, "write failed", e);
            }
        }
    }
}
```

Once you have established a connection to the accessory, you can begin with the actual sending and receiving of messages. As you may remember, a separate thread was started in the openAccessory method which is responsible for the message handling.

```
Thread thread = new Thread(null, commRunnable, TAG);
thread.start();
```

The Runnable object, which is passed to the thread, is also an anonymous inner class you have to implement. Its run method will be executed as long as you have an active inputstream from your accessory.

```
Runnable commRunnable = new Runnable() {

    @Override
    public void run() {
        int ret = 0;
        byte[] buffer = new byte[255];

        while (ret >= 0) {
            try {
```

```
                    ret = mInputStream.read(buffer);
                } catch (IOException e) {
                    break;
                }


                switch (buffer[0]) {
                case COMMAND_TEXT:
                    final StringBuilder textBuilder = new StringBuilder();
                    int textLength = buffer[2];
                    int textEndIndex = 3 + textLength;
                    for (int x = 3; x < textEndIndex; x++) {
                        textBuilder.append((char) buffer[x]);
                    }

                    runOnUiThread(new Runnable() {

                        @Override
                        public void run() {
                            textView.setText(textBuilder.toString());
                        }
                    });
                    sendText(COMMAND_TEXT, TARGET_DEFAULT, "Hello World from Android!");
                    break;

                default:
                    Log.d(TAG, "unknown msg: " + buffer[0]);
                    break;
                }
            }
        }
    }
};
```

In each iteration step, the content of the inputstream is read into a byte array. If the first byte depicts that you received a message of the type COMMAND_TEXT, a StringBuilder will be used to build the message from the remaining bytes that were sent.

Now that you have crafted the message, you need to display it to the user. Remember that you are still in a separate thread. The system only allows UI updates to happen on the UI thread. To update the text of your TextView UI element you use the convenience method runOnUiThread, which executes the given Runnable object on the system UI thread.

That's all for the receiving part of the message handling. After a message is received, another one is immediately sent back to the board. For that purpose you will write your own method called sendText, which takes the first two identifier bytes and the actual message to build your message data structure, which you can send via the outputstream to the accessory.

```
public void sendText(byte command, byte target, String text) {
    int textLength = text.length();
    byte[] buffer = new byte[3 + textLength];
    if (textLength <= 252) {
        buffer[0] = command;
        buffer[1] = target;
        buffer[2] = (byte) textLength;
```

```
            byte[] textInBytes = text.getBytes();
            for (int x = 0; x < textLength; x++) {
                buffer[3 + x] = textInBytes[x];
            }
            if (mOutputStream != null) {
                try {
                    mOutputStream.write(buffer);
                } catch (IOException e) {
                    Log.e(TAG, "write failed", e);
                }
            }
        }
    }
}
```

Congratulations! You have finished implementing both sides of the communication. Now upload the Arduino sketch to your ADK board and deploy the Android application onto your device. If you connect your Android device to your ADK board, you should see that your Android application is started automatically and that it will print the messages sent by the ADK board. If you open the Serial Monitor while your board is connected to your PC you can see the incoming messages from your Android device. Each device shows the other's message, as shown in Figure 2-18 and Figure 2-19.

Figure 2-18. The HelloWorld application on the Android device receiving messages

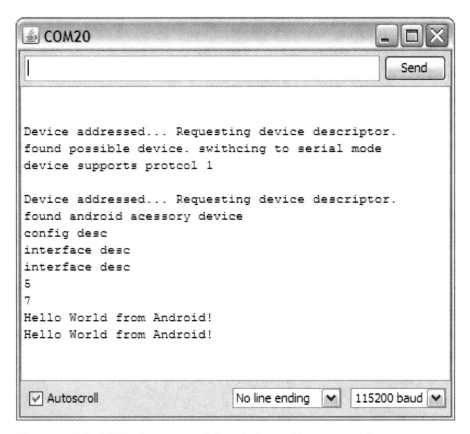

Figure 2-19. Serial Monitor output of the Arduino application receiving messages

Summary

You have learned how an Android device and an Arduino accessory recognize each other when they are connected. You learned what is necessary to implement the Open Accessory protocol on the Arduino side as well as on the Android side of the communication. The implementation on the Arduino side is rather simple, as most of the work is already done with the help of the AndroidAccessory Arduino library. You have already seen that the software challenge lies rather in the coding for the Android device since a lot more work has to be done there. This chapter showed you how you can transmit text messages across both platforms by using a self-defined data structure. The next chapters will build on what you have already learned to enable you to read sensor values or control actuators with your ADK board. The project you completed here will be the foundation for upcoming examples in this book.

CHAPTER 3

Outputs

An ADK board derived from the original Arduino design has several pins and connectors. The majority of those pins are digital pins. The digital pins on such an ADK board are capable of being configured as inputs or outputs. This chapter describes how the digital pins can be used when configured as output pins.

What does *output* mean in this particular case? It means that a pin will emit power when set to output mode. The digital pins on an Arduino-derived ADK board can emit up to 5V. They can be used in a digital context where they can take two states, HIGH and LOW. To set an output pin to HIGH means that it will emit 5V. If it is set to LOW it emits 0V, so no voltage at all. Some output pins can also be used in an analog context. This means that they are able to emit a range of output values from 0V to 5V.

The following two projects will explain both use cases in a practical application.

Project 1: Toggle an LED

This is the first of many projects in which you will use additional hardware parts. You will utilize a digital pin of the ADK board as an output port to power a light-emitting diode (LED) and you will write an Android application with which you can turn on and off this LED.

The Parts

You will use the following hardware in this project (shown in Figure 3-1):

- ADK board
- Breadboard
- LED operating at 5V
- 220Ω resistor
- Some wires

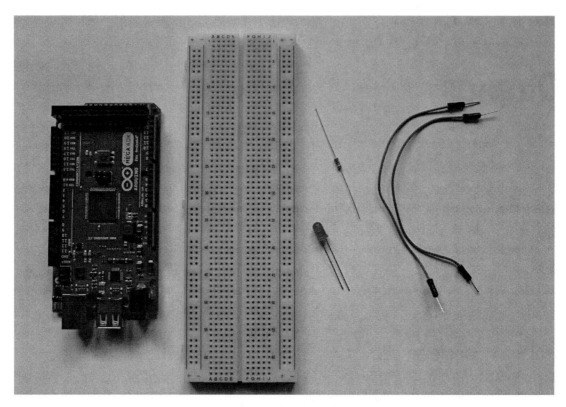

Figure 3-1. *Project 1 parts (ADK board, breadboard, resistor, LED, wires)*

LED

A *light-emitting diode* (LED) is a small semiconductor that acts as a light source (see Figure 3-2). LEDs can be found on nearly all electronic devices in your household. Mostly they are used as status indicators. LEDs are designed to be very energy efficient and reliable. That's why they have also found their way into art installations, car headlights, and normal home lighting solutions, just to name a few uses.

Figure 3-2. 5mm red LED

There are numerous types of LEDs. They differentiate in size, color spectrum, and operating voltage. LEDs are directional, which means it matters how you connect them in a circuit. Normal LEDs have an anode (positive connector) and a cathode (negative connector). You must connect the positive end of your energy source to the anode and the negative end to the cathode. If you connect it the other way around you will damage it permanently. On a normal LED you can differentiate the connectors in several ways. You may notice that the legs of the LED have different lengths. The long leg is the anode (positive connector) and the short leg is the cathode (negative connector). If you have a transparent LED lens you might see that both LED connectors have a different form at their embedded end. The smaller one that looks like a half of an arrow is the so-called *post*. The post is the embedded end of the anode connector. The cathode embedded part is called the *anvil*. Some LEDs also have a flattened spot on one side of their lens. This side marks the cathode. You see that a lot has been done to differentiate both connectors so that you don't accidentally destroy your LED by connecting it in the wrong way.

In this project you will use a digital output port of the ADK board which operates at 5V when it is set to HIGH and 0V when it is set to LOW. You should use an LED which also operates at 5V so that it has a longer lifespan. You could also use a lower-rated LED for 3.3V, but the higher voltage level will wear out that LED much more quickly. LEDs usually operate at a current of 20mA to 30mA and you should limit the current that is flowing so that the LED won't be damaged by a higher current. To limit the current flow, you use a resistor. LEDs should never be used without such a current-limiting resistor.

Resistor

A resistor is an electrical component used to limit the current flowing in a circuit. The resistance is the ratio of the voltage applied across the resistor in direct proportion to the current flowing through it. This ratio is defined in Ohm's law. *Ohm's law* is one of the most important formulas in electrical engineering. You will need it very often to decide which resistor to use in a circuit to limit the current so that you don't end up frying your components. The formula is defined in the following way:

$V = R \times I$

As you can see, the voltage is the product of the resistance and the current. Voltage is measured in volts and has the unit-symbol V. Current is measured in amperes and has the unit-symbol A. Resistance is measured in ohms and as a unit-symbol it has the greek letter Ω. In a simple example the formula can be applied like that:

$5V = 250\Omega \times 0.02A$

The standard 3mm and 5mm LEDs operate at a current limit of 20mA to 30mA. You want to limit the current to about 30mA and your digital output ports supply a voltage of 5V when they are set to HIGH. If you apply Ohm's law and rearrange it you can calculate the resistance value of your needed resistor.

$$R = \frac{5V}{30mA}$$
$$R = \frac{5V}{0.03A}$$
$$R = 166\Omega$$

Resistors come in standardized ranges and you won't find specific values like 166Ω. You should always use the next higher resistance value available and never a lower value as you don't want to damage your components permanently from overload. The next higher resistance value that can be found is the 220Ω resistor.

You have already learned how to determine which resistance value you will need in this project. Now let's have a look at the kind of resistors that are common and how you can identify their value by looking at them.

Resistors come in many forms and sizes but the most commonly used resistors besides the small surface mount devices (SMDs) are carbon-compound resistors and film resistors, shown in Figure 3-3.

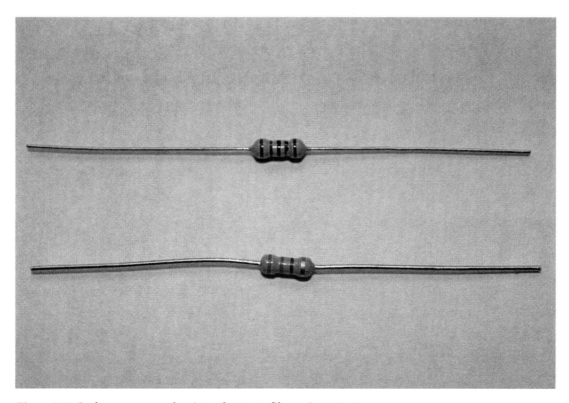

Figure 3-3. Carbon-compound resistor (bottom), film resistor (top)

Carbon-compound resistors consist of carbon and other compounds, hence the name. The resistance value depends on the amount of carbon in that mix. Carbon-compound resistors are generally more robust than other resistors as they can handle high pulses better without long lasting effects on their resistive value. The downside to that is that they are not the most accurate resistors.

A film resistor has an insulating ceramic rod or substrate covered by a film of metal. The thickness of the metal coating determines the resistive property of the resistor. Film resistors are less robust than the carbon-compound resistors as they are vulnerable to high pulses and overloads that can damage their resistive capabilities. The upside with those resistors is that they are more accurate than the carbon-compound resistors.

The criteria mentioned above should be considered in productive circuit designs but are not applicable to our simple projects.

Both resistor types have colored bands painted on their surface. Those bands help to identify the resistance value of a resistor. Carbon-compound resistors have a 4-band color coding whereas film resistors have a 5-band color coding.

Table 3-1 gives you an overview of color coding.

Table 3-1. Resistor Color Coding (* 3rd Band Is Only Used for Film Resistors)

Color	1st Band	2nd Band	3rd Band*	Multiplier	Tolerance
Black	0	0	0	1Ω	-
Brown	1	1	1	10Ω	+- 1%
Red	2	2	2	100Ω	+- 2%
Orange	3	3	3	1KΩ	-
Yellow	4	4	4	10KΩ	-
Green	5	5	5	100KΩ	+- 0.5%
Blue	6	6	6	1MΩ	+- 0.25%
Violet	7	7	7	10MΩ	+- 0.1%
Grey	8	8	8	-	+- 0.05%
White	9	9	9	-	-
Gold	-	-	-	0.1	+- 5%
Silver	-	-	-	0.01	+- 10%

You might wonder from which end of the resistor you should read the colored bands. If you look closely you can see that one band has a slightly bigger distance to the other ones. This is the tolerance band. Figure 3-4 shows a 4-band carbon-compound 220 Ω resistor with a +- 5% tolerance. The first band is red (2), the second band is red (2), and the multiplier band is brown (10), which translates to 22 × 10Ω = 220Ω. The tolerance band is gold (+- 5%).

Figure 3-4. 220Ω +- 5% carbon-compound resistor

Breadboard

A *breadboard,* also called protoboard, is a prototyping board that doesn't require soldering. It is usually a block of plastic with perforated holes in it. Those holes usually have a standardized spacing of 0.1" (2.54 mm).

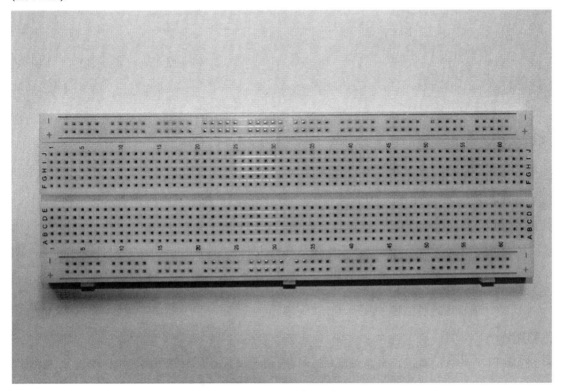

Figure 3-5. Breadboard/protoboard

Embedded into the board are conductive contact points aligned in a special layout. Those boards allow a plug-and-play mechanism so that you can concentrate on your circuit setup instead of soldering everything together. This way you can quickly adjust the circuit if you made mistakes in the setup. The boards come in many forms and sizes but the basic layout is mostly the same. The contacts at the top and bottom rail are mostly used for connecting the positive and the negative port of the power supply. The area in the middle of the board is the actual prototyping area. The connection layout embedded into the breadboard looks like Figure 3-6.

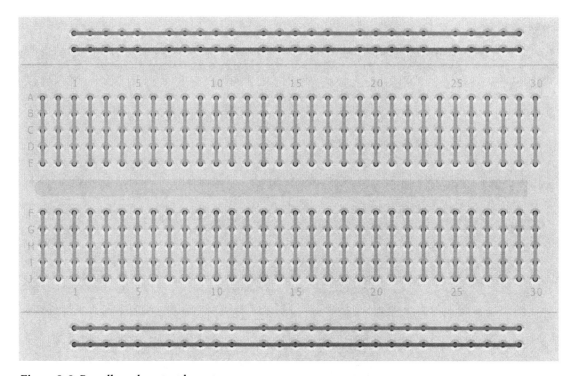

Figure 3-6. *Breadboard contact layout*

ADK Board

In Chapter 1 you learned about the specifications of your ADK board. The Arduino-derived ADK boards have several digital input and output pins. You will use one of those pins as an output port to switch the LED on and off. The output ports can provide a voltage of up to 5V. You will be using the digital output pin 2 which is seen in Figure 3-7 and you will set the output value in a digital context (HIGH/LOW).

Figure 3-7. *Digital output pin 2*

Wires

You will need some wires to connect the resistor and the LED on the breadboard to the ADK board. For prototyping and for work with a breadboard there are special breadboard or jumper wires. The advantage of using those wires is that you don't have to strip them yourself, they come in different lengths, and they are available with male and female connectors.

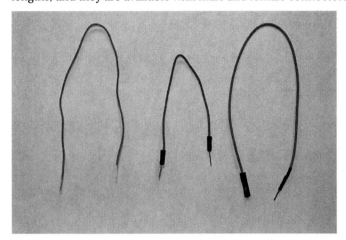

Figure 3-8. From left: electronics wire, jumper wire (male to male), jumper wire (female to male)

If you don't want to buy prepared wires you can also use electronics or bell wire. You will have to strip the wire ends on those wires to expose about 3/16" to 5/16" (5mm to 8mm) of the wire to enable a good contact to the contacts embedded in the breadboard. You can use a knife to carefully cut around the wire insulator and strip it off, but I would highly recommend using a cable stripper which is a much safer tool and easier to apply. You just get a grip around the wire, apply some soft pressure, and strip the isolator off of the wire. (See Figure 3-9.)

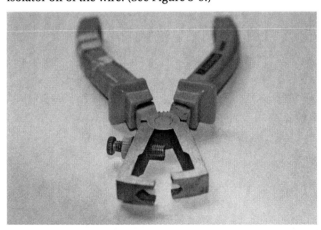

Figure 3-9. Wire stripper

The Setup

You need to connect the resistor in series to the LED. The digital output pin 2 of the ADK board will be connected to your resistor, the resistor is connected to the anode of the LED, and ground (GND) of the ADK board will be connected to the cathode (the negative lead) of the LED. Connect everything as shown in Figure 3-10.

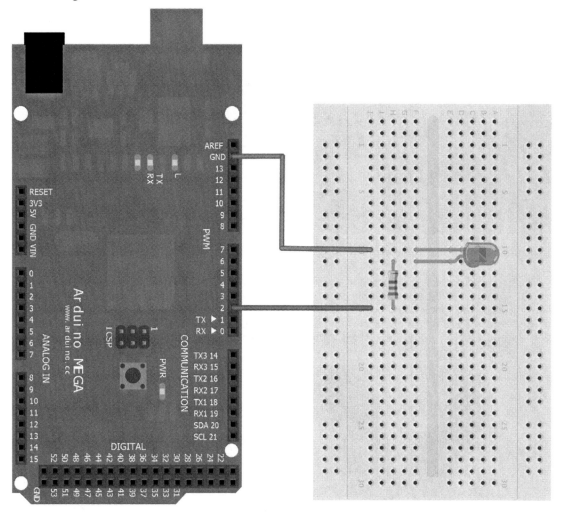

Figure 3-10. *Project 1 setup*

The Software

The hardware setup has been made and it is time to write the code that controls the LED. You will write an Arduino sketch that receives the switching command and toggles the LED according to the command sent by an Android application. The Android application will consist of a single toggle button to control the switching state.

The Arduino Sketch

Take the Arduino sketch written in Chapter 2 as a foundation for this sketch. You already implemented the ADK-specific part in it and you only need to change the communication part by defining another data protocol for the LED switching scenario. Create a new sketch and type in the code shown in Listing 3-1. Afterward, I will explain what has been changed.

Listing 3-1. Project 1: Arduino Sketch

```
#include <Max3421e.h>
#include <Usb.h>
#include <AndroidAccessory.h>

#define COMMAND_LED 0x2
#define TARGET_PIN_2 0x2
#define VALUE_ON 0x1
#define VALUE_OFF 0x0

#define PIN 2

AndroidAccessory acc("Manufacturer",
                     "Model",
                     "Description",
                     "Version",
                     "URI",
                     "Serial");

byte rcvmsg[3];

void setup() {
  Serial.begin(19200);
  acc.powerOn();
  pinMode(PIN, OUTPUT);
}

void loop() {
  if (acc.isConnected()) {
    //read the received data into the byte array
    int len = acc.read(rcvmsg, sizeof(rcvmsg), 1);
    if (len > 0) {
      if (rcvmsg[0] == COMMAND_LED) {
        if (rcvmsg[1] == TARGET_PIN_2){
          //get the switch state
          byte value = rcvmsg[2];
          //set output pin to according state
          if(value == VALUE_ON) {
            digitalWrite(PIN, HIGH);
```

```
      } else if(value == VALUE_OFF) {
        digitalWrite(PIN, LOW);
      }
    }
   }
  }
 }
}
```

The first thing you might notice is that the text message–specific code from Chapter 2 has been deleted. You won't need to send text in this project so the code has been changed to support the 3-byte data protocol, which was also mentioned in Chapter 2. To evaluate the received data from the Android device you'll have to define a command byte, a target byte, and a value byte constant. The meaning of the defined data protocol byte constants COMMAND_LED, TARGET_PIN_2, VALUE_ON, and VALUE_OFF should be self explanatory. You also define a PIN constant which reflects the pin that should be controlled.

Besides the already known accessory initializations which have to be made in the setup method, you also need to configure the mode of the digital pin you want to use. Because you want the pin to work as an output you need to set the pin mode with pinMode(PIN, OUTPUT).

In the loop method you check for an established connection and read the incoming data. The third byte is then evaluated for its value. If you have received a 0x1 byte you set the pin to HIGH to output 5V and if you have received a 0x0 byte you set the pin to LOW so that its output is 0V. You'll use the digitalWrite method for that. Its parameters are the pin to be set and the state it should switch to, HIGH or LOW.

That's all for the Arduino part. Let's continue with the Android software part.

The Android Application

For the Android part you will also build on the principles you learned from your Android application in Chapter 2. You will also have to adjust the data protocol and introduce a new UI element, a ToggleButton, which lets the user switch the LED on and off. Let's have a look at the class Listing 3-2 and the changes you'll have to make.

Listing 3-2. Project 1: ProjectOneActivity.java

```java
package project.one.adk;

import java.io.FileDescriptor;
import java.io.FileInputStream;
import java.io.FileOutputStream;
import java.io.IOException;

import android.app.Activity;
import android.app.PendingIntent;
import android.content.BroadcastReceiver;
import android.content.Context;
import android.content.Intent;
import android.content.IntentFilter;
import android.os.AsyncTask;
import android.os.Bundle;
import android.os.ParcelFileDescriptor;
```

```java
import android.util.Log;
import android.widget.CompoundButton;
import android.widget.CompoundButton.OnCheckedChangeListener;
import android.widget.ToggleButton;

import com.android.future.usb.UsbAccessory;
import com.android.future.usb.UsbManager;

public class ProjectOneActivity extends Activity {

    private static final String TAG = ProjectOneActivity.class.getSimpleName();

    private PendingIntent mPermissionIntent;
    private static final String ACTION_USB_PERMISSION = "com.android.example.USB_PERMISSION";
    private boolean mPermissionRequestPending;

    private UsbManager mUsbManager;
    private UsbAccessory mAccessory;
    private ParcelFileDescriptor mFileDescriptor;
    private FileInputStream mInputStream;
    private FileOutputStream mOutputStream;

    private static final byte COMMAND_LED = 0x2;
    private static final byte TARGET_PIN_2 = 0x2;
    private static final byte VALUE_ON = 0x1;
    private static final byte VALUE_OFF = 0x0;

    private ToggleButton ledToggleButton;

    /** Called when the activity is first created. */
    @Override
    public void onCreate(Bundle savedInstanceState) {
        super.onCreate(savedInstanceState);

        mUsbManager = UsbManager.getInstance(this);
        mPermissionIntent = PendingIntent.getBroadcast(this, 0, new Intent(
            ACTION_USB_PERMISSION), 0);
        IntentFilter filter = new IntentFilter(ACTION_USB_PERMISSION);
        filter.addAction(UsbManager.ACTION_USB_ACCESSORY_DETACHED);
        registerReceiver(mUsbReceiver, filter);

        setContentView(R.layout.main);
        ledToggleButton = (ToggleButton) findViewById(R.id.led_toggle_button);
        ledToggleButton.setOnCheckedChangeListener(toggleButtonCheckedListener);
    }

    /**
     * Called when the activity is resumed from its paused state and immediately
     * after onCreate().
     */
    @Override
```

```java
public void onResume() {
    super.onResume();

    if (mInputStream != null && mOutputStream != null) {
        return;
    }

    UsbAccessory[] accessories = mUsbManager.getAccessoryList();
    UsbAccessory accessory = (accessories == null ? null : accessories[0]);
    if (accessory != null) {
        if (mUsbManager.hasPermission(accessory)) {
            openAccessory(accessory);
        } else {
            synchronized (mUsbReceiver) {
                if (!mPermissionRequestPending) {
                    mUsbManager.requestPermission(accessory, mPermissionIntent);
                    mPermissionRequestPending = true;
                }
            }
        }
    } else {
        Log.d(TAG, "mAccessory is null");
    }
}

/** Called when the activity is paused by the system. */
@Override
public void onPause() {
    super.onPause();
    closeAccessory();
}

/**
 * Called when the activity is no longer needed prior to being removed from
 * the activity stack.
 */
@Override
public void onDestroy() {
    super.onDestroy();
    unregisterReceiver(mUsbReceiver);
}

OnCheckedChangeListener toggleButtonCheckedListener = new OnCheckedChangeListener() {

    @Override
    public void onCheckedChanged(CompoundButton buttonView, boolean isChecked) {
        if (buttonView.getId() == R.id.led_toggle_button) {

            new AsyncTask<Boolean, Void, Void>() {

                @Override
                protected Void doInBackground(Boolean... params) {
```

```
                    sendLedSwitchCommand(TARGET_PIN_2, params[0]);
                    return null;
                }
            }.execute(isChecked);
        }
    }
};
private final BroadcastReceiver mUsbReceiver = new BroadcastReceiver() {
    @Override
    public void onReceive(Context context, Intent intent) {
        String action = intent.getAction();
        if (ACTION_USB_PERMISSION.equals(action)) {
            synchronized (this) {
                UsbAccessory accessory = UsbManager.getAccessory(intent);
                if (intent.getBooleanExtra(UsbManager.EXTRA_PERMISSION_GRANTED, false)) {
                    openAccessory(accessory);
                } else {
                    Log.d(TAG, "permission denied for accessory " + accessory);
                }
                mPermissionRequestPending = false;
            }
        } else if (UsbManager.ACTION_USB_ACCESSORY_DETACHED.equals(action)) {
            UsbAccessory accessory = UsbManager.getAccessory(intent);
            if (accessory != null && accessory.equals(mAccessory)) {
                closeAccessory();
            }
        }
    }
};

private void openAccessory(UsbAccessory accessory) {
    mFileDescriptor = mUsbManager.openAccessory(accessory);
    if (mFileDescriptor != null) {
        mAccessory = accessory;
        FileDescriptor fd = mFileDescriptor.getFileDescriptor();
        mInputStream = new FileInputStream(fd);
        mOutputStream = new FileOutputStream(fd);
        Log.d(TAG, "accessory opened");
    } else {
        Log.d(TAG, "accessory open fail");
    }
}

private void closeAccessory() {
    try {
        if (mFileDescriptor != null) {
            mFileDescriptor.close();
        }
    } catch (IOException e) {
    } finally {
        mFileDescriptor = null;
```

```
            mAccessory = null;
        }
    }

    public void sendLedSwitchCommand(byte target, boolean isSwitchedOn) {
        byte[] buffer = new byte[3];
        buffer[0] = COMMAND_LED;
        buffer[1] = target;
        if (isSwitchedOn) {
            buffer[2] = VALUE_ON;
        } else {
            buffer[2] = VALUE_OFF;
        }
        if (mOutputStream != null) {
            try {
                mOutputStream.write(buffer);
            } catch (IOException e) {
                Log.e(TAG, "write failed", e);
            }
        }
    }
}
```

If you change the activity name and the package name as it was done here, make sure that you change the AndroidManifest.xml entries as well to reflect that renaming.

Listing 3-3. Project 1: AndroidManifest.xml

```
<manifest xmlns:android="http://schemas.android.com/apk/res/android"
    package="project.one.adk" android:versionCode="1" android:versionName="1.0">
...
    <activity android:name=".ProjectOneActivity" android:label="@string/app_name"
        android:screenOrientation="portrait">
...
</manifest>
```

The data protocol constants have been changed from the 4-byte protocol to the 3-byte protocol. As you have done in the Arduino sketch, you also define the constants for the LED switching data message.

```
private static final byte COMMAND_LED = 0x2;
private static final byte TARGET_PIN_2 = 0x2;
private static final byte VALUE_ON = 0x1;
private static final byte VALUE_OFF = 0x0;
```

The scope of this project is to switch an LED on and off, so you won't need to display any text. Therefore the TextView UI element has been replaced by a ToggleButton.

```
private ToggleButton ledToggleButton;

@Override
public void onCreate(Bundle savedInstanceState) {
    super.onCreate(savedInstanceState);

    ...
    setContentView(R.layout.main);
    ledToggleButton = (ToggleButton) findViewById(R.id.led_toggle_button);
    ledToggleButton.setOnCheckedChangeListener(toggleButtonCheckedListener);
}
```

You can see that an OnCheckedChangeListener is assigned to the ledToggleButton which implements a callback method that is triggered every time the button is pressed. The ToggleButton is a special stateful implementation of a Button, which means that it knows if it is checked or unchecked. The implementation of the OnCheckedChangeListener is done in an anonymous inner class. The only method that has to be implemented is the onCheckedChange method which has two parameters: the button that triggered the event and a Boolean flag indicating the new state of the button.

```
OnCheckedChangeListener toggleButtonCheckedListener = new OnCheckedChangeListener() {

    @Override
    public void onCheckedChanged(CompoundButton buttonView, boolean isChecked) {
        if (buttonView.getId() == R.id.led_toggle_button) {
            new AsyncTask<Boolean, Void, Void>() {

                @Override
                protected Void doInBackground(Boolean... params) {
                    sendLedSwitchCommand(TARGET_PIN_2, params[0]);
                    return null;
                }
            }.execute(isChecked);
        }
    }
};
```

If you have more than one button using the same listener you should always validate if the correct button has been pressed. That's what's done here. In this particular project you wouldn't need to check that because you only use one button, but it is a good practice if you plan to use the listener for more components. After validating that the correct button triggered the event, you can start sending the command to the ADK board to toggle the LED. The sendText method has been removed because you don't need it in this project. A new method was implemented to send the 3-byte data message to the board named sendLedSwitchCommand. It has two parameters, the target pin of the ADK board where the LED is connected and the state it should be switched to.

You may wonder what this AsyncTask is all about. The event callback method is executed on the UI thread. If you were to just send the message there you would do the outputstream operations in the UI thread as well. This generally works but it is a bad practice. Longer operations may block the UI which is very frustrating for the user. To avoid those situations you can do several things: open another Thread, utilize the Android Handler mechanism or, as done in this case, use an AsyncTask for concurrency. Explaining the pros and cons of each of these is beyond the scope of this book, but you can read a lot about them in the Android Dev Guide at http://developer.android.com/guide/topics/fundamentals/processes-and-threads.html. What AsyncTask basically does is open another thread to handle your operations in the background while your

UI thread is running to serve the user. Here only the doInBackground method is implemented because it is all you need. Additionally, the AsyncTask has callback methods that are running on the UI thread to visualize the progress of a background operation or to update the UI elements when it is finished.

The sendLedSwitchCommand method looks similar to the sendText method you already know but it implements the 3-byte data protocol.

```
public void sendLedSwitchCommand(byte target, boolean isSwitchedOn) {
    byte[] buffer = new byte[3];
    buffer[0] = COMMAND_LED;
    buffer[1] = target;
    if (isSwitchedOn) {
        buffer[2] = VALUE_ON;
    } else {
        buffer[2] = VALUE_OFF;
    }
    if (mOutputStream != null) {
        try {
            mOutputStream.write(buffer);
        } catch (IOException e) {
            Log.e(TAG, "write failed", e);
        }
    }
}
```

That's all for the code changes. You remember that a ToggleButton should be shown to the user, so you need to make some changes in the layout file main.xml as well (Listing 3-4).

Listing 3-4. Project 1: main.xml

```
<?xml version="1.0" encoding="utf-8"?>
<LinearLayout xmlns:android="http://schemas.android.com/apk/res/android"
    android:orientation="vertical"
    android:layout_width="fill_parent"
    android:layout_height="fill_parent"
    android:gravity="center">
    <ToggleButton android:id="@+id/led_toggle_button"
        android:layout_width="wrap_content"
        android:layout_height="wrap_content"
        android:textOn="@string/led_on"
        android:textOff="@string/led_off" />
</LinearLayout>
```

As you can see, the TextView element was replaced by the ToggleButton element. It is defined to be only as wide and as high as its own content; the text that is displayed when it is checked or unchecked is referenced in the strings.xml file. If you switch to the graphical layout editor in Eclipse you can already see the button in the middle of your layout (Figure 3-11).

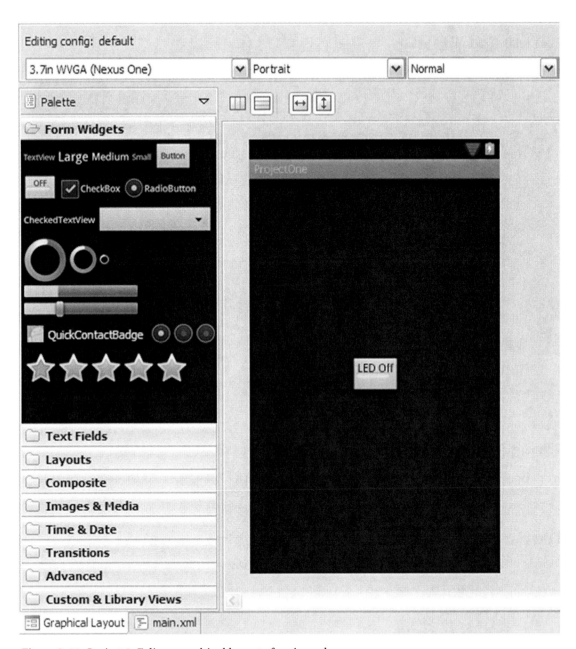

Figure 3-11. Project 1: Eclipse graphical layout of main.xml

That's all there is to do for the Android part of this project. Project 1 is now finished and ready to be tested. Upload the applications for both devices, connect them together, and you should end up with something like what you see in Figure 3-12.

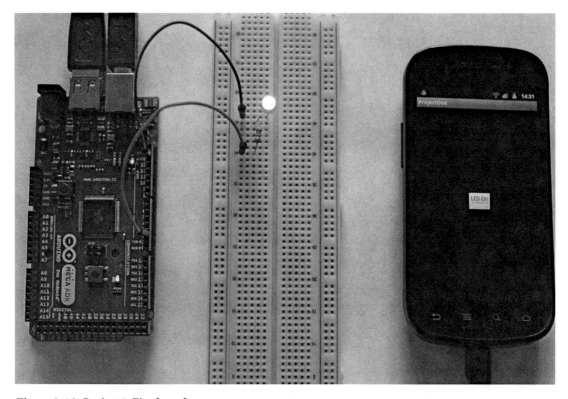

Figure 3-12. Project 1: Final result

Project 2: Dim an LED

In this project you will learn about another feature of the digital IO pins on your ADK board, the pulse-width modulation. You will learn what pulse-width modulation is and how you can dim an LED with it. You will write an Android application to control the dimming process with the help of a slider.

The Parts

The parts for this project are exactly the same as in project 1. You won't need any new hardware parts.

- ADK board
- Breadboard
- LED operating at 5V
- 220Ω resistor
- Some wires

These parts were already explained in project 1 but you will use one new feature of your ADK board, which I will explain next.

ADK Board

Some digital IO pins of the ADK boards have an additional feature called PWM. PWM stands for pulse-width modulation. Pins having that feature are marked on Arduino-derived ADK boards as shown in Figure 3-13.

Figure 3-13. PWM marking on Arduino boards

PWM can be described as a very fast back and forth HIGH-LOW switching of a digital output. When switched, the digital pin produces a square wave signal (see Figure 3-14).

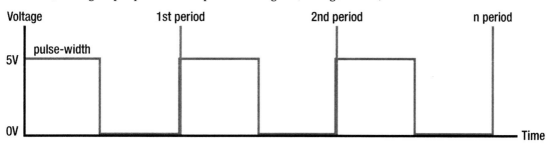

Figure 3-14. Pulse-width modulation example with 50% duty cycle

The time the signal spends in an on state compared to the time it is in the off state is referred to as the duty cycle. The time the signal is in the on state is referred to as the pulse width. So in Figure 3-14 you have a duty cycle of 50%.

The fast-paced state changing of the pin directly affects the analog characteristics, that is, the voltage supplied by the pin. With a duty cycle of 100%, the pin generates an analog value of about 5V. An Arduino-derived board maps 256 values to the range between 0V and 5V. So a value of 127 would cause the pin to generate a square wave with a duty cycle of 50% generating about 2.5V.

To control the pulse-width of a pin in an Arduino sketch, the `analogWrite` method is used with its parameters being the digital pin to use and a value between 0 and 256.

The Setup

The circuit setup is exactly the same as in project 1 and can be seen in Figure 3-10 for reference.

The Software

Most of the code for both platforms can stay as it is. You will only change minor details for transmitting a broader value range for the pulse-width and you will introduce a new UI element, the SeekBar, in the Android code for choosing the PWM value.

The Arduino Sketch

The changed Arduino code to support PWM output can be seen in Listing 3-5.

Listing 3-5. Project 2: Arduino Sketch

```
#include <Max3421e.h>
#include <Usb.h>
#include <AndroidAccessory.h>

#define COMMAND_LED 0x2
#define TARGET_PIN_2 0x2

#define PIN 2

AndroidAccessory acc("Manufacturer",
                     "Model",
                     "Description",
                     "Version",
                     "URI",
                     "Serial");

byte rcvmsg[3];

void setup() {
  Serial.begin(19200);
  acc.powerOn();
  pinMode(PIN, OUTPUT);
}

void loop() {
  if (acc.isConnected()) {
    //read the received data into the byte array
    int len = acc.read(rcvmsg, sizeof(rcvmsg), 1);
    if (len > 0) {
      if (rcvmsg[0] == COMMAND_LED) {
        if (rcvmsg[1] == TARGET_PIN_2){
```

```
                //get the analog value
                byte value = rcvmsg[2];
                //set output pin to according analog value
                analogWrite(PIN, value);
            }
          }
        }
      }
    }
```

What you can see is that the constants for the LED state (VALUE_ON/VALUE_OFF) have been deleted because you are working with analog values now instead of digital states. The byte value transmitted by the Android application is read and directly fed into the analogWrite method. This method triggers digital pins to generate square waves with a certain duty cycle if they are PWM capable. As parameters it takes the pin to be used and a byte value of 0 to 255 which is mapped to an analog value ranging from 0V to 5V.

The Android Application

The Android application from project 1 can also be used as the basis for this project. You won't need to change a lot of things in this project. You will introduce a new UI element to your application: the SeekBar. After having a look at the complete code listing for ProjectTwoActivity, I will explain the parts that have changed which enable you to transmit the value range used by the ADK board for PWM later on. Because most parts of the code haven't changed and are described in the previous listings, I will hide their implementation part with three dots (…) to concentrate on the important part only (see Listing 3-6). However, the full code reference can be found at www.apress.com, as usual.

Listing 3-6. Project 2: ProjectTwoActivity.java

```
package project.two.adk;

import java.io.FileDescriptor;
import java.io.FileInputStream;
import java.io.FileOutputStream;
import java.io.IOException;

import android.app.Activity;
import android.app.PendingIntent;
import android.content.BroadcastReceiver;
import android.content.Context;
import android.content.Intent;
import android.content.IntentFilter;
import android.os.AsyncTask;
import android.os.Bundle;
import android.os.ParcelFileDescriptor;
import android.util.Log;
import android.widget.SeekBar;
import android.widget.SeekBar.OnSeekBarChangeListener;
import android.widget.TextView;
```

91

```
import com.android.future.usb.UsbAccessory;
import com.android.future.usb.UsbManager;

public class ProjectTwoActivity extends Activity {

    private static final String TAG = ProjectTwoActivity.class.getSimpleName();

    private PendingIntent mPermissionIntent;
    private static final String ACTION_USB_PERMISSION = "com.android.example.USB_PERMISSION";
    private boolean mPermissionRequestPending;

    private UsbManager mUsbManager;
    private UsbAccessory mAccessory;
    private ParcelFileDescriptor mFileDescriptor;
    private FileInputStream mInputStream;
    private FileOutputStream mOutputStream;

    private static final byte COMMAND_LED = 0x2;
    private static final byte TARGET_PIN_2 = 0x2;

    private TextView ledIntensityTextView;
    private SeekBar ledIntensitySeekBar;

    @Override
    public void onCreate(Bundle savedInstanceState) {
        super.onCreate(savedInstanceState);
        ...
        setContentView(R.layout.main);
        ledIntensityTextView = (TextView) findViewById(R.id.led_intensity_text_view);
        ledIntensitySeekBar = (SeekBar) findViewById(R.id.led_intensity_seek_bar);
        ledIntensitySeekBar.setOnSeekBarChangeListener(ledIntensityChangeListener);
        ledIntensityTextView.setText("LED intensity: " + ledIntensitySeekBar.getProgress());
    }

    @Override
    public void onResume() {
        super.onResume();
        ...
    }

    @Override
    public void onPause() {
        super.onPause();
        ...
    }

    @Override
    public void onDestroy() {
        super.onDestroy();
        ...
    }
```

```
OnSeekBarChangeListener ledIntensityChangeListener = new OnSeekBarChangeListener() {
    @Override
    public void onProgressChanged(SeekBar seekBar, int progress, boolean fromUser) {
        ledIntensityTextView.setText("LED intensity: " +
            ledIntensitySeekBar.getProgress());
        new AsyncTask<Byte, Void, Void>() {

            @Override
            protected Void doInBackground(Byte... params) {
                sendLedIntensityCommand(TARGET_PIN_2, params[0]);
                return null;
            }
        }.execute((byte) progress);
    }

    @Override
    public void onStartTrackingTouch(SeekBar seekBar) {
        // not implemented
    }

    @Override
    public void onStopTrackingTouch(SeekBar seekBar) {
        // not implemented
    }
};

private final BroadcastReceiver mUsbReceiver = new BroadcastReceiver() {
    …
};

private void openAccessory(UsbAccessory accessory) {
    …
}

private void closeAccessory() {
    …
}

public void sendLedIntensityCommand(byte target, byte value) {
    byte[] buffer = new byte[3];
    buffer[0] = COMMAND_LED;
    buffer[1] = target;
    buffer[2] = value;
    if (mOutputStream != null) {
        try {
            mOutputStream.write(buffer);
        } catch (IOException e) {
            Log.e(TAG, "write failed", e);
        }
    }
}
```

```
        }
    }
```

You can see that the byte constants for the on and off state of the LED have been removed here also. Two UI elements are shown to the user in this project. The first one is a TextView which should show the currently selected value transmitted to the ADK board. The second element is a SeekBar which is a slider control that lets the user easily select a value in a predefined range.

```
private TextView ledIntensityTextView;
private SeekBar ledIntensitySeekBar;

@Override
public void onCreate(Bundle savedInstanceState) {
    super.onCreate(savedInstanceState);

    ...
    setContentView(R.layout.main);
    ledIntensityTextView = (TextView) findViewById(R.id.led_intensity_text_view);
    ledIntensitySeekBar = (SeekBar) findViewById(R.id.led_intensity_seek_bar);
    ledIntensitySeekBar.setOnSeekBarChangeListener(ledIntensityChangeListener);
    ledIntensityTextView.setText("LED intensity: " + ledIntensitySeekBar.getProgress());
}
```

The SeekBar, like every other View element, can register a broad set of listeners that are notified if certain events occur. A dedicated listener for the SeekBar is the OnSeekBarChangeListener which gets registered here in the onCreate method. It gets notified if the slider receives the first touch gesture, if the slider changes its value, and if the touch is released. You only care about the changing state of the SeekBar, so the implementation looks like this:

```
OnSeekBarChangeListener ledIntensityChangeListener = new OnSeekBarChangeListener() {

    @Override
    public void onProgressChanged(SeekBar seekBar, int progress, boolean fromUser) {
        ledIntensityTextView.setText("LED intensity: " + ledIntensitySeekBar.getProgress());
        new AsyncTask<Byte, Void, Void>() {

            @Override
            protected Void doInBackground(Byte... params) {
                sendLedIntensityCommand(TARGET_PIN_2, params[0]);
                return null;
            }
        }.execute((byte) progress);
    }

    @Override
    public void onStartTrackingTouch(SeekBar seekBar) {
        // not implemented
    }

    @Override
    public void onStopTrackingTouch(SeekBar seekBar) {
        // not implemented
    }
};
```

When the onProgressChanged method is called it receives three parameters from the system. The first one is the actual SeekBar element that triggered the event, the second one is the current progress of the SeekBar, and the third one is a Boolean flag to indicate if the change in progress was made by the user by sliding over the SeekBar or if the progress was set programmatically. The implementation is very straightforward. You display the change of the value to the user with the help of the TextView and after that you transmit the value to the ADK board. Note that the progress is of the datatype byte. You will see later on that the range of the SeekBar is configured to be from 0 to 255. The datatype byte however has a range from -128 to 127. What happens is that the progress value is cast into a byte and if the value is larger than 127 it becomes negative. That has to do with bit-arithmetic and the so called sign-bit. This should not concern you at the moment because on the Arduino side, a possible negative byte value will be translated back to its original representation when it is given into the analogWrite method. Just note that in general this cast would not be safe, although it works in this example.

You already learned that IO operations should be made in a UI-separate thread so you will use an AsyncTask for that purpose once again. The actual communication logic is encapsulated in the sendLedIntensityCommand method.

```
public void sendLedIntensityCommand(byte target, byte value) {
    byte[] buffer = new byte[3];
    buffer[0] = COMMAND_LED;
    buffer[1] = target;
    buffer[2] = value;
    if (mOutputStream != null) {
        try {
            mOutputStream.write(buffer);
        } catch (IOException e) {
            Log.e(TAG, "write failed", e);
        }
    }
}
```

The implementation is almost equal to the sendLedSwitchCommand from project 1. Instead of transmitting only two possible states, you will transmit the current value of the SeekBar, which has a range from 0 to 255.

That's all about the code implementation for project 2. You still need to change the main.xml file to actually display the TextView and the SeekBar to the user. The new main.xml file looks like Listing 3-7.

Listing 3-7. Project 2 – main.xml

```
<?xml version="1.0" encoding="utf-8"?>
<LinearLayout xmlns:android="http://schemas.android.com/apk/res/android"
    android:orientation="vertical"
    android:layout_width="fill_parent"
    android:layout_height="fill_parent"
    android:gravity="center">
    <TextView android:id="@+id/led_intensity_text_view"
        android:layout_width="wrap_content"
        android:layout_height="wrap_content"
        android:text="LED intensity: 0"/>
    <SeekBar android:id="@+id/led_intensity_seek_bar"
        android:layout_width="fill_parent"
        android:layout_height="wrap_content"
        android:max="255" />
```

```
</LinearLayout>
```

You have already learned about the attributes of the TextView element so let's see what's special about the SeekBar. Apart from the already known attributes such as id, layout_width, and layout_height, you see an attribute called max. This attribute defines the maximum value the SeekBar can reach. The starting value of 0 is a default and you don't have to define it yourself. So in the layout you already defined the range from 0 to 255. If you switch to the graphical layout editor you can already see a preview of that user interface (Figure 3-15).

Figure 3-15. Project 2: Eclipse graphical layout of main.xml

Project 2 is now finished and ready for testing. Upload the applications to your devices and start them up. Your completed project should look like Figure 3-16.

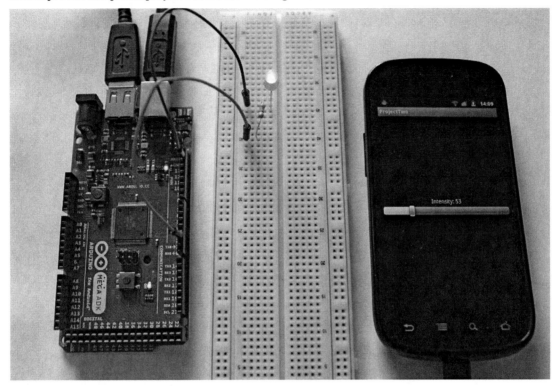

Figure 3-16. Project 2: Final result

Summary

In this chapter you learned what an output pin on an ADK board is and what it is capable of. In the first project of this chapter you saw how to use an output pin in a digital context to switch a simple LED on and off by providing either 5V or 0V when the output is switched to HIGH or LOW. The second project introduced the PWM or pulse-width modulation mode of digital outputs where an output pin can emit a range of output voltages from 0V to 5V. To give the user the control about the value transmitted to the ADK board you used two different Android UI elements: the ToggleButton to switch the LED on and off in a digital context, and the SeekBar to pick from a range of values to dim the LED in an analog context.

CHAPTER 4

Inputs

In the context of the ADK board, *inputs* are pins and connectors on the board with which you can receive data or measurements. Although the common USB-type connectors are technically also inputs, this chapter will only concentrate on the inputs with which you can take measurements or detect digital state changes. The inputs in that sense are the pins of the ADK board.

The majority of the pins on an ADK board are capable of being used as input pins. You remember that digital pins can be configured to work as outputs and inputs. Digital pins are configured as input pins by default. You can set them into input mode by using the pinMode method, but you don't necessarily need to.

Additionally, an ADK board has dedicated analog input pins. With analog input pins you can measure changes in the applied voltage on those pins. The measured analog voltage is mapped to a digital representation you can process in your code.

Both input pin types and their use cases are described in the following two projects.

Project 3: Reading the State of a Button

In this project you will learn how the digital input pins on the ADK board can be used to detect the state of a button or a switch. For additional hardware you will need a button or a switch and a resistor. You can use a button or a switch in this project because they basically work the same way. Both components can be used to close or open a circuit. You will write an Arduino sketch that reads the current state of a button and transmits the state change to an Android application. The Android application receiving the state change will propagate the change in a TextView and your Android device's vibrator will be triggered to vibrate whenever the button is pressed.

The Parts

You already know most of the parts for this project by now. However, I will explain the principle of a button or switch, the use of a so-called pull-up resistor, and the use of a digital pin configured as an input pin. You will need the following hardware in this project (shown in Figure 4-1):

- ADK board
- Breadboard
- Button or switch
- 10kΩ pull-up resistor
- Some wires

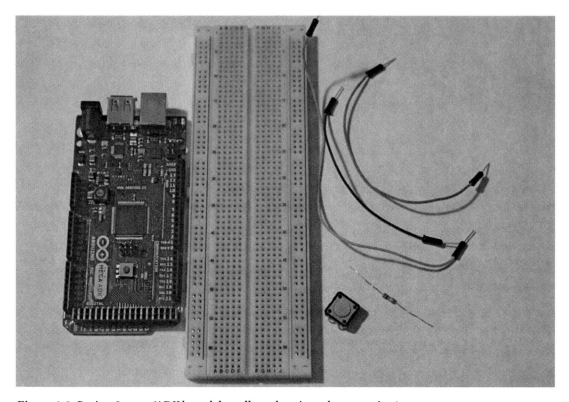

Figure 4-1. Project 3 parts (ADK board, breadboard, resistor, button, wires)

Button or Switch

A *button* or a *switch* is a component used to control the state of a circuit. A circuit can be either closed, which means that the power source has a return path, or it can be open, which means that the circuit's return path is blocked or not connected to the circuit. To achieve the change from an open circuit to a closed one, a button or a switch is used. In its ON state, a button or switch ideally has no voltage drop across itself and no current-limiting properties. In its OFF state, a button or switch ideally has no voltage limit and an infinite resistance value. In a simple circuit diagram, a closed circuit would look like the one shown in Figure 4-2.

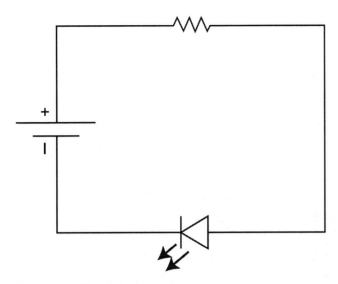

Figure 4-2. Closed circuit

As you can see, the power can flow through the circuit's components to its return path. If you connect a switch or a button to that circuit you can control whether the circuit should be open or closed. By pressing the button or switching the switch to its ON position, you close the circuit so that power can flow through the circuit. If you release the button or switch the switch back to its OFF position, you disconnect the circuit, thus leaving it open. The circuit diagram symbol for a button or a switch is displayed as an open part in the circuit. The symbol for a switch can be seen in the circuit diagram in Figure 4-3.

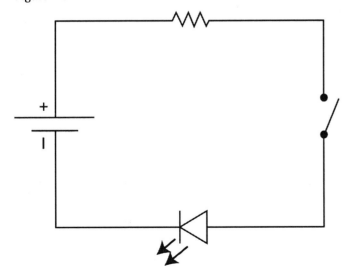

Figure 4-3. Circuit with switch

Buttons and switches come in numerous types and sizes. Typical buttons can be *push buttons*, which you need to press and hold to close a circuit and release to open a circuit, or they can be *toggle buttons*, which reside in their current state after being pushed. Switches also have several shapes and application types, but the most common are the well known ON/OFF switch, which defines two states, and the toggle switch, which can switch between many states (see Figure 4-4).

Figure 4-4. Buttons and switches

Pull-up Resistor

You already used a resistor to limit the current in a circuit. In this project you will use a resistor in combination with a button or switch to pull the input pin to either LOW (0V) or HIGH (5V). This can be achieved by a special circuit setup.

There are certain situations in which you would want the input pin to be in a defined state. So, for example, when a digital pin is configured as an input and no component is connected to it you will still measure a voltage fluctuation. Those fluctuations are a result of external signals or other electrical disturbances. The voltage measured on the pin will be anywhere between 0V and 5V, which causes a continuous change in the digital readings of the pin state (LOW/HIGH). To eliminate those disturbances you will pull the voltage on that input pin up. In this kind of use case the resistor is called a *pull-up resistor.*

The pull-up resistor has to be placed between the voltage source and the input pin within the circuit. The button or switch is placed between the input pin and ground. A simple schematic for this setup looks like that shown in Figure 4-5.

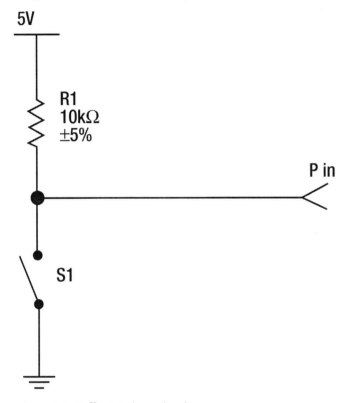

Figure 4-5. *Pull-up resistor circuit*

An easy explanation of what happens here is that if the switch or the button is not pressed, the input is only connected to Vcc (5V), the line is pulled up, and the input is set to HIGH. When the switch or the button is pressed and the input is connected to Vcc and GND (0V), the current flow has more resistance at the 10kΩ resistor than at the switch or button, which has a very low resistance (usually way below 1Ω). In this case the input is set to LOW as the connection to GND is stronger than to Vcc.

The high-valued resistor is also needed to limit the overall current flow in the circuit. If you press the switch or button you directly connect Vcc to GND. Without a high value resistor you would let too much current flow directly to GND and you would cause a short circuit. The high current flow would cause heat to build up which, most of the time, will damage your components permanently.

ADK Board

You have already worked with the digital pins of the ADK board configured as output pins. For this project you will use the pins in their input mode. By using the digital pins as input pins you have the capability of measuring digital signals: a digital HIGH expresses a voltage of around 5V across the input pin, while a digital LOW is somewhere close to 0V. You have already learned that pull-up resistors can be used to stabilize the input pin so that it isn't influenced by disturbances by steadily pulling the pin up to the supply voltage of 5V. One specialty of the ADK boards is that the embedded ATmega chip has integrated pull-up resistors that can be activated by code. To activate an integrated pull-up resistor you only have to set the pin to input mode and set it to HIGH.

```
pinMode(pin, INPUT);        // set digital pin to input mode
digitalWrite(pin, HIGH);    // turn on pullup resistor for pin
```

I do not recommend using this technique in this project, however, so that you can learn the fundamentals of pull-up resistors firsthand. If you have no high-valued resistor at hand you can still change this project's code as shown above to activate the internal pull-up resistors. Note that you only have to use the pinMode method to define an input pin if it was used as an output pin before in the code . Per default, all digital pins are configured to act as inputs, so you won't have to explicitly set the pinMode if the pin is only used as an input the entire time.

The Setup

You have just learned that you need to connect your digital input pin which you want to use to a pull-up resistor circuit. You can see in Figure 4-6 that the +5V Vcc pin of the ADK board has to be connected to one lead of the 10kΩ pull-up resistor. The other lead is connected to the digital input pin 2. The digital pin 2 also connects to one lead of the switch or button. The opposite lead is connected to ground. It's as easy as that. With this setup you pull the input pin up to 5V when the button or switch is not pressed, causing the digital input pin to measure a digital HIGH. If the button or switch is now pressed, the digital input pin is pulled down to GND, causing the input to measure a digital LOW.

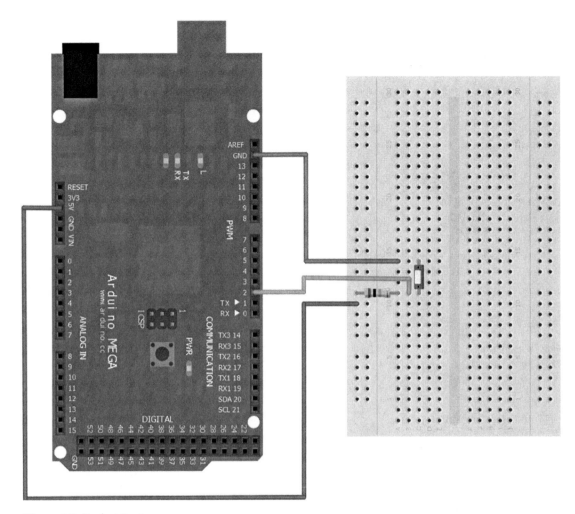

Figure 4-6. Project 3 setup

The Software

As described in the project description at the beginning of the chapter, you will write an Arduino sketch that continuously monitors the state of a digital input pin. Each time the pin changes its state from HIGH to LOW, or vice versa, you will send a message to the connected Android device. The Android application will listen to incoming state changes and it will show the current state in a TextView. Additionally, the vibrator of the Android device will be activated as long as the button is pressed.

105

The Arduino Sketch

As before, the Arduino sketch implementation is very straightforward. Have a look at Listing 4-1 and I will explain the details afterward.

Listing 4-1. Project 3: Arduino Sketch

```
#include <Max3421e.h>
#include <Usb.h>
#include <AndroidAccessory.h>

#define COMMAND_BUTTON 0x1
#define TARGET_BUTTON 0x1
#define VALUE_ON 0x1
#define VALUE_OFF 0x0
#define INPUT_PIN 2

AndroidAccessory acc("Manufacturer",
                     "Model",
                     "Description",
                     "Version",
                     "URI",
                     "Serial");

byte sntmsg[3];
int lastButtonState;
int currentButtonState;

void setup() {
  Serial.begin(19200);
  acc.powerOn();
  sntmsg[0] = COMMAND_BUTTON;
  sntmsg[1] = TARGET_BUTTON;
}

void loop() {
  if (acc.isConnected()) {
    currentButtonState = digitalRead(INPUT_PIN);
    if(currentButtonState != lastButtonState) {
      if(currentButtonState == LOW) {
        sntmsg[2] = VALUE_ON;
      } else {
        sntmsg[2] = VALUE_OFF;
      }
      acc.write(sntmsg, 3);
      lastButtonState = currentButtonState;
    }
    delay(100);
  }
}
```

The first thing to do here is to define some new message bytes for the button state message.

```
#define COMMAND_BUTTON 0x1
#define TARGET_BUTTON 0x1
#define VALUE_ON 0x1
#define VALUE_OFF 0x0
#define INPUT_PIN 2
```

Since the first two bytes of your message won't change, you can already set them in your setup method.

```
sntmsg[0] = COMMAND_BUTTON;
sntmsg[1] = TARGET_BUTTON;
```

Note that it is not necessary to call the pinMode method within the setup method because the digital pin is an input pin per default.

The first new method here is the digitalRead method, which measures the applied voltage on an input pin and translates it to two possible digital states, HIGH or LOW. The only parameter that is supplied to that method is the pin, which should be read.

```
currentButtonState = digitalRead(INPUT_PIN);
```

The next thing you see is that the current state is compared to the previous one so that a message is only sent to the Android device if the state has changed.

```
if(currentButtonState != lastButtonState) {
  if(currentButtonState == LOW) {
    sntmsg[2] = VALUE_ON;
  } else {
    sntmsg[2] = VALUE_OFF;
  }
  acc.write(sntmsg, 3);
  lastButtonState = currentButtonState;
}
```

Now let's have a look at the Android application.

The Android Application

The Android application for this project introduces no new UI element. You will visualize the state change of the button or switch with the help of the already known TextView. However, you will be learning how to call system services to address certain system or hardware features. For this project the vibrator service of the Android device will be responsible for controlling the vibrator motor in the device. First, have a look at the code in Listing 4-2. I will explain the new functionalities afterward. Again, the already known code parts that haven't changed are shortened so that you can focus on the important parts.

Listing 4-2. Project 3: ProjectThreeActivity.java

```
package project.three.adk;

import …;
```

```java
public class ProjectThreeActivity extends Activity {

    ...

    private static final byte COMMAND_BUTTON = 0x1;
    private static final byte TARGET_BUTTON = 0x1;
    private static final byte VALUE_ON = 0x1;
    private static final byte VALUE_OFF = 0x0;

    private static final String BUTTON_PRESSED_TEXT = "The Button is pressed!";
    private static final String BUTTON_NOT_PRESSED_TEXT = "The Button is not pressed!";

    private TextView buttonStateTextView;

    private Vibrator vibrator;
    private boolean isVibrating;

    @Override
    public void onCreate(Bundle savedInstanceState) {
        super.onCreate(savedInstanceState);

        ...

        setContentView(R.layout.main);
        buttonStateTextView = (TextView) findViewById(R.id.button_state_text_view);

        vibrator = ((Vibrator) getSystemService(VIBRATOR_SERVICE));
    }

    @Override
    public void onResume() {
        super.onResume();
        ...
    }

    @Override
    public void onPause() {
        super.onPause();
        closeAccessory();
        stopVibrate();
    }

    @Override
    public void onDestroy() {
        super.onDestroy();
        unregisterReceiver(mUsbReceiver);
    }

    private final BroadcastReceiver mUsbReceiver = new BroadcastReceiver() {
        @Override
        public void onReceive(Context context, Intent intent) {
```

```
        ...
    }
};

private void openAccessory(UsbAccessory accessory) {
    mFileDescriptor = mUsbManager.openAccessory(accessory);
    if (mFileDescriptor != null) {
        mAccessory = accessory;
        FileDescriptor fd = mFileDescriptor.getFileDescriptor();
        mInputStream = new FileInputStream(fd);
        mOutputStream = new FileOutputStream(fd);
        Thread thread = new Thread(null, commRunnable, TAG);
        thread.start();
        Log.d(TAG, "accessory opened");
    } else {
        Log.d(TAG, "accessory open fail");
    }
}

private void closeAccessory() {
    ...
}

Runnable commRunnable = new Runnable() {

    @Override
    public void run() {
        int ret = 0;
        final byte[] buffer = new byte[3];

        while (ret >= 0) {
            try {
                ret = mInputStream.read(buffer);
            } catch (IOException e) {
                break;
            }

            switch (buffer[0]) {
            case COMMAND_BUTTON:

                if(buffer[1] == TARGET_BUTTON) {
                    if(buffer[2] == VALUE_ON) {
                        startVibrate();
                    } else if(buffer[2] == VALUE_OFF){
                        stopVibrate();
                    }
                    runOnUiThread(new Runnable() {

                        @Override
                        public void run() {
```

```
                                buttonStateTextView.setText(buffer[2] == VALUE_ON ?
                                    BUTTON_PRESSED_TEXT : BUTTON_NOT_PRESSED_TEXT);
                        }
                    });
                }
                break;

            default:
                Log.d(TAG, "unknown msg: " + buffer[0]);

                break;
            }
        }
    }
};

public void startVibrate() {
    if(vibrator != null && !isVibrating) {
        isVibrating = true;
        vibrator.vibrate(new long[]{0, 1000, 250}, 0);
    }
}

public void stopVibrate() {
    if(vibrator != null && isVibrating) {
        isVibrating = false;
        vibrator.cancel();
    }
}
}
```

Have a look at the variables that have been added for this project:

```
private static final byte COMMAND_BUTTON = 0x1;
private static final byte TARGET_BUTTON = 0x1;
private static final byte VALUE_ON = 0x1;
private static final byte VALUE_OFF = 0x0;

private static final String BUTTON_PRESSED_TEXT = "The Button is pressed!";
private static final String BUTTON_NOT_PRESSED_TEXT = "The Button is not pressed!";

private TextView buttonStateTextView;

private Vibrator vibrator;
private boolean isVibrating;
```

You should already recognize the protocol bytes needed to verify the sent message later on. Then you see two String constants which are used to update the text of the TextView if the state of the button or switch has changed. The last two variables are used to have a reference to the system vibrator service and to check if the vibrator has been activated.

In the onCreate method you request the system service for the device's vibrator:

```
vibrator = ((Vibrator) getSystemService(VIBRATOR_SERVICE));
```

The getSystemService method returns a handle to a system service of the Android device. This method can be called from each subclass of the Context class or from a Context reference directly. So you have access to system services from within an Activity or a Service, and from an Application subclass. The Context class also defines the constants for accessing the system services.

You already know the implementation details for receiving data messages from your HelloWorld application in Chapter 2. A separate thread checks for incoming data and processes the messages. Depending on the received button state value, either the startVibrate or stopVibrate method is called. The startVibrate method checks if you still have a valid handle to the system service and if the vibrator is not already vibrating. Then it sets the Boolean flag to depict that the vibrator is activated and it defines a vibration pattern to be started immediately.

```
public void startVibrate() {
    if(vibrator != null && !isVibrating) {
        isVibrating = true;
        vibrator.vibrate(new long[]{0, 1000, 250}, 0);
    }
}
```

The vibrate method of the vibrator system service takes two parameters. The first one is an array of the data type long. It contains three values: the time to wait before the vibration starts, the time to vibrate, and the time to turn off the vibrating. The second parameter for the vibrate method defines the index in the pattern where the pattern should be repeated. Passing in a value of 0 means to start at the beginning over and over again. If you don't want to repeat the pattern, just pass in a value of -1. The time unit for the values is milliseconds. So what the pattern does is to start immediately, vibrate for a second, turn off for 250 milliseconds, and than start all over again.

If your application gets paused you should make sure to not leave resources unnecessarily allocated, so make sure to stop the vibrator if that happens. That's why the stopVibrate method is called in the onPause lifecycle method. The implementation is simple.

```
public void stopVibrate() {
    if(vibrator != null && isVibrating) {
        isVibrating = false;
        vibrator.cancel();
    }
}
```

First check if you still have a valid reference to the service and if the vibrator is still vibrating. Then reset the Boolean flag and cancel the vibrating.

Now upload the Arduino sketch to your ADK board and deploy the Android application onto your device. If you did everything correctly your project should look like that shown in Figure 4-7 and your Android device should vibrate and change its TextView each time you press the button or switch connected to your ADK board.

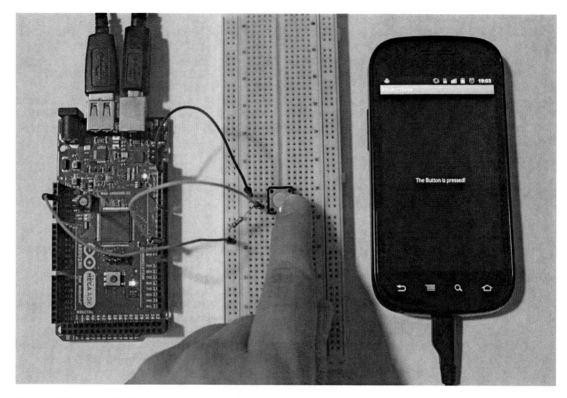

Figure 4-7. Project 3: Final result

Project 4: Adjusting Analog Input with a Potentiometer

Analog input measurements are used to recognize changes in the applied voltage on analog input pins. Many sensors and components express value changes by altering their output voltage. This project will teach you how to work with the analog input pins of your board and how the analog input is mapped to digital values with which you can work in your code. To achieve a change in the analog input you will utilize a new component called a potentiometer. You will change the analog value which is converted into a digital value to be transmitted to an Android application. In the Android application you will use a ProgressBar UI element to visualize the change in the value received.

The Parts

For this project you'll only need a potentiometer and some wires as additional hardware components (shown in Figure 4-8):

- ADK board
- Breadboard
- Potentiometer

- Some wires

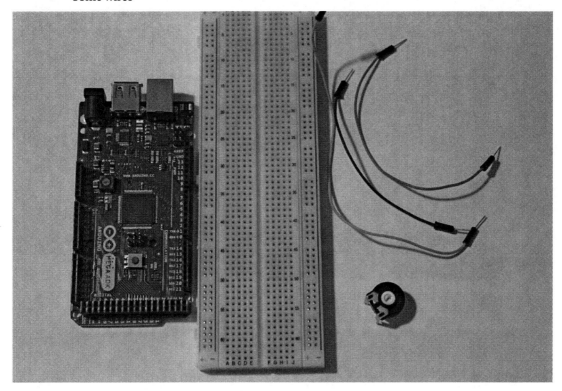

Figure 4-8. *Project 4 parts (ADK board, breadboard, potentiometer, wires)*

ADK Board

This is the first time you won't be using the digital IO pins of your ADK board. Instead, you will be using the analog input pins on your board. As their name already implies, they can only be used as inputs. The special thing about those pins is that they can measure analog values, meaning changes in the applied voltage. The ADK board is capable of translating those measured values into digital values. This procedure is called *analog to digital conversion*. This is done by an internal component called ADC, an *analog to digital converter*. In the case of the ADK board, it means that the values from 0V to 5V are mapped to digital values from 0 to 1023, so it is able to visualize the change in value in a 10-bit range. The analog input pins are placed on the opposite side of the digital pins on the board and are for the most part properly labeled with ANALOG IN and the pin number prefix A. So the analog pin 5 would be labeled A5. You can see those pins in Figure 4-9.

Figure 4-9. Analog input pins

Potentiometer

A potentiometer is a variable resistor. It has three leads you can connect to a circuit. It has two functionalities, depending on how you connect it. If you just connect one of the outer terminals and the middle terminal to your circuit, it only serves as a simple variable resistor as shown in Figure 4-10.

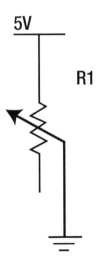

Figure 4-10. Potentiometer as variable resistor

If you also connect the third lead, it serves as a so-called voltage divider. A *voltage divider* (also called a *potential divider*) is a special circuit setup which, as the name implies, is capable of dividing the voltage in a circuit into different voltage levels among the circuit's components. A typical voltage divider circuit consists of two resistors in series or one potentiometer. A circuit visualization can be seen in Figure 4-11.

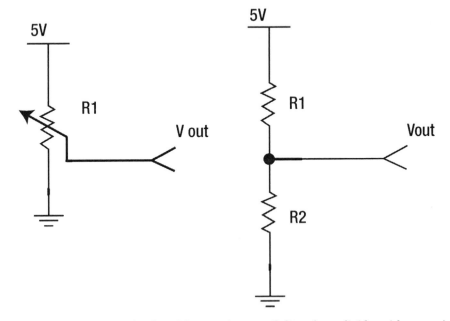

Figure 4-11. Voltage divider with potentiometer (left), voltage divider with two resistors in series (right)

Vin is the voltage which is applied across both resistors in series and Vout is the voltage across the second resistor (R2). The formula to determine the output voltage is as follows:

$$Vout = \frac{R2}{(R1+ R2\ )} \times Vin$$

Let's see that in an example. Consider the use case in which you have a 9V battery but one of your electrical components only operates at a voltage level of 5V. You have already determined your Vin, which is 9V, and your Vout, which is 5V. The only thing missing is the resistor values, which you will need.

Let's try using a 27kΩ resistor for R2. The only thing missing now is R1. Put the values into the formula and it looks like this:

$$5V = \frac{27000\Omega}{(R1+27000\Omega)} \times 9V$$

Rearrange the formula so that you can determine the missing variable R1.

$$R1 = \frac{R2 \times Vin}{Vout} - R2$$

$$R1 = \frac{27000\Omega \times 9V}{5V} - 27000\Omega$$

$$R1 = 21600\Omega$$

$$R1 = 21.6k\Omega$$

Since you won't find such a specific resistor value you can take the next higher one, which is 22kΩ. With that value for R1 you will end up with 4.96V, which is very close to the targeted 5V.

If you twist the potentiometer, you basically change its internal resistance proportion, meaning that if the resistance between the left terminal and the middle terminal decreases, the resistance between the right terminal and the middle terminal increases and vice versa. So if you apply that principle on the voltage divider formula, this would mean that if the value of R1 increases, it decreases at R2 and vice versa. So when the resistance proportion changes within the potentiometer, it causes a change in Vout. Potentiometers come in several shapes and resistance ranges. The most common types are the *trimmer*, which is adjusted by using a screwdriver or similar fitting object, and the *rotary potentiometers*, which have a shaft or knob to adjust the resistance value (shown in Figure 4-12). In this project I used the trimmer type because it is usually a bit cheaper than a rotary potentiometer.

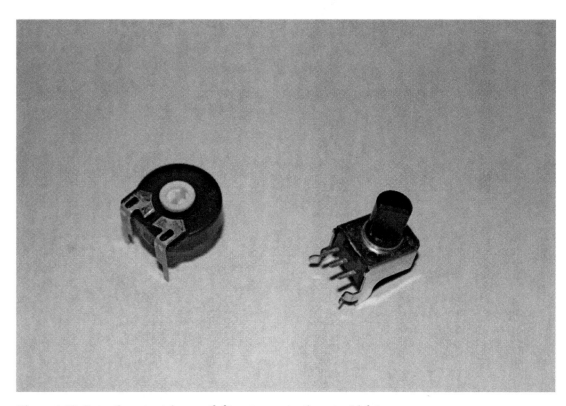

Figure 4-12. Potentiometer: trimmer (left), rotary potentiometer (right)

The Setup

The setup for this project is simple. Just connect the +5V pin to one of the outer leads of the potentiometer and a GND pin to the opposite outer lead. Connect analog pin A0 to the middle lead of the potentiometer and you're already done. Your setup should look like Figure 4-13. If you adjust your potentiometer, the measured value at the analog pin will change.

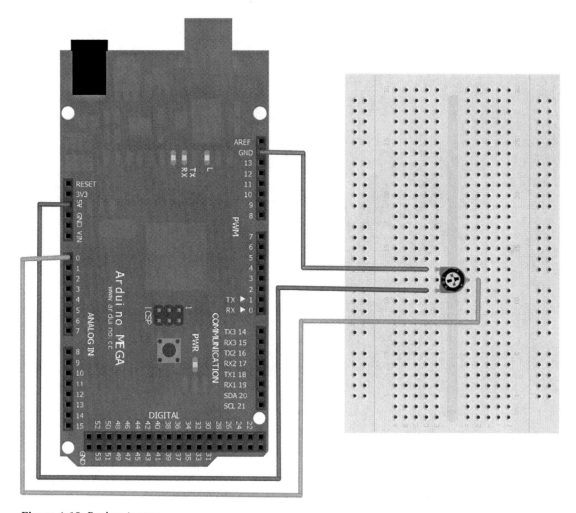

Figure 4-13. Project 4 setup

The Software

The Arduino sketch is responsible for reading the ADC value of the analog pin. The transmitted 10-bit value will be received by the Android application and the value change will be shown in a TextView and in a ProgressBar UI element. You will also learn a conversion technique to transmit large values.

The Arduino Sketch

Have a look at the complete Arduino sketch in Listing 4-3. I'll discuss what's new afterward.

Listing 4-3. Project 4: Arduino Sketch

```
#include <Max3421e.h>
#include <Usb.h>
#include <AndroidAccessory.h>

#define COMMAND_ANALOG 0x3
#define TARGET_PIN 0x0
#define INPUT_PIN A0

AndroidAccessory acc("Manufacturer",
                     "Model",
                     "Description",
                     "Version",
                     "URI",
                     "Serial");

byte sntmsg[6];
int analogPinReading;

void setup() {
  Serial.begin(19200);
  acc.powerOn();
  sntmsg[0] = COMMAND_ANALOG;
  sntmsg[1] = TARGET_PIN;
}

void loop() {
  if (acc.isConnected()) {
    analogPinReading = analogRead(INPUT_PIN);
    sntmsg[2] = (byte) (analogPinReading >> 24);
    sntmsg[3] = (byte) (analogPinReading >> 16);
    sntmsg[4] = (byte) (analogPinReading >> 8);
    sntmsg[5] = (byte) analogPinReading;
    acc.write(sntmsg, 6);
    delay(100);
  }
}
```

The first new method that can be seen is the analogRead method. It converts the analog voltage value to a 10-bit digital value. Since it is a 10-bit value it is too big to be stored in a byte variable. That's why you have to store it in an integer typed variable.

analogPinReading = analogRead(INPUT_PIN);

The problem is that you only can transmit bytes, so you have to transform and split the integer value into several bytes. The size of an integer as a data type is as big as 4 bytes, that's why you'll have to transform the integer to four single bytes which you can transmit later on. To transform the value, a technique called bit-shifting is used here. Bit-shifting means that the value is processed in its binary representation, which consists of single bits, and that you shift all the bits to a certain direction.

To better understand what bit-shifting is, have a look at an example. Imagine that you want to transmit the value 300. As you can already tell, this value is an integer. The binary representation of that value looks like this:

00000000 00000000 00000001 00101100 = 300

The mathematical correct expression for that is even shorter and would not require you to write all the leading zeros. It is just prefixed with 0b.

0b100101100 = 300

If you cast this value simply to a byte, only the last eight bits will form the byte value. In this case you would end up with a value of 44.

00101100 = 44

That's only one part of the whole value. To transform the rest of the bits, you need to get them into the proper places first. That's where bit-shifting is used. You can shift bits in both directions using either the operator <<, to shift them to the left side, or >>, to shift them to the right side. In this case you need a right shift, so you use the >> operator. You need to shift the value eight times to the right before you can cast it to a new byte. Since you need to shift it several times to construct all four bytes, the complete syntax would be this:

```
(byte) (300 >> 24)
(byte) (300 >> 16)
(byte) (300 >> 8)
(byte) 300
```

In its new binary representation, the above values look like this:

```
00000000
00000000
00000001
00101100
```

You can see that the shifted-out bits are simply dismissed. Now you can transmit all four data bytes and retransform them on the other side back to the initial integer.

The Android Application

In the Android application, the received four-byte value will be converted back to an integer value and the change in the measured value will be visualized by a TextView, which presents the current value. A second visual indicator will be the ProgressBar UI element. It looks similar to the already introduced SeekBar, but here the user has no possibility to interact with the bar. Have a look at the code in Listing 4-4. I'll explain the specifics afterward.

Listing 4-4. Project 4: ProjectFourActivity.java

```
package project.four.adk;
```

```
import …;

public class ProjectFourActivity extends Activity {

    …

    private static final byte COMMAND_ANALOG = 0x3;
    private static final byte TARGET_PIN = 0x0;

    private TextView adcValueTextView;
    private ProgressBar adcValueProgressBar;

    @Override
    public void onCreate(Bundle savedInstanceState) {
        super.onCreate(savedInstanceState);

        …

        setContentView(R.layout.main);
        adcValueTextView = (TextView) findViewById(R.id.adc_value_text_view);
        adcValueProgressBar = (ProgressBar) findViewById(R.id.adc_value_bar);
    }

    @Override
    public void onResume() {
        super.onResume();
        …
    }

    @Override
    public void onPause() {
        super.onPause();
        …
    }

    @Override
    public void onDestroy() {
        super.onDestroy();
        …
    }

    private final BroadcastReceiver mUsbReceiver = new BroadcastReceiver() {
        @Override
        public void onReceive(Context context, Intent intent) {
            …
        }
    };

    private void openAccessory(UsbAccessory accessory) {
        mFileDescriptor = mUsbManager.openAccessory(accessory);
        if (mFileDescriptor != null) {
            mAccessory = accessory;
```

```
        FileDescriptor fd = mFileDescriptor.getFileDescriptor();
        mInputStream = new FileInputStream(fd);
        mOutputStream = new FileOutputStream(fd);
        Thread thread = new Thread(null, commRunnable, TAG);
        thread.start();
        Log.d(TAG, "accessory opened");
    } else {
        Log.d(TAG, "accessory open fail");
    }
}

private void closeAccessory() {
    …
}

Runnable commRunnable = new Runnable() {

    @Override
    public void run() {
        int ret = 0;
        byte[] buffer = new byte[6];

        while (ret >= 0) {
            try {
                ret = mInputStream.read(buffer);
            } catch (IOException e) {
                Log.e(TAG, "IOException", e);
                break;
            }

            switch (buffer[0]) {
            case COMMAND_ANALOG:

                if (buffer[1] == TARGET_PIN) {
                    final int adcValue = ((buffer[2] & 0xFF) << 24)
                                       + ((buffer[3] & 0xFF) << 16)
                                       + ((buffer[4] & 0xFF) << 8)
                                       + (buffer[5] & 0xFF);
                    runOnUiThread(new Runnable() {

                        @Override
                        public void run() {
                            adcValueProgressBar.setProgress(adcValue);
                            adcValueTextView.setText(getString(R.string.adc_value_text,
                                adcValue));
                        }
                    });
                }
                break;

            default:
```

```
                    Log.d(TAG, "unknown msg: " + buffer[0]);
                    break;
                }
            }
        }
    };
}
```

As you can see, the new variables in this code snippet are the same message definition bytes as in the Arduino sketch and the two UI elements I described at the beginning.

```
private static final byte COMMAND_ANALOG = 0x3;
private static final byte TARGET_PIN = 0x0;

private TextView adcValueTextView;
private ProgressBar adcValueProgressBar;
```

Have a look at the UI element definition that needs to be made in the main.xml layout file shown in Listing 4-5. In addition to the usual layout attributes of both elements, you have to define the max value attribute of the ProgressBar so that the graphical visualization can be made in the correct range from 0 to 1023.

You can see that there is a second attribute of importance. The style attribute tells the system to render the UI elements' appearance in a certain style. If the attribute is omitted, the ProgressBar will render in its default style, which is a loading-type spinning wheel. That's not what you want here so you can overwrite the style with another one. The syntax for that particular style lookup looks a little bit strange. The ?android: prefix means that this particular resource cannot be found in the current project's res folder but in the Android system resources.

Listing 4-5. Project 4: main.xml

```
<?xml version="1.0" encoding="utf-8"?>
<LinearLayout xmlns:android="http://schemas.android.com/apk/res/android"
    android:orientation="vertical"
    android:layout_width="fill_parent"
    android:layout_height="fill_parent"
    android:gravity="center">
    <TextView android:id="@+id/adc_value_text_view"
        android:layout_width="wrap_content"
        android:layout_height="wrap_content"/>
    <ProgressBar android:id="@+id/adc_value_bar"
        android:layout_width="fill_parent"
        android:layout_height="wrap_content"
        android:max="1023"
        style="?android:attr/progressBarStyleHorizontal"/>
</LinearLayout>
```

As in project 3 you are interested in the received input, so the logic of receiving data stays pretty much the same. A separate thread is responsible for reading the inputstream and processing the received message. You can see that the last four bytes of the received message are reconverted into an integer value again by using the bit-shifting technique—only this time, the shift happens in the other direction.

```
final int adcValue = ((buffer[2] & 0xFF) << 24)
    + ((buffer[3] & 0xFF) << 16)
    + ((buffer[4] & 0xFF) << 8)
    + (buffer[5] & 0xFF);
```

You also see that the byte values are altered before they are bit-shifted. This operation is called bitwise AND. By applying the value 0xFF you eliminate possible sign-bit errors when dealing with negative and positive numbers.

If you consider the example from before and imagine that the value that was measured is 300, then the four received bytes would have the following values without the bit-shifting:

00000000 = 0
00000000 = 0
00000001 = 1
00101100 = 44

To reconstruct the original integer value you need to left-shift the byte values as done above.

00000000 << 24 = 00000000 00000000 00000000 00000000 = 0
00000000 << 16 = 00000000 00000000 00000000 00000000 = 0
00000001 << 8 = 00000000 00000000 00000001 00000000 = 256
00101100   = 00000000 00000000 00000000 00101100 = 44

Now if you add the received byte values you end up with the original integer value again.

0 + 0 + 256 + 44 = 300

The last thing to do is to visualize the value to the user. With the helper method runOnUiThread, both UI elements are updated. The TextView gets its text set accordingly and the ProgressBar sets its new progress value.

Upload both the Arduino sketch and the Android application and see how the value changes if you adjust the potentiometer. The final result is shown in Figure 4-14

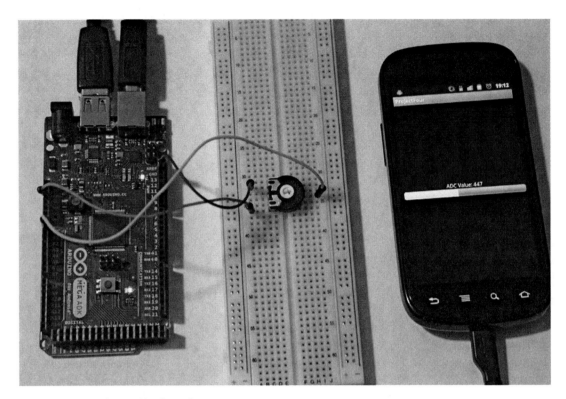

Figure 4-14. Project 4: Final result

Summary

This chapter showed how you can read values from the input pins of your ADK board. You used the digital pins in their input configuration to read digital inputs of HIGH and LOW. A button or switch was used to toggle between those two states and an Android application expressed the current state by vibrating whenever the button was pressed or the switch got closed. You also learned about a second possibility to measure a range of values by converting analog voltage readings on the analog input pins of the ADK board to digital expressions in the range from 0 to 1023. An Android application visualized the current reading with a new UI element, the ProgressBar. You changed the appearance of a UI element by applying a different style. Along the way you learned about the principles of a voltage divider and a pull-up resistor and you learned that bit-shifting can serve as a way for data conversion.

CHAPTER 5

Sounds

The ADK board on its own is not capable of generating or detecting sounds. Luckily there is one component that can help with both of these tasks: the piezo buzzer.

What is the definition of sound? *Sound*, in general is a set of waves of pressure that can be transmitted through solids, liquids, and gases. A piezo buzzer transmits sound through the air by oscillating at different frequencies. The different frequencies of those waves make up the different sounds you are able to hear. A human being is capable of hearing frequencies in the range of 20Hz up to 20,000Hz. The unit for frequencies is Hz (Hertz). It defines the number of cycles per second. So the more sound waves the human ear detects per second, the higher the perceived sound is. If you have ever stood close to a big audio speaker box you may have seen the membrane of the speaker vibrating. That's essentially the speaker producing pressure waves at different frequencies.

In the following two projects you will learn how to use the piezo buzzer to generate sound and how to detect sound in the proximity. The first project will provide you with a way to generate sound for your own projects so that you can build audio alarm systems, notification devices, or simple musical instruments. The second project will show you a way to detect sound in close range or even vibrations. Those capabilities are used, for example, in knock sensor projects or to measure vibrations that could harm sensitive goods.

Project 5: Generating Sound with a Piezo Buzzer

This project will show you how to use a piezo buzzer to generate sound. It will explain the principle of the reverse piezoelectric effect. You will use your Android device to select a note's frequency value which will be transmitted to your ADK board to generate a sound with the piezo buzzer.

The Parts

For this project you will need one new component: a piezoelectric component, that is, a piezo buzzer. Other than that, you only need the following components (shown in Figure 5-1):

- ADK board
- Breadboard
- Piezo buzzer
- Some wires

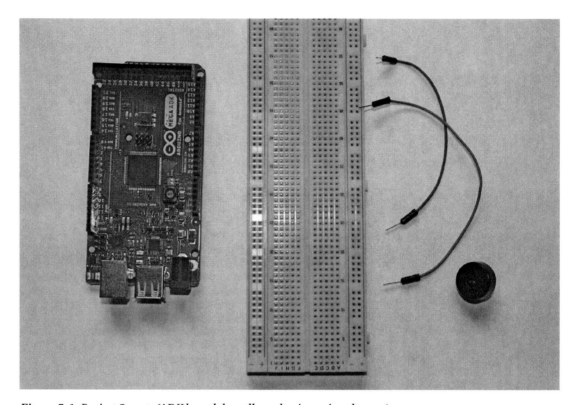

Figure 5-1. Project 5 parts (ADK board, breadboard, wires, piezo buzzer)

ADK Board

You will use one of the digital pins of your ADK board capable of supporting pulse-width modulation (PWM). You already used the PWM capability of the digital pins to dim an LED. Again you are using the PWM feature to generate square waves, which will be applied to the piezo buzzer later on. The change of the square wave characteristics will cause the piezo buzzer to produce different frequencies of oscillation and therefore produce different sounds.

Piezo Buzzer

A *piezo buzzer* is a piezoelectric component that can utilize both the piezoelectric effect and the reverse piezoelectric effect. This means that it can sense and generate sound. A typical piezo buzzer consists of a ceramic wafer placed on a metal plate. The ceramic wafer contains piezo crystals, which are sensitive to oscillation.

The *piezoelectric effect* describes that a mechanical force such as pressure leads to a generation of electrical charge across the piezo element. The pressure waves let the ceramic wafer expand and contract. Together with the metal plate it causes an oscillation and the resulting deformation of the piezo crystals generates a measurable electrical charge. (See Figure 5-2.) In the second project, the piezoelectric effect is used to sense vibrations in its proximity.

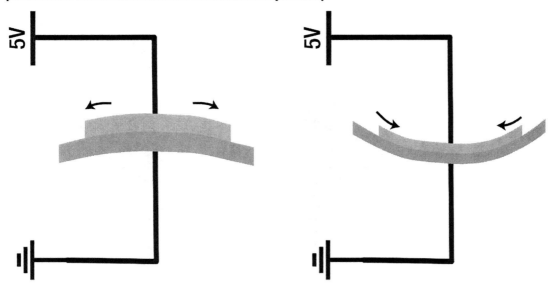

Figure 5-2. Piezoelectric effect (expansion and contraction of the piezo element)

The reverse piezoelectric effect describes the effect of the piezo element which generates a mechanical force such as pressure waves when an electrical potential is applied. Stimulated by the electrical potential, the piezo element again contracts and expands and the resulting oscillation produces sound waves which can be even amplified by a resonating hollow casing. The different sound waves being produced depend on the frequency of the oscillation. This effect will be demonstrated in this chapter's first project to generate sounds in different frequencies.

The most common piezo buzzers come in a plastic casing, but you also can find them as ceramic piezo buzzer plates (Figure 5-3).

Figure 5-3. Piezo buzzer

Piezo buzzers are used in household appliances, industrial machines, and even musical equipment. You may have heard them in fire alarm systems, accessibility systems, or when your washing machine or dryer tries to tell you that their work is done. Sometimes you see them attached to acoustic guitars as a pickup to convert the vibration of the resonating guitar body to electrical signals.

The Setup

This project's setup is very easy (see Figure 5-4). You only need to connect one connection of the piezo buzzer to GND and the other one to digital pin 2 of your ADK board. Keep in mind that some piezo buzzers may have a certain polarity. Normally they are marked accordingly or they already have the corresponding wires attached. In that case, connect the negative wire to GND and the positive wire to digital pin 2.

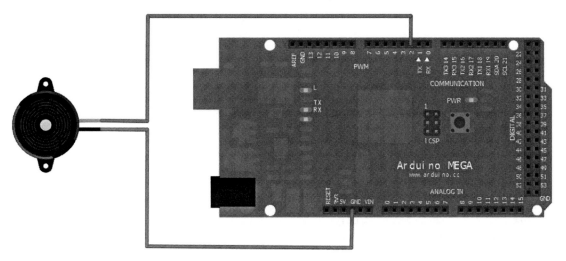

Figure 5-4. Project 5 setup

The Software

For this project you will write an Android application that lets the user choose a note via the Spinner UI element, which is something like a drop-down list, something you might know from the Web. The note will be mapped to its representing frequency and its value will be transmitted to the ADK board. On the Arduino side, you utilize the Arduino tone method, which is part of the Arduino IDE, to generate the corresponding sound on the connected piezo buzzer.

The Arduino Sketch

The Arduino sketch for this project is very similar to the one used in Project 2. Only this time, instead of writing to the output pin directly with the analogWrite method, you will be using the tone method, which generates the necessary waveform to produce the desired sound. Internally, it uses the capability of the addressed digital PWM pin to create the waveform. Have a look at the complete Listing 5-1. I will explain what the tone method does afterward.

Listing 5-1. Project 5: Arduino Sketch

```
#include <Max3421e.h>
#include <Usb.h>
#include <AndroidAccessory.h>

#define COMMAND_ANALOG 0x3
#define TARGET_PIN_2 0x2

AndroidAccessory acc("Manufacturer",
                     "Model",
                     "Description",
                     "Version",
```

```
                    "URI",
                    "Serial");

byte rcvmsg[6];

void setup() {
  Serial.begin(19200);
  pinMode(TARGET_PIN_2, OUTPUT);
  acc.powerOn();
}

void loop() {
  if (acc.isConnected()) {
    int len = acc.read(rcvmsg, sizeof(rcvmsg), 1);
    if (len > 0) {
      if (rcvmsg[0] == COMMAND_ANALOG) {
        if (rcvmsg[1] == TARGET_PIN_2){
          int output = ((rcvmsg[2] & 0xFF) << 24)
                     + ((rcvmsg[3] & 0xFF) << 16)
                     + ((rcvmsg[4] & 0xFF) << 8)
                     + (rcvmsg[5] & 0xFF);
          //set the frequency for the desired tone in Hz
          tone(TARGET_PIN_2, output);
        }
      }
    }
  }
}
```

The Arduino IDE provides an overloaded special method called tone for generating square waves, which can be used to produce sounds with a speaker or a piezo buzzer. In its first variant the tone method accepts two parameters, the digital PWM pin to which the buzzer is connected to and the frequency in Hz.

```
tone(pin, frequency);
```

Its second variant takes even a third parameter where you can specify the duration of the tone in milliseconds.

```
tone(pin, frequency, duration);
```

Internally, the tone method implementation uses the analogWrite method to utilize the PWM functionality of the ADK board to produce the waveforms. As you can see, the two-parameter variant of the tone method has been used in this example to produce a steady continuous tone. The received frequency value is converted by using the bit-shifting technique before it is fed to the tone method.

The Android Application

For the Android part, you will use a drop-down list–like UI element called Spinner to let the user chose a note which will be mapped to its corresponding frequency. You will learn how list-like UI elements are initialized and how to work with them. Have a look at the complete Listing 5-2 before I explain the specifics.

Listing 5-2. Project 5: ProjectFiveActivity.java

```java
package project.five.adk;

import …;

public class ProjectFiveActivity extends Activity {

    …

    private static final byte COMMAND_ANALOG = 0x3;
    private static final byte TARGET_PIN_2 = 0x2;

    private Spinner notesSpinner;
    private ArrayAdapter<CharSequence> adapter;
    private int[] notes = {/*C3*/ 131, /*D3*/ 147, /*E3*/ 165,
                        /*F3*/ 175, /*G3*/ 196, /*A3*/ 220, /*B3*/ 247};

    /** Called when the activity is first created. */
    @Override
    public void onCreate(Bundle savedInstanceState) {
        super.onCreate(savedInstanceState);

        …

        setContentView(R.layout.main);
        notesSpinner = (Spinner) findViewById(R.id.spinner);
        notesSpinner.setOnItemSelectedListener(onItemSelectedListener);
        adapter = ArrayAdapter.createFromResource(this, R.array.notes,
                            android.R.layout.simple_spinner_item);
        adapter.setDropDownViewResource(android.R.layout.simple_spinner_dropdown_item);
        notesSpinner.setAdapter(adapter);
    }

    /**
     * Called when the activity is resumed from its paused state and immediately
     * after onCreate().
     */
    @Override
    public void onResume() {
        super.onResume();
        …
    }

    /** Called when the activity is paused by the system. */
    @Override
    public void onPause() {
        super.onPause();
        closeAccessory();
    }
```

```
/**
 * Called when the activity is no longer needed prior to being removed from
 * the activity stack.
 */
@Override
public void onDestroy() {
    super.onDestroy();
    unregisterReceiver(mUsbReceiver);
}

OnItemSelectedListener onItemSelectedListener = new OnItemSelectedListener() {

    @Override
    public void onItemSelected(AdapterView<?> adapterView, View view, int position,
        long id) {
        new AsyncTask<Integer, Void, Void>() {

            @Override
            protected Void doInBackground(Integer... params) {
                sendAnalogValueCommand(TARGET_PIN_2, notes[params[0]]);
                return null;
            }
        }.execute(position);
    }

    @Override
    public void onNothingSelected(AdapterView<?> arg0) {
        // not implemented
    }
};

private final BroadcastReceiver mUsbReceiver = new BroadcastReceiver() {
    @Override
    public void onReceive(Context context, Intent intent) {
        ...
    }
};

private void openAccessory(UsbAccessory accessory) {
    ...
}

private void closeAccessory() {
    ...
}

public void sendAnalogValueCommand(byte target, int value) {
    byte[] buffer = new byte[6];
    buffer[0] = COMMAND_ANALOG;
    buffer[1] = target;
    buffer[2] = (byte) (value >> 24);
```

```
        buffer[3] = (byte) (value >> 16);
        buffer[4] = (byte) (value >> 8);
        buffer[5] = value;
        if (mOutputStream != null) {
            try {
                mOutputStream.write(buffer);
            } catch (IOException e) {
                Log.e(TAG, "write failed", e);
            }
        }
    }
}
```

Let's first have a look at the variables that are new.

```
private Spinner notesSpinner;
private ArrayAdapter<CharSequence> adapter;
              notes = {/*C3*/ 131, /*D3*/ 147, /*E3*/ 165,
                  /*F3*/ 175, /*G3*/ 196, /*A3*/ 220, /*B3*/ 247};
```

e a UI element called Spinner to give the user the possibility of selecting a note. The
element that is very similar to a drop-down list. It is an input element that unfolds a list
he elements in the list are the possible input values that can be selected. List-like UI
ge their content with adapters. Those adapters are responsible for filling the list with
accessing it later on. The ArrayAdapter you see here is such an adapter and can hold a
ontent elements. The last thing here is a mapping array that maps the selected note to its
esentation later on. The values are close approximations of the corresponding note's
rtz (Hz).

Before you can assign the new view element to the variable, you'll have to define it in your layout
main.xml file (see Listing 5-3).

Listing 5-3. Project 5: main.xml

```
<?xml version="1.0" encoding="utf-8"?>
<LinearLayout xmlns:android="http://schemas.android.com/apk/res/android"
        android:orientation="vertical"
        android:layout_width="fill_parent"
        android:layout_height="fill_parent"
        android:gravity="center">
        <Spinner android:id="@+id/spinner"
        android:layout_width="fill_parent"
        android:layout_height="wrap_content"
        android:prompt="@string/notes_prompt"/>
</LinearLayout>
```

The Spinner has one new attribute called prompt which defines the prompt shown when the list
content of the Spinner is shown. You can define a short descriptive label in the strings.xml file that can
be referenced in that attribute.

```
<string name="notes_prompt">Choose a note</string>
```

Now you can properly initialize the view element in the onCreate method.

```
/** Called when the activity is first created. */
@Override
public void onCreate(Bundle savedInstanceState) {
    super.onCreate(savedInstanceState);

    …

    setContentView(R.layout.main);
    notesSpinner = (Spinner) findViewById(R.id.spinner);
    notesSpinner.setOnItemSelectedListener(onItemSelectedListener);
    adapter = ArrayAdapter.createFromResource(this, R.array.notes,
                        android.R.layout.simple_spinner_item);
    adapter.setDropDownViewResource(android.R.layout.simple_spinner_dropdown_item);
    notesSpinner.setAdapter(adapter);
}
```

To get notified and to react if a new value was selected you'll have to set a listener on the Spinner. In this case you will be using an OnItemSelectedListener, which you will implement later. The ArrayAdapter responsible for the content management can be initialized easily with a static method called createFromResource. As the name implies, it constructs the content out of a resource definition. This definition is made in the strings.xml file. You just need to define an array of string items as shown here.

```
<string-array name="notes">
    <item>C3</item>
    <item>D3</item>
    <item>E3</item>
    <item>F3</item>
    <item>G3</item>
    <item>A3</item>
    <item>B3</item>
</string-array>
```

It has to be given a name attribute so that it can be referenced later on. The initializing method call takes three parameters. The first one is a context object. Here you can use the current Activity itself because it extends the Context class. The second parameter is the resource id of the content definition. Here you'll use the notes array you defined before. The last parameter is the resource id of the layout for the drop-down box itself. You can use a custom layout or just take the default system spinner item layout as done here by using the identifier android.R.layout.simple_spinner_item.

```
ArrayAdapter.createFromResource(this, R.array.notes,
                        android.R.layout.simple_spinner_item);
```

You should also set the appearance of the single content items in the list. This is done by calling the setDropDownViewResource method with a layout id as well. Again, you can just use the system default here.

```
adapter.setDropDownViewResource(android.R.layout.simple_spinner_dropdown_item);
```

Finally you can associate the configured adapter with the Spinner.

```
notesSpinner.setAdapter(adapter);
```

The initial steps have been done and it is time to implement the listener responsible for handling the case in which a value has been selected.

```
OnItemSelectedListener onItemSelectedListener = new OnItemSelectedListener() {

    @Override
    public void onItemSelected(AdapterView<?> adapterView, View view, int position,
        long id) {
        new AsyncTask<Integer, Void, Void>() {

            @Override
            protected Void doInBackground(Integer... params) {
                sendAnalogValueCommand(TARGET_PIN_2, notes[params[0]]);
                return null;
            }
        }.execute(position);
    }

    @Override
    public void onNothingSelected(AdapterView<?> arg0) {
        // not implemented
    }
};
```

When implementing the OnItemSelectedListener, you will have to address two methods. One is the onNothingSelected method, which is not of interest in this case; the other is the onItemSelected method, which gets triggered when a user makes a selection. When it gets called by the system it supplies four parameters: the AdapterView with its underlying adapter, the view element that was selected, the position of the selected item in the list, and the id of that list item. Now that you know which item has been selected, you can map the note to its actual frequency and send the value to the ADK board. This is done in an AsyncTask so that the IO operation does not happen on the UI thread.

```
new AsyncTask<Integer, Void, Void>() {

    @Override
    protected Void doInBackground(Integer... params) {
        sendAnalogValueCommand(TARGET_PIN_2, notes[params[0]]);
        return null;
    }
}.execute(position);
```

The frequency integer value has to be bit-shifted in the sendAnalogValueCommand method before transmitting it as a four-byte data packet.

Everything is set and you are good to go (Figure 5-5). Deploy both the Android application and the Arduino sketch and listen to the sound of the piezo buzzer. You can even extend this project and play melodies with the piezo buzzer. A tutorial on how to do just that can be found in the tutorial area on the Arduino home page at http://www.arduino.cc/en/Tutorial/PlayMelody.

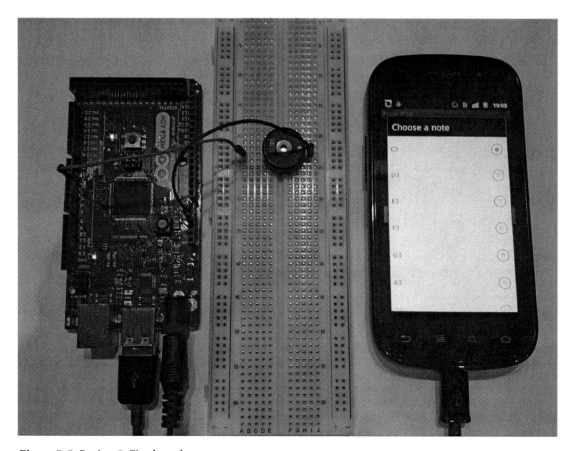

Figure 5-5. Project 5: Final result

Project 6: Sensing Sound with a Piezo Buzzer

This chapter's second project will show you the principle of the piezoelectric effect. You will use the piezo buzzer to build a knock sensor that produces an electrical charge when the piezo element is oscillating. You will write an Android application in which the background changes each time a knock has been sensed. A simple `ProgressBar` UI element will visualize the current ADC value that has been sensed.

The Parts

The only additional part you will need for this project is a high value resistor. You will use a 1MΩ pull-down resistor. The other components have already been used in the previous projects (See Figure 5-6):

- ADK board
- Breadboard

- 1MΩ pull-down resistor
- Piezo buzzer
- Some wires

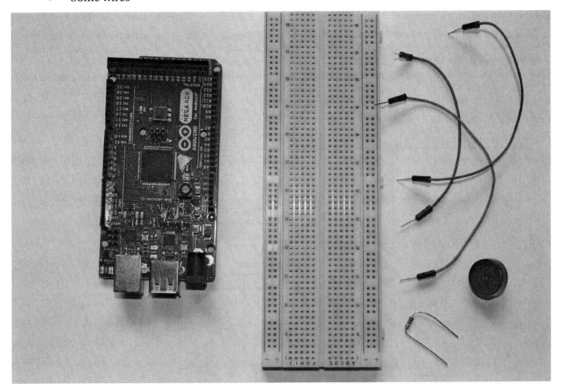

Figure 5-6. Project 6 parts (ADK board, breadboard, wires, 1MΩ Resistor, piezo buzzer)

ADK Board

Since you need to measure the change in voltage when the piezo buzzer oscillates, you need to use one of the analog input pins on your ADK board. The analog input will be converted into a digital value (ADC), which can be processed in your Android application later on.

Piezo Buzzer

As already mentioned, you will utilize the piezoelectric effect of the piezo buzzer in this project. A knock or a sudden pressure wave influences the piezo element in a way that makes it oscillate. The frequency of that oscillation has an effect on the electrical charge that is produced across the piezo element. So the frequency of the oscillation stands in direct proportion to the charge produced.

Pull-down Resistor

In the previous chapter you used a pull-up resistor to pull a digital input pin steadily to the state HIGH (+5V) to avoid static noise when the circuit was in an idle state. When the connected button was pressed and the circuit was connected to GND (0V), the path of least resistance led to GND and the input pin was set to 0V.

Since you need to measure the applied voltage on an analog pin now, it makes no sense to pull the input pin up to 5V. You just wouldn't be able to properly measure the change in voltage caused by the piezo buzzer because the input pin would constantly float around 5V. To continue to avoid the static noise that is caused in an idle state while also able to measure the changes in voltage, you can pull the input pin down to GND (0V) and measure the voltage if the piezo element generates a load. The simple circuit schematic for this use case is shown in Figure 5-7.

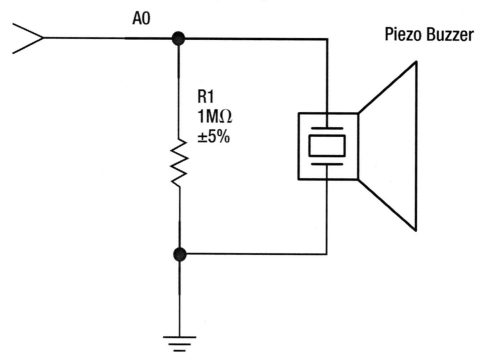

Figure 5-7. Pull-down resistor circuit for piezo buzzer input measurement

The Setup

This project's setup (shown in Figure 5-8) changes only slightly from the one before. You only need to connect the high value resistor in parallel to the piezo buzzer. The positive lead of the piezo buzzer is connected to one end of the resistor and the analog input pin A0 of your ADK board. The negative lead is connected to the other end of the resistor and GND.

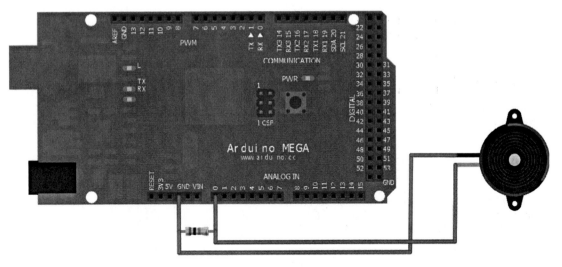

Figure 5-8. *Project 6 setup*

The Software

You will write an Arduino sketch that reads the analog input pin A0. If the piezo buzzer oscillates and a voltage is measured on that pin, the corresponding value will be converted to a digital value and can be transmitted to the Android device. The Android application will visualize the transmitted value via a `ProgressBar` UI element and, if a certain threshold is reached, the background color of the container view element will change to a random color. So each knock will eventually produce a new background color.

The Arduino Sketch

This project's Arduino sketch is essentially the same as in project 4. You will measure the analog input on pin A0 and transmit the converted ADC values, in the range of 0 to 1023, to the connected Android device. See the complete Listing 5-4.

Listing 5-4. *Project 6: Arduino Sketch*

```
#include <Max3421e.h>
#include <Usb.h>
#include <AndroidAccessory.h>

#define COMMAND_ANALOG 0x3
#define INPUT_PIN_0 0x0

AndroidAccessory acc("Manufacturer",
                     "Model",
                     "Description",
                     "Version",
                     "URI",
```

```
                             "Serial");

byte sntmsg[6];

void setup() {
  Serial.begin(19200);
  acc.powerOn();
  sntmsg[0] = COMMAND_ANALOG;
  sntmsg[1] = INPUT_PIN_0;
}

void loop() {
  if (acc.isConnected()) {
    int currentValue = analogRead(INPUT_PIN_0);
    sntmsg[2] = (byte) (currentValue >> 24);
    sntmsg[3] = (byte) (currentValue >> 16);
    sntmsg[4] = (byte) (currentValue >> 8);
    sntmsg[5] = (byte) currentValue;
    acc.write(sntmsg, 6);
    delay(100);
  }
}
```

Again you can see that you have to use the bit-shifting technique to encode the analog-to-digital converted integer value into bytes before you can transmit them to the Android device via the predefined message protocol.

The Android Application

The Android application decodes the received message and transforms the received bytes back into the measured integer value. If a threshold of 100 is reached, the LinearLayout view container will change its background color randomly. As a second visualization element you will add a ProgressBar to the LinearLayout so that a spike in the measurements can be seen if the user knocks in proximity of the piezo buzzer.

Listing 5-5. Project 6: ProjectSixActivity.java

```
package project.six.adk;

import …;

public class ProjectSixActivity extends Activity {

    …

    private static final byte COMMAND_ANALOG = 0x3;
    private static final byte TARGET_PIN = 0x0;

    private LinearLayout linearLayout;
    private TextView adcValueTextView;
    private ProgressBar adcValueProgressBar;
```

```java
private Random random;
private final int THRESHOLD = 100;

/** Called when the activity is first created. */
@Override
public void onCreate(Bundle savedInstanceState) {
    super.onCreate(savedInstanceState);

    …

    setContentView(R.layout.main);
    linearLayout = (LinearLayout) findViewById(R.id.linear_layout);
    adcValueTextView = (TextView) findViewById(R.id.adc_value_text_view);
    adcValueProgressBar = (ProgressBar) findViewById(R.id.adc_value_bar);

    random = new Random(System.currentTimeMillis());
}

/**
 * Called when the activity is resumed from its paused state and immediately
 * after onCreate().
 */
@Override
public void onResume() {
    super.onResume();
    …
}

/** Called when the activity is paused by the system. */
@Override
public void onPause() {
    super.onPause();
    closeAccessory();
}

/**
 * Called when the activity is no longer needed prior to being removed from
 * the activity stack.
 */
@Override
public void onDestroy() {
    super.onDestroy();
    unregisterReceiver(mUsbReceiver);
}

private final BroadcastReceiver mUsbReceiver = new BroadcastReceiver() {
    @Override
    public void onReceive(Context context, Intent intent) {
        …
    }
};
```

```
    private void openAccessory(UsbAccessory accessory) {
        mFileDescriptor = mUsbManager.openAccessory(accessory);
        if (mFileDescriptor != null) {
            mAccessory = accessory;
            FileDescriptor fd = mFileDescriptor.getFileDescriptor();
            mInputStream = new FileInputStream(fd);
            mOutputStream = new FileOutputStream(fd);
            Thread thread = new Thread(null, commRunnable, TAG);
            thread.start();
            Log.d(TAG, "accessory opened");
        } else {
            Log.d(TAG, "accessory open fail");
        }
    }

    private void closeAccessory() {
        try {
            if (mFileDescriptor != null) {
                mFileDescriptor.close();
            }
        } catch (IOException e) {
        } finally {
            mFileDescriptor = null;
            mAccessory = null;
        }
    }

    Runnable commRunnable = new Runnable() {

        @Override
        public void run() {
            int ret = 0;
            byte[] buffer = new byte[6];

            while (ret >= 0) {
                try {
                    ret = mInputStream.read(buffer);
                } catch (IOException e) {
                    Log.e(TAG, "IOException", e);
                    break;
                }

                switch (buffer[0]) {
                case COMMAND_ANALOG:

                    if (buffer[1] == TARGET_PIN) {
                        final int adcValue = ((buffer[2] & 0xFF) << 24)
                                            + ((buffer[3] & 0xFF) << 16)
                                            + ((buffer[4] & 0xFF) << 8)
                                            + (buffer[5] & 0xFF);
                        runOnUiThread(new Runnable() {
```

```
            @Override
            public void run() {
                adcValueProgressBar.setProgress(adcValue);
                adcValueTextView.setText(getString(R.string.adc_value_text,
                    adcValue));
                if(adcValue >= THRESHOLD) {
                    linearLayout.setBackgroundColor(Color.rgb(
                        random.nextInt(256), random.nextInt(256),
                        random.nextInt(256)));
                }
            }
        });
    }
    break;

default:
    Log.d(TAG, "unknown msg: " + buffer[0]);
    break;
    }
   }
  }
 };
}
```

The only thing that might be new to you here is the Random class. The Random class provides methods that return pseudo-random numbers for all kinds of numerical data types. The nextInt method in particular has one overloaded method signature that accepts an upper bound integer n so that it returns only values from 0 to n. After the received value from the ADK knock sensor is reconverted into an integer, it is checked against a threshold value. If the value exceeds the threshold then the nextInt method of the random object is called to generate three random integer numbers. Those numbers are used to produce an RGB Color (red, green, blue) where each integer defines the intensity of the corresponding color spectrum to form a new color. The screen's linearLayout view container is updated with that new color so that its background color is changed each time a knock occurs.

If you have finished writing both the Arduino sketch and the Android application, deploy them onto the devices and see your final result. It should look like Figure 5-9.

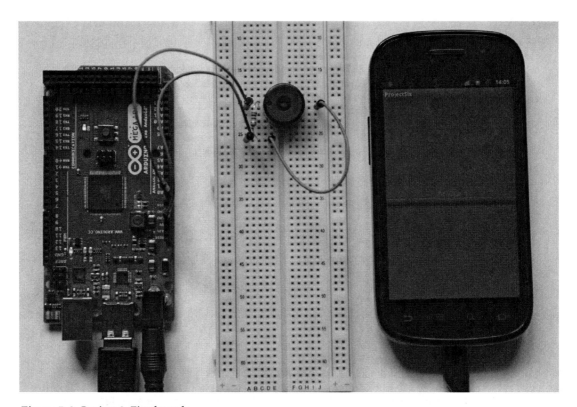

Figure 5-9. Project 6: Final result

Summary

In this chapter you learned about the principles of the piezoelectric effect and the reverse piezoelectric effect to be able to sense and to generate sound. You influenced the frequency of the oscillation of a piezo buzzer to produce sounds. You also used the piezo buzzer to detect oscillation of the piezo element caused by waves of pressure or vibration in proximity of the buzzer. Along the way, you learned about the Arduino tone method and how to work with the Android Spinner UI element. Once again you utilized the analog features of your ADK board for reading analog values and converting them into digital ones to sense sound or vibration in your proximity. You can use all this learning in further projects of your own to, for example, give audible feedback or sense vibration.

CHAPTER 6

Light Intensity Sensing

In this chapter you will learn how to sense the intensity of light in your close environment. In order to do that you will need another new component, called a photoresistor or light dependent resistor (LDR). I will explain the operating principle of this component later in the section "The Parts." But first you'll need to understand the description of light itself.

So what is light, anyway? It surrounds us everywhere in our daily life. The complete ecosystem of our planet relies on light. It is the source of all life and yet most of us have never really bothered to understand what light really is. I am not a physicist and don't claim to offer the best explanation of its physical principle but I want to at least provide a brief description of what light is to give you a sense of the goals of this chapter's project.

Light is physically described as electromagnetic radiation. *Radiation* is the term for energetic waves or particles moving through a medium. Light in that context is any wavelength of energetic waves. The human eye is only capable of seeing a certain range of wavelengths. It can respond to light in the wavelength of 390nm to 750nm. Different light colors are perceived when light is detected at a certain wavelength and frequency. Table 6-1 gives an overview of the color spectrum of light the human eye can see.

Table 6-1. Visible Light Color Ranges

Color	Wavelength	Frequency
Violet	380 – 450 nm	668 – 789 THz
Blue	450 – 475 nm	631 – 668 THz
Cyan	476 – 495 nm	606 – 630 THz
Green	495 – 570 nm	526 – 606 THz
Yellow	570 – 590 nm	508 – 526 THz
Orange	590 – 620 nm	484 – 508 THz
Red	620 – 750 nm	400 – 484 THz

A very good example of light that can't be seen by the human eye is the small infrared LED on your TV remote control. The infrared light spectrum is in the range of 700nm to 1000nm. The LED's light wavelength is usually in the area of about 980nm and therefore exceeds the light spectrum visible to the human eye. The LED communicates in manufacturer-dependent patterns with the receiver unit of the TV. Since sunlight covers a wide range of wavelengths and infrared light is part of that range, it would normally interfere with the communication. To avoid that problem, TV manufacturers use the infrared light at a certain frequency which cannot be found in sunlight.

Infrared light has a wavelength higher than that of visible light, but there is also a light with a wavelength below visible light, called ultraviolet light. *Ultraviolet light*, or UV light for short, is in the range of 10nm to 400nm. UV light is essentially electromagnetic radiation which can cause chemical reactions and can even damage biological systems. A good example of that effect is the sunburn you typically get when exposed to a lot of UV light for a long time without any protective lotion. This dangerous wavelength is lower than 300nm. With decreasing wavelength, the energy per photon increases. The high power of the photons in that wavelength has an effect on substances and organisms on a molecular level. Due to its ability to cause chemical reactions, UV light is often used for detecting certain substances. Some substances react by literally glowing. This effect is often used in crime investigations to detect counterfeit money, counterfeit passports, or even bodily fluids.

Project 7: Sensing Light Intensity with a Photoresistor

This chapter's project should provide you with a way to easily sense changes in the lighting of your surroundings. You will measure the voltage changes resulting from the intensity of exposure to light of a photoresistor on an analog input pin of your ADK board. The resulting converted digital value will be sent to the Android device to adjust the screen brightness of the Android device according to the surrounding light conditions. Most Android devices have such a sensor already built in to do exactly that, but this project should help you to understand how your device operates and how you can influence its light settings yourself.

The Parts

The new part for this project is a photoresistor. The remaining parts are not new to you (see Figure 6-1):

- ADK board
- Breadboard
- Photoresistor
- 10kΩ resistor
- Some wires

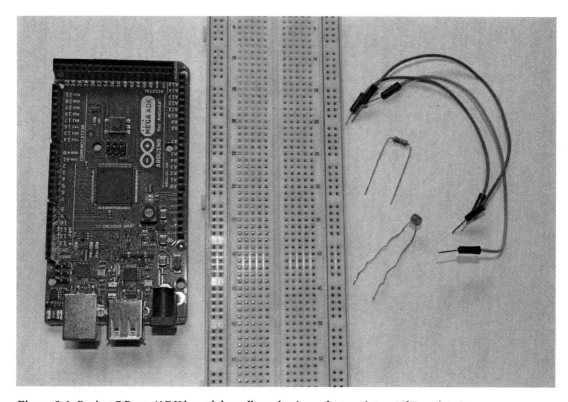

Figure 6-1. Project 7 Parts (ADK board, breadboard, wires, photoresistor, 10kΩ resistor)

ADK Board

Again it's time to use an analog input pin of your ADK board to measure voltage changes. This project's circuit setup will eventually build a voltage divider in conjunction with the photoresistor. When voltage changes are measured on an analog input pin they will be expressed with digital ADC values. You will work with the digital values later on to make assumptions about the relative ambient lighting.

Photoresistor

A *photoresistor* is a resistor whose resistance decreases if it is exposed to light (see Figure 6-2). This behavior is caused by the so-called *photoelectric effect*.

Figure 6-2. Photoresistor

The electrons of a semiconductor such as the photoresistor can have different states. Those states are described by *energy bands*. The bands consist of the *valence band,* where the electrons are bound to individual atoms, the *band gap,* where no electron states exist, and the *conduction band,* where electrons can move freely. If electrons get enough energy from the absorbed light's photons, they get knocked off their atoms and move from the valence band into the conduction band where they can move freely now. This process has a direct effect on the resistive value of the photoresistor. That's the principle of the photoelectric effect, as shown in Figure 6-3.

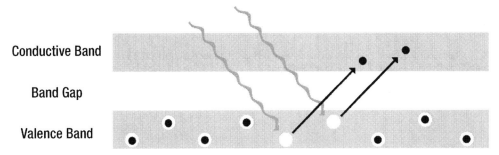

Figure 6-3. Photoelectric effect

Photoresistors are commonly used for projects that require sensing a change in lighting. A night light, for example, is a perfect use case for a photoresistor. You want the night light to turn on when the ambient lighting is very dark so that people have better orientation at night and don't have to switch on their main light. At day time, when the lighting situation is much better, you'll want the night light to switch off to save energy. A photoresistor can be used here to propagate the lighting changes to a microcontroller which in turn could switch on or off the little night light.

Another scenario would be to use the photoresistor along with other environmental sensors to build a weather station to monitor weather changes throughout the day. You could determine if it is cloudy or sunny, for example. If you were to use this kind of weather station in conjunction with an Android device, you could persist your data and even send it to remote locations. As you can see, the possibilities are limitless.

Resistor

The additional resistor is needed to create a voltage divider circuit. You learned about the principles of a voltage divider circuit in Chapter 4. The voltage divider is needed to measure voltage changes when the photoresistor is exposed to light. The circuit's output voltage changes if the resistance of the photoresistor changes. If you just connected the photoresistor on its own to the analog input pin you would measure no change in voltage on the pin because the exposure to light only changes the resistive property of the photoresistor and therefore only has an effect on the current let through. You could also end up damaging your ADK board if too much current were let through because the unused energy would manifest in a lot of heat building up.

The Setup

As described, you need to build a voltage divider circuit for this project. In order to do that, you need to connect one lead of the photoresistor to +5V and the other lead to the additional resistor and to analog input pin A0. The resistor is connected with one lead to the photoresistor and the analog input pin A0, and with the other lead to GND. The project setup can be seen in Figure 6-4.

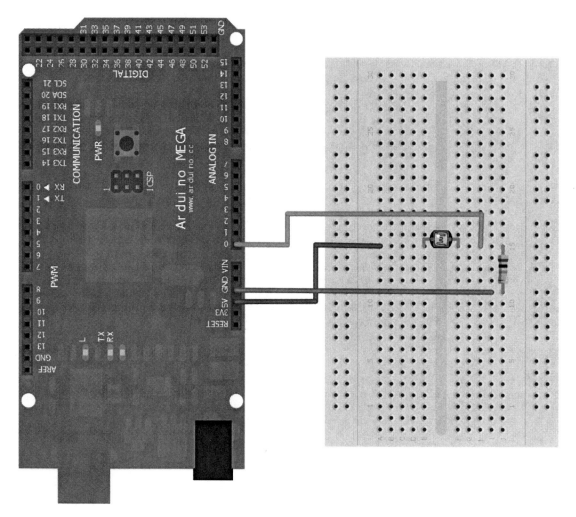

Figure 6-4. Project 7 setup

The Software

You will write an Arduino sketch that takes an analog reading at the analog input pin A0 and converts it into a digital 10-bit value. The value is mapped to a lower-range value between 0 and 100, and sent to the Android device. The Android application will calculate the new screen brightness according to the received value.

The Arduino Sketch

Again, you will take a reading of an analog pin, only this time you won't utilize the bit-shifting technique to transmit the ADC value. You will use the utility map method to transform your measured value first, but more on that later. First have a look at the complete Listing 6-1.

Listing 6-1. Project 7: Arduino Sketch

```
#include <Max3421e.h>
#include <Usb.h>
#include <AndroidAccessory.h>

#define COMMAND_LIGHT_INTENSITY 0x5
#define INPUT_PIN_0 0x0

AndroidAccessory acc("Manufacturer",
                     "Model",
                     "Description",
                     "Version",
                     "URI",
                     "Serial");

byte sntmsg[3];

void setup() {
  Serial.begin(19200);
  acc.powerOn();
  sntmsg[0] = COMMAND_LIGHT_INTENSITY;
  sntmsg[1] = INPUT_PIN_0;
}

void loop() {
  if (acc.isConnected()) {
    int currentValue = analogRead(INPUT_PIN_0);
    sntmsg[2] = map(currentValue, 0, 1023, 0, 100);
    acc.write(sntmsg, 3);
    delay(100);
  }
}
```

As you can see, a new command byte and the used analog input pin are defined at the beginning.

```
#define COMMAND_LIGHT_INTENSITY 0x5
#define INPUT_PIN_0 0x0
```

In this project you'll only need a three-byte message because you don't need to bit-shift the measured ADC value. You won't need to bit-shift the value because you will use the map method before transmitting the message. What the map method does is to translate a range of values into another range of values. You will map the ADC value, which is in the range of 0 to 1023, to a range of 0 to 100. An ADC value of 511, for example, will be translated to the value 50. When transformed, the measured value will not be bigger than 100, which is small enough to fit in one byte. After constructing the whole three-byte message you can simply transmit it to the Android device.

```
int currentValue = analogRead(INPUT_PIN_0);
sntmsg[2] = map(currentValue, 0, 1023, 0, 100);
acc.write(sntmsg, 3);
delay(100);
```

That's it for the Arduino part. Let's see what has to be done on the Android side.

The Android Application

Once again the Android application is responsible for receiving messages from the ADK board. When the Android application receives the value it calculates the new intensity of the screen brightness. Afterward, the new screen brightness is set. Listing 6-2 only emphasizes the important parts; the code has been kept short as you should know it by now.

Listing 6-2. Project 7: ProjectSevenActivity.java

```java
package project.seven.adk;

import …;

public class ProjectSevenActivity extends Activity {

    …

    private static final byte COMMAND_LIGHT_INTENSITY = 0x5;
    private static final byte TARGET_PIN = 0x0;

    private TextView lightIntensityTextView;
    private LayoutParams windowLayoutParams;

    /** Called when the activity is first created. */
    @Override
    public void onCreate(Bundle savedInstanceState) {
        super.onCreate(savedInstanceState);

        …

        setContentView(R.layout.main);
        lightIntensityTextView = (TextView) findViewById(R.id.light_intensity_text_view);
    }

    /**
     * Called when the activity is resumed from its paused state and immediately
     * after onCreate().
     */
    @Override
    public void onResume() {
        super.onResume();
        …
    }
```

```java
/** Called when the activity is paused by the system. */
@Override
public void onPause() {
    super.onPause();
    closeAccessory();
}

/**
 * Called when the activity is no longer needed prior to being removed from
 * the activity stack.
 */
@Override
public void onDestroy() {
    super.onDestroy();
    unregisterReceiver(mUsbReceiver);
}

private final BroadcastReceiver mUsbReceiver = new BroadcastReceiver() {
    @Override
    public void onReceive(Context context, Intent intent) {
        …
    }
};

private void openAccessory(UsbAccessory accessory) {
    mFileDescriptor = mUsbManager.openAccessory(accessory);
    if (mFileDescriptor != null) {
        mAccessory = accessory;
        FileDescriptor fd = mFileDescriptor.getFileDescriptor();
        mInputStream = new FileInputStream(fd);
        mOutputStream = new FileOutputStream(fd);
        Thread thread = new Thread(null, commRunnable, TAG);
        thread.start();
        Log.d(TAG, "accessory opened");
    } else {
        Log.d(TAG, "accessory open fail");
    }
}

private void closeAccessory() {
    try {
        if (mFileDescriptor != null) {
            mFileDescriptor.close();
        }
    } catch (IOException e) {
    } finally {
        mFileDescriptor = null;
        mAccessory = null;
    }
}

Runnable commRunnable = new Runnable() {
```

```java
@Override
public void run() {
    int ret = 0;
    byte[] buffer = new byte[3];

    while (ret >= 0) {
        try {
            ret = mInputStream.read(buffer);
        } catch (IOException e) {
            Log.e(TAG, "IOException", e);
            break;
        }

        switch (buffer[0]) {
        case COMMAND_LIGHT_INTENSITY:
            if (buffer[1] == TARGET_PIN) {
                final byte lightIntensityValue = buffer[2];
                runOnUiThread(new Runnable() {

                    @Override
                    public void run() {
                        lightIntensityTextView.setText(
                            getString(R.string.light_intensity_value,
                                lightIntensityValue));
                        windowLayoutParams = getWindow().getAttributes();
                        windowLayoutParams.screenBrightness =
                            lightIntensityValue / 100.0f;
                        getWindow().setAttributes(windowLayoutParams);
                    }
                });
            }
            break;

        default:
            Log.d(TAG, "unknown msg: " + buffer[0]);
            break;
        }
    }
};
}
```

First you have to define the same command byte and pin byte to match the received message later on.

```java
private static final byte COMMAND_LIGHT_INTENSITY = 0x5;
private static final byte TARGET_PIN = 0x0;

private TextView lightIntensityTextView;
private LayoutParams windowLayoutParams;
```

You declare the only UI element here, a TextView that shows the user the current lighting level in arbitrary units. You also see the declaration of a LayoutParams object. LayoutParams define how a view should be laid out by its parent. The WindowManager.LayoutParams class additionally defines a field called screenBrightness which instructs the current Window to override the user's preferred lighting settings when set.

The inner class of the type Runnable implements the screen brightness adjustment logic described above. After you have received the value from the ADK board you update the TextView UI element to give textual feedback to the user.

```
lightIntensityTextView.setText(getString(R.string.light_intensity_value,
                                          lightIntensityValue));
```

In order to adjust the screen's brightness, you first have to get a reference to the LayoutParams object of the current Window.

```
windowLayoutParams = getWindow().getAttributes();
```

The screenBrightness attribute of the LayoutParams class defines, as the name already implies, the screen's brightness. Its value is of the numerical data-type Float. The range of the value is from 0.0 to 1.0. Since you receive a value between 0 and 100, you'll have to divide that value by 100.0f to be in the required range.

```
windowLayoutParams.screenBrightness = lightIntensityValue / 100.0f;
```

When you have finished setting the brightness value you update the LayoutParams of the current Window object.

```
getWindow().setAttributes(windowLayoutParams);
```

Now it's time to see how the Android device responds to the light sensor you have built. Deploy both applications on the corresponding devices and find out. If everything worked out, your final result should look like Figure 6-5.

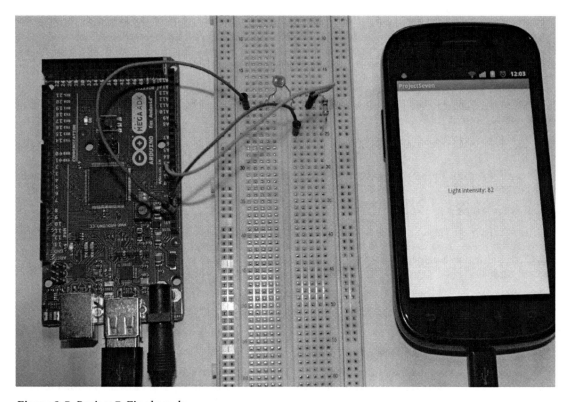

Figure 6-5. Project 7: Final result

Bonus: Measure Illuminance in Lux with Android

Sometimes it is not enough to work with relative values as has been done in this project. A more scientific approach to the measurement of light intensity is to measure the illuminance of a given area. The unit for illuminance is *lux*; its symbol is lx.

Many Android devices have built-in light sensors to adjust the screen brightness to its surrounding ambient lighting. Those sensors return their measurement values in lux (lx). To request those values, you first have to get a reference to the SensorManager class which serves as a kind of a registry for your device's sensors. After, you can get a reference to the light sensor itself by calling the getDefaultSensor method on the SensorManager with the sensor type constant for the light sensor Sensor.TYPE_LIGHT.

```
SensorManager sensorManager = (SensorManager) getSystemService(Context.SENSOR_SERVICE);
Sensor lightSensor = sensorManager.getDefaultSensor(Sensor.TYPE_LIGHT);
```

What you'll want now is to get notified whenever the current illuminance value changes. To achieve this, you register a SensorEventListener at the sensorManager and associate the corresponding sensor with this listener.

```
sensorManager.registerListener(lightSensorEventListener, lightSensor,
    SensorManager.SENSOR_DELAY_NORMAL);
```

The implementation of the `lightSensorEventListener` is as follows:

```
SensorEventListener lightSensorEventListener = new SensorEventListener(){

    @Override
    public void onAccuracyChanged(Sensor sensor, int accuracy) {
        // nothing to implement here
    }

    @Override
    public void onSensorChanged(SensorEvent sensorEvent) {
        if(sensorEvent.sensor.getType() == Sensor.TYPE_LIGHT){
            Log.i("Light in lx", sensorEvent.values[0]);
        }
    }
};
```

You only need to implement the `onSensorChanged` method since that is the event you are interested in here. The `SensorEvent` object passed into the method by the system contains an array of values. Depending on which sensor type you are reading you get different values in that array. The value for the sensor type light is at index 0 of that array and it reflects the current ambient light in lux.

You can convert your measurements taken by the photoresistor into lux as well. This, however, requires a deeper understanding of datasheets and the use of logarithmic functions if the photoresistor is nonlinear, which most of them are. Since this goes into too much detail I won't cover it here. However, you can find detailed information and tutorials on the Web if you search for "calculate lux photoresistor" with your search engine of choice.

If you aren't a big fan of math you could also use a simple pragmatic approach. You could experiment with the lighting conditions and compare the results received from your Android device's light sensor with the results from the measurements taken with the photoresistor in project 7. You could then map the lux values to your relative values and define your own lookup table for future reference. Just note that this is more of an approximation than an exact calculation.

Summary

This chapter showed you the principle of the photoelectric effect and how, with the help of a photoresistor, to utilize it to measure changes in light intensity. For that purpose you applied a voltage divider circuit layout. You also learned how to map a range of values to another range of values on the Arduino platform and you changed the brightness of your Android device's screen depending on the surrounding light intensity. As a little bonus you saw how to request the current ambient illuminance in lux on your Android device's built-in light sensor.

CHAPTER 7

Temperature Sensing

Temperature sensors are broadly used in many household devices and industrial machinery. Their purpose is to measure the current temperature in their proximity. Often they are used for precautionary reasons—to keep sensitive components from overheating, for example—or just to monitor changes in temperature.

There are several very common kinds of low-cost components to measure ambient temperature. One such component is a called a thermistor. It is a variable temperature–dependent resistor that has to be set up with a voltage divider circuit (see Chapter 6) to measure the change in a circuit's voltage. Other kinds are small integrated circuits (ICs), such as the LM35 found on the Google ADK Demo Shield, or sensors that can usually be connected directly to a microcontroller without a special circuit setup.

This chapter will show you how to use the thermistor because it is the cheapest and most widely available component to measure the temperature. You will learn how to calculate the temperature with the help of your component's datasheet and some formulas. You will write an Android application that visualizes changes in temperature by directly drawing shapes and text on the device's screen using a customized view component.

Project 8: Sensing the Temperature with a Thermistor

Project 8 will guide you through the process of building a temperature sensor. You will use a thermistor to calculate the temperature in correspondence to its resistance value. In order to do that you will have to set up a voltage divider circuit and connect it to an analog input pin of your ADK board. You will measure the change in voltage and apply some formulas to calculate the temperature. You will learn how to calculate the temperature with the help of your component's datasheet and the Steinhart-Hart equation. After that, you will transmit the determined value to the Android device. An Android application will visualize the measured temperature by drawing a thermometer and the textual value to its screen.

The Parts

Beside the aforementioned thermistor you will need an additional 10kΩ resistor, your ADK board, a breadboard, and some wires. I will use a 4.7kΩ thermistor in this project description. The 4.7kΩ resistance value is the resistance at 25° Celsius. It is not important which resistance value you choose but it is important if the thermistor has a negative or positive coefficient and which specification values its datasheet provides (but more on that later). The parts you will need for this project are shown in Figure 7-1:

- ADK board
- Breadboard

- 4.7kΩ thermistor
- 10kΩ resistor
- Some wires

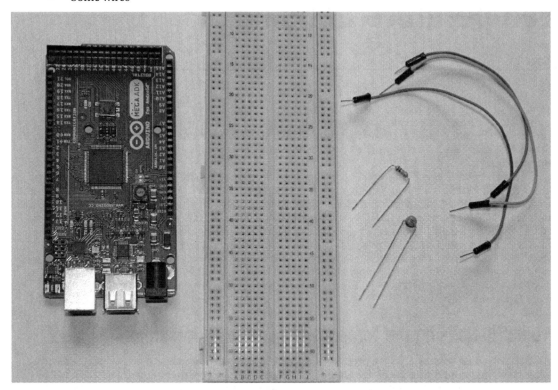

Figure 7-1. Project 8 parts (ADK board, breadboard, wires, 4.7kΩ thermistor, 10kΩ resistor)

Thermistor

A *thermistor* is a variable resistor whose resistance value is dependent on the ambient temperature. Its name is a composition of the words *thermal* and *resistor*. Thermistors are not directional, meaning that it doesn't matter which way you connect them to your circuit, just as with common resistors. They can have a negative or a positive coefficient, which means that their resistance in correspondence to the temperature increases when they have a negative coefficient and that it decreases if they have a positive coefficient. As photoresistors do, they rely on the band theory, described in Chapter 6 in the section on photoresistors. The temperature change has a direct effect on a thermistor's electrons, promoting them into the conductive band and causing a change in conductivity and resistance. Thermistors come in different shapes, but the most common is the leaded disc thermistor which resembles a typical ceramic capacitor. (See Figure 7-2.)

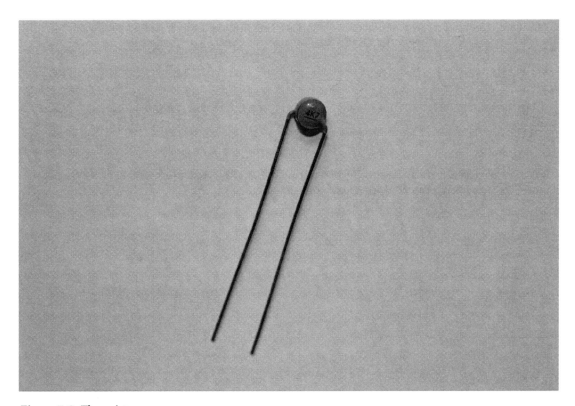

Figure 7-2. Thermistor

The most important thing to do when choosing a thermistor is to have a look into its datasheet first. The datasheet needs to contain some important details for the temperature calculation. Some datasheets contain lookup tables where each resistance value is mapped to a temperature value. Although you could work with such a table, it is a tedious task to transfer it into your code.

A better approach is to calculate the current temperature with the Steinhart-Hart equation. The following abstract will show you the necessary equations for calculating the temperature. Don't be afraid of the math here. Once you know which values you have to put into the equations, it's fairly easy.

The Steinhart-Hart Equation

The Steinhart-Hart equation describes a model where a semiconductor's resistance is dependent of the current temperature T. The formula looks like this:

$$\frac{1}{T} = a + b \times \ln(R) + c \times \ln(R)^3$$

In order to apply this formula you'll need three coefficients—a, b, and c—and, additionally, the current resistance R value of your thermistor. If your thermistor's datasheet contains those values you can work with them just fine, but most of the datasheets only provide a so called B or *Beta* coefficient.

Luckily there is another representation of the Steinhart-Hart equation which works with this B parameter and a pair of temperature $T0$ and resistance $R0$ for a specific temperature T.

$$\frac{1}{T} = \frac{1}{T_0} + \frac{1}{B} \times \ln(\frac{R}{R_0})$$

The different parameters in this equation are just representations of a, b and c.

a = (1 / T0) - (1 / B)×ln(R0)
b = 1 / B
c = 0

R_0 is specified as the resistance at T_0 which is usually 298.15 Kelvin and equal to 25° Celsius. The following is a simplified formula of the B parameter equation:

$$R = R\infty \times e^{B/T}$$

$R\infty$ describes the resistance tending to infinity and can be calculated with:

$$R\infty = R_0 \times e^{-B/T0}$$

Now that you can calculate all necessary values you can rearrange the previous formula to finally calculate the temperature.

$$T = \frac{B}{\ln(R/R\infty)}$$

The equations will be applied in the Arduino sketch later on so you will encounter them again later.

The Setup

You'll have to set up a voltage divider circuit to measure the change in voltage when the resistance of the thermistor changes. The composition of the voltage divider depends on the type of thermistor you use. If you are using a negative coefficient thermistor (NTC) your basic circuit setup looks like the one shown in Figure 7-3.

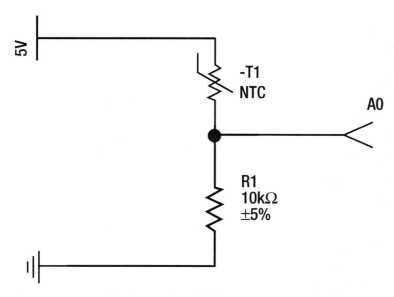

Figure 7-3. *NTC thermistor voltage divider*

If you are using a positive coefficient thermistor (PTC) you'll need a circuit as shown in Figure 7-4.

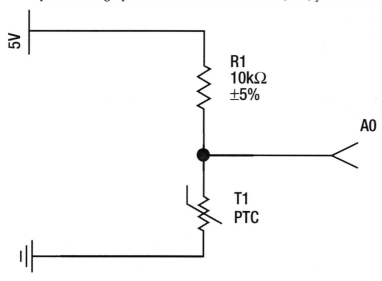

Figure 7-4. *PTC thermistor voltage divider*

For this project you'll need to see an increase in voltage measured on the analog input pin when the temperature goes up and a decrease in the measured voltage when the temperature goes down. So make sure to build your voltage divider circuit according to the thermistor you use, as shown above. Figure 7-5 shows the project setup for an NTC thermistor.

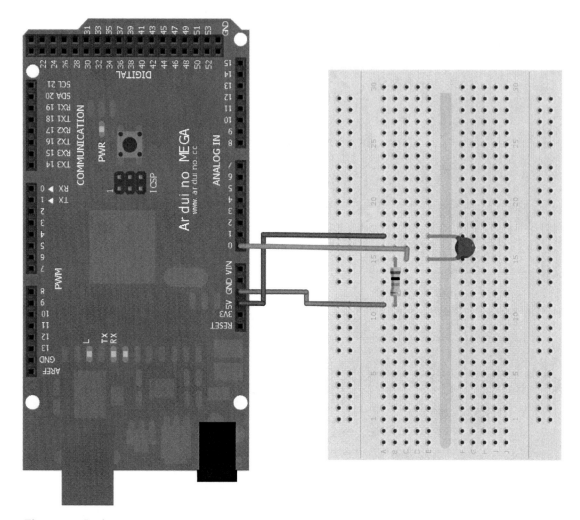

Figure 7-5. Project 8 setup

The Software

The Arduino sketch for this project will use some of the mathematical functions of the Arduino platform. You will use self-written methods to express formulas to calculate the current temperature. The temperature value will be transmitted to the Android device afterward. The Android application will demonstrate how to draw simple shapes and text to the Android device's screen to visualize the measured temperature.

The Arduino Sketch

For the first time you will be writing your own custom methods in an Arduino sketch. Custom methods must be written outside of the mandatory setup and loop method. They can have a return type and input parameters.

Additionally, you will use some of the Arduino platform's mathematical functions. You will need the log and exp function to apply the Steinhart-Hart equation for calculating the temperature. The calculated temperature value needs to be bit-shifted for proper transmission to the Android device. Have a look at the complete Listing 7-1; I describe the details after the listing.

Listing 7-1. Project 8: Arduino Sketch

```
#include <Max3421e.h>
#include <Usb.h>
#include <AndroidAccessory.h>

#define COMMAND_TEMPERATURE 0x4
#define INPUT_PIN_0 0x0
//-----
//change those values according to your thermistor's datasheet
long r0 = 4700;
long beta = 3980;
//-----

double t0 = 298.15;
long additional_resistor = 10000;
float v_in = 5.0;
double r_inf;
double currentThermistorResistance;

AndroidAccessory acc("Manufacturer",
                     "Model",
                     "Description",
                     "Version",
                     "URI",
                     "Serial");

byte sntmsg[6];

void setup() {
  Serial.begin(19200);
  acc.powerOn();
  sntmsg[0] = COMMAND_TEMPERATURE;
  sntmsg[1] = INPUT_PIN_0;
  r_inf = r0 * (exp((-beta) / t0));
}

void loop() {
  if (acc.isConnected()) {
    int currentADCValue = analogRead(INPUT_PIN_0);
```

```
    float voltageMeasured = getCurrentVoltage(currentADCValue);
    double currentThermistorResistance = getCurrentThermistorResistance(voltageMeasured);
    double currentTemperatureInDegrees =
      getCurrentTemperatureInDegrees(currentThermistorResistance);

    // multiply the float value by 10 to retain one value behind the decimal point before
    // converting to an integer for better value transmission
    int convertedValue = currentTemperatureInDegrees * 10;

    sntmsg[2] = (byte) (convertedValue >> 24);
    sntmsg[3] = (byte) (convertedValue >> 16);
    sntmsg[4] = (byte) (convertedValue >> 8);
    sntmsg[5] = (byte) convertedValue;
    acc.write(sntmsg, 6);
    delay(100);
  }
}

// "reverse ADC calculation"
float getCurrentVoltage(int currentADCValue) {
  return v_in * currentADCValue / 1024;
}

// rearranged voltage divider formula for thermistor resistance calculation
double getCurrentThermistorResistance(float voltageMeasured) {
  return ((v_in * additional_resistor) - (voltageMeasured * additional_resistor)) /
    voltageMeasured;
}

//Steinhart-Hart B equation for temperature calculation
double getCurrentTemperatureInDegrees(double currentThermistorResistance) {
  return (beta / log(currentThermistorResistance / r_inf)) - 273.15;
}
```

Let's have a look at the variables defined at the top of the sketch. The first variables you see here are the definitions for the data protocol. To confirm that temperature data is transmitted, the byte constant COMMAND_TEMPERATURE 0x4 has been chosen. The analog input pin for taking measurements is defined as being INPUT_PIN_0 0x0.

Now the datasheet-specific values are defined:

```
long r0 = 4700;
long beta = 3980;
```

I used a 4.7kΩ thermistor in this project, which means that the thermistor's resistance at 25° Celsius (*R0*) is 4.7kΩ. That's why r0 is defined as 4700. The thermistor's datasheet only defined the *B* value in my case, which was 3980. Have a look into your thermistor's datasheet and adjust those values if necessary.

Next you'll see some definitions of constant values for calculation purposes:

```
double t0 = 298.15;
long additional_resistor = 10000;
float v_in = 5.0;
```

You need the temperature in Kelvin at 25° Celsius (*T0*) for calculating *R∞*. Additionally, you need the second resistor value in the voltage divider circuit, which is 10kΩ, and the input voltage to calculate the current resistance of the thermistor.

The last two variables are needed in the *B* parameter variation of the Steinhart-Hart equation when you calculate the current temperature.

Now let's see what happens in the program flow. In the setup method, you will calculate the value for *R∞*, as it only needs to be calculated once at the beginning.

```
r_inf = r0 * (exp((-beta) / t0));
```

The repeating steps in the loop method can be described as follows:

1. Read current ADC value.

2. Calculate the actual voltage on the pin from the ADC value.

3. Calculate the current thermistor resistance.

4. Calculate the current temperature.

5. Convert the temperature to an integer number for easier transmission.

6. Transmit the data.

Now let's see the detailed description of the single steps.

The analogRead method returns the currently read ADC value. You will use it to calculate the actual voltage applied to the analog input pin. For that purpose you use a self-written custom method:

```
float getCurrentVoltage(int currentADCValue) {
  return v_in * currentADCValue / 1024;
}
```

The getCurrentVoltage method takes the currentADCValue as an input parameter and returns the calculated voltage as a float. Since the Arduino platform maps the voltage range of 0V to 5V to 1024 values, you simply multiply the currentADCValue with 5.0V and divide it by 1024 to calculate the current voltage.

Now that you have the measured voltage you can calculate the actual resistance of the thermistor with the self-written method getCurrentThermistorResistance.

```
double getCurrentThermistorResistance(float voltageMeasured) {
  return ((v_in * additional_resistor) - (voltageMeasured * additional_resistor)) /
    voltageMeasured;
}
```

The getCurrentThermistorResistance method takes the measured voltage as an input parameter, calculates the resistance, and returns it as a double.

Finally, the most important calculation can be made. To calculate the temperature you use the self-written method getCurrentTemperatureInDegrees.

```
double getCurrentTemperatureInDegrees(double currentThermistorResistance) {
  return (beta / log(currentThermistorResistance / r_inf)) - 273.15;
}
```

The method takes the current thermistor resistance as an input parameter. It uses the *B* parameter variant of the Steinhart-Hart equation to calculate the current temperature in Kelvin. To convert it into degrees Celsius you have to subtract a value of 273.15. The method returns the current temperature in degrees Celsius as a double. The Arduino log function used here is the natural logarithmic function ln used in the formulas above.

The last remaining step before transmitting the data to the Android device is to convert the temperature value for easier transmission. For example, you might have calculated a double value of 22.52 degrees Celsius. Since you are transmitting only bytes you have to convert the value into a non-floating point number. A precision of one number after the decimal point should be sufficient so the conversion is as easy as just multiplying the value by 10, causing the value to be 225.

```
int convertedValue = currentTemperatureInDegrees * 10;
```

During the multiplication the decimal point is shifted one position to the right. Since the multiplication also converts the value to a non-floating number, the number after the decimal point is used to round the preceding number up or down before being dropped. So a value of 22.52 would become 225 and a value of 22.56 would become 226.

Now that you have an integer value, you need the bit-shifting technique again to convert it into a four-byte array.

```
sntmsg[2] = (byte) (convertedValue >> 24);
sntmsg[3] = (byte) (convertedValue >> 16);
sntmsg[4] = (byte) (convertedValue >> 8);
sntmsg[5] = (byte) convertedValue;
acc.write(sntmsg, 6);
```

That's it for the Arduino part, so let's have a look at the Android application.

The Android Application

As you already know, the first steps in the Android application are to establish the communication with the ADK board, reading the transmitted data and converting it back to its original integer value. Once you've done that you will visualize the current temperature by drawing 2D graphics onto the device's screen. This application will show you how to use some of the 2D graphics classes and methods to draw simple shapes to the screen's canvas. Listing 7-2 shows a snippet of the current project's activity with the emphasis on the new and important parts.

Listing 7-2. Project 8: ProjectEightActivity.java

```
package project.eight.adk;

import …;

public class ProjectEightActivity extends Activity {

    …

    private static final byte COMMAND_TEMPERATURE = 0x4;
    private static final byte TARGET_PIN = 0x0;

    private TemperatureView temperatureView;

    /** Called when the activity is first created. */
    @Override
    public void onCreate(Bundle savedInstanceState) {
```

```
    super.onCreate(savedInstanceState);

    …

    setContentView(R.layout.main);
    temperatureView = (TemperatureView) findViewById(R.id.temperature_view);
}

/**
 * Called when the activity is resumed from its paused state and immediately
 * after onCreate().
 */
@Override
public void onResume() {
    super.onResume();
    …
}

/** Called when the activity is paused by the system. */
@Override
public void onPause() {
    super.onPause();
    closeAccessory();
}

/**
 * Called when the activity is no longer needed prior to being removed from
 * the activity stack.
 */
@Override
public void onDestroy() {
    super.onDestroy();
    unregisterReceiver(mUsbReceiver);
}

private final BroadcastReceiver mUsbReceiver = new BroadcastReceiver() {
    @Override
    public void onReceive(Context context, Intent intent) {

    }
};

private void openAccessory(UsbAccessory accessory) {
    mFileDescriptor = mUsbManager.openAccessory(accessory);
    if (mFileDescriptor != null) {
        mAccessory = accessory;
        FileDescriptor fd = mFileDescriptor.getFileDescriptor();
        mInputStream = new FileInputStream(fd);
        mOutputStream = new FileOutputStream(fd);
        Thread thread = new Thread(null, commRunnable, TAG);
        thread.start();
        Log.d(TAG, "accessory opened");
```

```
        } else {
            Log.d(TAG, "accessory open fail");
        }
    }

    private void closeAccessory() {
        try {
            if (mFileDescriptor != null) {
                mFileDescriptor.close();
            }
        } catch (IOException e) {
        } finally {
            mFileDescriptor = null;
            mAccessory = null;
        }
    }
```

```
Runnable commRunnable = new Runnable() {

    @Override
    public void run() {
        int ret = 0;
        byte[] buffer = new byte[6];

        while (ret >= 0) {
            try {
                ret = mInputStream.read(buffer);
            } catch (IOException e) {
                Log.e(TAG, "IOException", e);
                break;
            }

            switch (buffer[0]) {
            case COMMAND_TEMPERATURE:
                if (buffer[1] == TARGET_PIN) {
                    final float temperatureValue = (((buffer[2] & 0xFF) << 24)
                                            + ((buffer[3] & 0xFF) << 16)
                                            + ((buffer[4] & 0xFF) << 8)
                                            + (buffer[5] & 0xFF))
                                            / 10;
                    runOnUiThread(new Runnable() {

                        @Override
                        public void run() {
                            temperatureView.setCurrentTemperature(temperatureValue);
                        }
                    });
                }
                break;

            default:
```

```
                        Log.d(TAG, "unknown msg: " + buffer[0]);
                        break;
                }
            }
        }
    };
}
```

First have a look at the variable definitions. The first two message bytes have to match the bytes defined in the Arduino sketch, so you define them as follows:

```
private static final byte COMMAND_TEMPERATURE = 0x4;
private static final byte TARGET_PIN = 0x0;
```

Then you can see another variable of the type TemperatureView.

```
private TemperatureView temperatureView;
```

TemperatureView, as the name implies, is a self-written custom View which extends the Android system View class. We will have a look into that class soon, but first let's continue with the remaining code of the activity class.

After reading the received message, you have to convert the byte array back into its original integer value. You just reverse the bit-shifting done in the Arduino part to get the integer value. Additionally you need to divide the integer number by ten to get the floating-point value you initially calculated.

```
final float temperatureValue = (((buffer[2] & 0xFF) << 24)
                            + ((buffer[3] & 0xFF) << 16)
                            + ((buffer[4] & 0xFF) << 8)
                            + (buffer[5] & 0xFF))
                            / 10;
```

A received value of 225 would now be converted to 22.5.

The last thing to do is to transfer the value to the TemperatureView so that you can draw a temperature visualization on its canvas.

```
runOnUiThread(new Runnable() {

    @Override
    public void run() {
        temperatureView.setCurrentTemperature(temperatureValue);
    }
});
```

Remember that you should update UI elements only on the UI thread. You have to set the temperature value on the TemperatureView within the runOnUIThread method because it will invalidate itself afterward to be redrawn.

The 2D drawings are implemented in the TemperatureView class itself so have a look at the complete Listing 7-3 first.

Listing 7-3. Project 8: TemperatureView.java

```
package project.eight.adk;

import android.content.Context;
import android.content.res.TypedArray;
```

```java
import android.graphics.Canvas;
import android.graphics.Color;
import android.graphics.Paint;
import android.graphics.RectF;
import android.util.AttributeSet;
import android.view.View;

public class TemperatureView extends View {
    private float currentTemperature;
    private Paint textPaint = new Paint();
    private Paint thermometerPaint = new Paint();
    private RectF thermometerOval = new RectF();
    private RectF thermometerRect = new RectF();

    private int availableWidth;
    private int availableHeight;

    private final float deviceDensity;

    private int ovalLeftBorder;
    private int ovalTopBorder;
    private int ovalRightBorder;
    private int ovalBottomBorder;

    private int rectLeftBorder;
    private int rectTopBorder;
    private int rectRightBorder;
    private int rectBottomBorder;

    public TemperatureView(Context context, AttributeSet attrs) {
        super(context, attrs);
        textPaint.setColor(Color.BLACK);
        thermometerPaint.setColor(Color.RED);
        deviceDensity = getResources().getDisplayMetrics().density;
        TypedArray attributeArray = context.obtainStyledAttributes(attrs,
            R.styleable.temperature_view_attributes);
        int textSize = attributeArray.getInt(
            R.styleable.temperature_view_attributes_textSize, 18);
        textSize = (int) (textSize * deviceDensity + 0.5f);
        textPaint.setTextSize(textSize);
    }

    @Override
    protected void onMeasure(int widthMeasureSpec, int heightMeasureSpec) {
        super.onMeasure(widthMeasureSpec, heightMeasureSpec);
        availableWidth = getMeasuredWidth();
        availableHeight = getMeasuredHeight();

        ovalLeftBorder = (availableWidth / 2) - (availableWidth / 10);
        ovalTopBorder = availableHeight - (availableHeight / 10) - (availableWidth / 5);
        ovalRightBorder = (availableWidth / 2) + (availableWidth / 10);
        ovalBottomBorder = availableHeight - (availableHeight / 10);
```

```
            //setup oval with its position centered horizontally and at the bottom of the screen
            thermometerOval.set(ovalLeftBorder, ovalTopBorder, ovalRightBorder, ovalBottomBorder);

            rectLeftBorder = (availableWidth / 2) - (availableWidth / 15);
            rectRightBorder = (availableWidth / 2) + (availableWidth / 15);
            rectBottomBorder = ovalBottomBorder - ((ovalBottomBorder - ovalTopBorder) / 2);
        }

    public void setCurrentTemperature(float currentTemperature) {
        this.currentTemperature = currentTemperature;
        //only draw a thermometer in the range of -50 to 50 degrees celsius
        float thermometerRectTop = currentTemperature + 50;
        if(thermometerRectTop < 0) {
            thermometerRectTop = 0;
        } else if(thermometerRectTop > 100){
            thermometerRectTop = 100;
        }
        rectTopBorder = (int) (rectBottomBorder - (thermometerRectTop *
            (availableHeight / 140)));
        //update rect borders
        thermometerRect.set(rectLeftBorder, rectTopBorder, rectRightBorder, rectBottomBorder);
        invalidate();
    }

    @Override
    protected void onDraw(Canvas canvas) {
        super.onDraw(canvas);
        //draw shapes
        canvas.drawOval(thermometerOval, thermometerPaint);
        canvas.drawRect(thermometerRect, thermometerPaint);
        //draw text in the upper left corner
        canvas.drawText(getContext().getString(
            R.string.temperature_value, currentTemperature),
            availableWidth / 10, availableHeight / 10, textPaint);
    }
}
```

Have a look at the variables first. The currentTemperature variable will be set by the activity containing the TemperatureView, as you've seen before.

```
private float currentTemperature;
```

Next you can see two Paint references. A Paint object defines things like color, size, strokewidth, and so on. When you are drawing shapes or text you can provide a Paint object for the corresponding method call for refining the drawing result. You'll use two Paint objects, one for the textual visualization and one for the shapes you will draw later on.

```
private Paint textPaint = new Paint();
private Paint thermometerPaint = new Paint();
```

The RectF objects can be understood as bounding boxes that are used to define the bounds of a shape.

```
private RectF thermometerOval = new RectF();
private RectF thermometerRect = new RectF();
```

You'll be drawing a thermometer, so you will draw two different shapes: an oval for the basis and a rectangle for the temperature bar (see Figure 7-6).

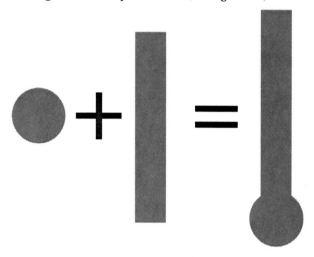

Figure 7-6. 2D shapes to create a thermometer (oval + rect = thermometer)

The next two variables will contain the View's width and height. They are used to calculate the position where you will draw the thermometer.

```
private int availableWidth;
private int availableHeight;
```

To be able to adjust the text size to your device's screen properties, you'll have to determine your screen density (but more on that later).

```
private final float deviceDensity;
```

The 2D graphics you will draw to depict a thermometer have defined boundaries. Those boundaries need to be calculated dynamically to fit to any screen size so you will save them in global variables as well.

```
private int ovalLeftBorder;
private int ovalTopBorder;
private int ovalRightBorder;
private int ovalBottomBorder;

private int rectLeftBorder;
private int rectTopBorder;
private int rectRightBorder;
private int rectBottomBorder;
```

That's it for the variables. Now we will have a look at the method implementations, starting with the constructor of the TemperatureView.

```
public TemperatureView(Context context, AttributeSet attrs) {
    super(context, attrs);
    textPaint.setColor(Color.BLACK);
    thermometerPaint.setColor(Color.RED);
    deviceDensity = getResources().getDisplayMetrics().density;
    TypedArray attributeArray = context.obtainStyledAttributes(attrs,
        R.styleable.temperature_view_attributes);
    int textSize = attributeArray.getInt(
        R.styleable.temperature_view_attributes_textSize, 18);
    textSize = (int) (textSize * deviceDensity + 0.5f);
    textPaint.setTextSize(textSize);
}
```

If you want to embed your custom View into an XML layout file you need to implement a constructor that takes not only a Context object but also an AttributeSet. Those will be set by the system once the View is inflated. The AttributeSet contains the XML definitions you can make such as width and height and even self-defined attributes. You also need to call the parent View's constructor for the attributes to be set properly. The constructor is also used to set up the Paint objects. This is only needed once, so you can set the colors and the text size in here.

When defining the text size, you have to consider that devices have different screen properties. They can come in different sizes from small to extra large, and each size can have a different density, as well, ranging from low density to extra-high density. The size describes the actual physical size measured as the screen's diagonal. The density describes the number of pixels in a defined physical area, mostly expressed as dots per inch (dpi). If you were to define a fixed pixel size for the text, it would show very differently across devices having the same size. It could be rendered very large on devices with a low density, whereas other devices of the same size would render it very small because they have a higher density.

▨ **Note** To learn more about screen sizes and densities visit the Android Developer Guide at

`http://developer.android.com/guide/practices/screens_support.html.`

To address that issue you'll have to do several things here. First, you'll have to determine the device's density to calculate the actual pixel size you need to set so that the text looks uniform across devices.

`deviceDensity = getResources().getDisplayMetrics().density;`

Now that you have the density, you only need the relative size of the text to calculate the actual pixel size. When writing your own View element you can also define custom attributes for that view. In this example you will define the attribute textSize for the TemperatureView. In order to do that you'll have to create a new file that defines all custom attributes the TemperatureView can have. Create an XML file called attributes.xml in res/values. The name of the file is not restricted, so you can choose to call it whatever you like; just make sure that it ends with .xml. Inside of this XML file you'll have to define the attribute as shown in Listing 7-4.

Listing 7-4. Project 8: attributes.xml

```xml
<?xml version="1.0" encoding="utf-8"?>
<resources>
    <declare-styleable name="temperature_view_attributes">
        <attr name="textSize" format="integer"/>
    </declare-styleable>
</resources>
```

Next, you'll need to add the TemperatureView to your layout and set its textSize attribute. If you use your own custom views in an XML layout file you have to define them with their fully qualified class name, which is their package name plus their class name. The main.xml layout file for this project looks like Listing 7-5.

Listing 7-5. Project 8: main.xml

```xml
<?xml version="1.0" encoding="utf-8"?>
<project.eight.adk.TemperatureView
    xmlns:android="http://schemas.android.com/apk/res/android"
    xmlns:temperatureview="http://schemas.android.com/apk/res/project.eight.adk"
    android:id="@+id/custom_view"
    android:layout_width="fill_parent"
    android:layout_height="fill_parent"
    android:background="#FFFFFF"
    temperatureview:textSize="18">
</project.eight.adk.TemperatureView>
```

Since you add not only system attributes but also your own attribute, you'll have to define your own namespace in addition to the standard system namespace.

```
xmlns:temperatureview="http://schemas.android.com/apk/res/project.eight.adk"
```

To define your own namespace you specify a name, as done here with temperatureview, and add the schema location. The schema location of the custom attribute you added earlier is http://schemas.android.com/apk/res/project.eight.adk. The important last part of the schema location reflects your package structure. Once the schema is added, you can define the custom attribute textSize by adding your namespace-name as a prefix.

```
temperatureview:textSize="18">
```

You have successfully configured the custom attribute textSize now. Let's see how you can access its value when you initialize the TemperatureView.

```
TypedArray attributeArray = context.obtainStyledAttributes(attrs,
    R.styleable.temperature_view_attributes);
int textSize = attributeArray.getInt(R.styleable.temperature_view_attributes_textSize, 18);
```

First, you'll have to get a reference to a TypedArray object that holds all attributes for a given styleable attribute set. To do that you call the obtainStyledAttributes method on the current Context object. This method takes two parameters, the current view's AttributeSet and the styleable attribute set you are interested in. Within the returned TypedArray you will find your textSize attribute. To access it, you call the type specific getter method on the TypedArray and provide the attribute's name you're interested in, along with a default value if that attribute cannot be found.

Finally you have the defined text size you can use to calculate the actual pixel size you need for your device's density.

```
textSize = (int) (textSize * deviceDensity + 0.5f);
```

That's it for the constructor of the TemperatureView. Next up is the onMeasure method.

```
@Override
protected void onMeasure(int widthMeasureSpec, int heightMeasureSpec) {
    super.onMeasure(widthMeasureSpec, heightMeasureSpec);
    availableWidth = getMeasuredWidth();
    availableHeight = getMeasuredHeight();

    ovalLeftBorder = (availableWidth / 2) - (availableWidth / 10);
    ovalTopBorder = availableHeight - (availableHeight / 10) - (availableWidth / 5);
    ovalRightBorder = (availableWidth / 2) + (availableWidth / 10);
    ovalBottomBorder = availableHeight - (availableHeight / 10);
    //setup oval with its position centered horizontally and at the bottom of the screen
    thermometerOval.set(ovalLeftBorder, ovalTopBorder, ovalRightBorder, ovalBottomBorder);

    rectLeftBorder = (availableWidth / 2) - (availableWidth / 15);
    rectRightBorder = (availableWidth / 2) + (availableWidth / 15);
    rectBottomBorder = ovalBottomBorder - ((ovalBottomBorder - ovalTopBorder) / 2);
}
```

The onMeasure method is inherited from the View system class. It is called by the system to calculate the necessary size to display the View. It's overridden here to get the current width and height of the View so that the shapes can be drawn in proper proportion later on. Note that it is important to also call the parent's onMeasure method or the system will throw an IllegalStateException. Once you have the width and height you can already define the bounding box for the oval shape because it will not change later on. You can also calculate three of the four borders of the rectangle shape. The only border that depends on the current temperature is the top border, so that will be calculated later. The calculations for the borders define shapes that will look proportional on each device.

To update the measured temperature value for visualization, you write a setter method called setCurrentTemperature, which takes the current temperature as a parameter. The setCurrentTemperature method is not just a simple variable setter. It is also used here to update the bounding box for the thermometer bar's rectangle and for invalidating the view so that it gets redrawn.

```
public void setCurrentTemperature(float currentTemperature) {
    this.currentTemperature = currentTemperature;
    //only draw a thermometer in the range of -50 to 50 degrees celsius
    float thermometerRectTop = currentTemperature + 50;
    if(thermometerRectTop < 0) {
        thermometerRectTop = 0;
    } else if(thermometerRectTop > 100){
        thermometerRectTop = 100;
    }
    rectTopBorder = (int) (rectBottomBorder - (thermometerRectTop *
        (availableHeight / 140)));
    //update rect borders
    thermometerRect.set(rectLeftBorder, rectTopBorder, rectRightBorder, rectBottomBorder);
    invalidate();
}
```

After updating the borders of the rectangle you need to invalidate the TemperatureView. The invalidate method, inherited from the TemperatureView's super class View, tells the system that this particular view element is invalid and needs to be redrawn.

The last method is the actual method responsible for the 2D graphical drawing. The onDraw method is called on a View each time it needs to be updated. You can tell the system that it needs redrawing by calling the invalidate method as was done in the setCurrentTemperature method. Let's have a look into its implementation.

```
@Override
protected void onDraw(Canvas canvas) {
    super.onDraw(canvas);

    //draw shapes
    canvas.drawOval(thermometerOval, thermometerPaint);
    canvas.drawRect(thermometerRect, thermometerPaint);

    //draw text in the upper left corner
    canvas.drawText(getContext().getString(
        R.string.temperature_value, currentTemperature),
        availableWidth / 10, availableHeight / 10, textPaint);
}
```

When the system calls the onDraw method it provides a Canvas object associated with the View. The Canvas object is used for drawing on its surface. The order of the draw method calls is important. You can think of it as an actual real-life canvas on which you would draw layer over layer. Here you can see that first an oval with its predefined RectF and Paint object is drawn. Next, the rectangle symbolizing the thermometer bar is drawn. At last the textual visualization is drawn by defining the text to draw, its coordinates with the origin being the top-left corner and its associated Paint object. That's it for the coding part.

After all those calculations, it is finally time to see if your self-built thermometer works. Deploy your applications and you should see an increase in temperature if you warm up the thermistor with your fingertips. The final result should look like Figure 7-7.

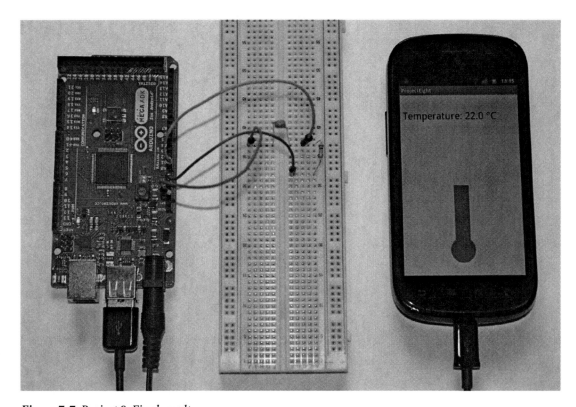

Figure 7-7. Project 8: Final result

Summary

In this chapter you learned how to build your own thermometer. You also learned the basics about thermistors and how to calculate the ambient temperature with the help of the Steinhart-Hart equation. For visualization purposes, you wrote your own custom UI element. You also used 2D graphical drawings to draw a virtual thermometer along with a textual representation of the currently measured temperature.

CHAPTER 8

A Sense of Touch

Touch user-interfaces have become increasingly part of our daily life. We see them on vending machines, home appliances, our phones, and our computers. Touch interfaces make day-to-day activities seem a little bit more futuristic and classy. When you are watching old science fiction movies you notice that, even back then, touch was the preferred way to imagine the user input of the future. Nowadays children are growing up with this kind of technology.

There are many different types of touch interface technology, each with its pros and cons. The three most widespread technologies are resistive touch sensing, capacitive touch sensing, and infrared (IR) touch sensing.

Resistive touch sensing is mostly realized by a system of two electrically resistive layers that, when pressed, touch each other at a certain point. One layer is responsible for detecting the position on the x-axis and the other is responsible for the position on the y-axis. Resistive touchscreens have been around for quite some time, reaching their peak with business smartphones of an earlier generation. Nevertheless new smartphones are still coming out that work on the principle of resistive touch. Resistive touch has the advantage of allowing you to use not only your finger as an input instrument but any object as well. The disadvantage is that you have to apply force to the touch interface's surface which, over time, can damage the system or wear it out.

Capacitive touch is another approach to touch sensing that was adopted by more modern devices such as newer smartphones. Its principle relies on the capacitive property of the human body. The capacitive touch surface forms an electrical field that is distorted by the human body when touched and is measured as a change in capacitance. Capacitive touch systems have the advantage that you don't necessarily have to touch the surface in order to sense the touch. When the system has no substantially high insulation you can influence the sensor when you are in its proximity. Touchscreens, however, have a glass insulation which requires you to touch them directly. Capacitive touch systems don't require force to sense input. The disadvantage is that not every object can interact with a capacitive touch system. You might have noticed that you can't control your smartphone when you have your normal winter gloves on. That's because you have no conductivity and too much insulation wrapped around your fingers. Aside from your fingers, you can only control capacitive touch systems with a special stylus or an equivalent.

The last system you may have heard of is the *infrared (IR) touch system*. This touch system is mainly used in outdoor kiosks or in large multi-touch tables, which you may have heard about. The IR system works on the principle that infrared light, emitted by IR LEDs, is projected into the edges of a screen or glass surface. The IR beams are reflected inside the screen in a certain pattern which gets disrupted when an object is placed on its surface. The IR LEDs are positioned to cover the x-axis and the y-axis so that the proper location of the object being placed on the screen can be determined. The advantage of the IR system is that every object can be used to interact with the system because the system has no requirements for properties like conductivity or capacitance. One disadvantage is that cheap systems can be influenced by direct sunlight, which contains the IR light spectrum. However, most industrial or consumer systems have proper filter mechanisms to avoid these disturbances.

Project 9: DIY Capacitive Touch Game Show Buzzer

This project will unleash your do-it-yourself (DIY) spirit so that you are able to build your own custom capacitive touch sensor. The capacitive touch sensor is by far the easiest and cheapest to build for yourself which is why you will be using it in this chapter's project. You will build a custom sensor out of aluminum foil, which will later be part of your project's circuit. You will use one of the ADK board's digital input pins to sense when a user touches the sensor or influences its electrical field. The touch information will be propagated to an Android application that lets your Android device become a game show buzzer by vibrating and playing a simple sound file at the same time.

The Parts

As you know, you won't use a pre-built sensor for this chapter's project. This time you will build your own sensor out of parts that can be found in any household. In order to build a capacitive touch sensor you can connect to your circuit, you will need adhesive tape, aluminum foil, and a wire. Here is the complete part list for this project (shown in Figure 8-1):

- ADK board
- Breadboard
- Aluminum foil
- Adhesive tape
- 10kΩ resistor
- Some wires

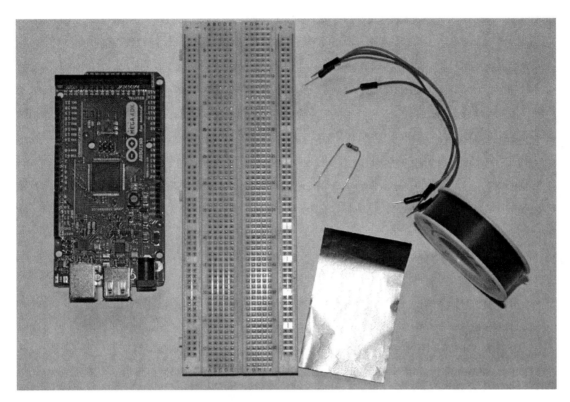

Figure 8-1. *Project 9 parts (ADK board, breadboard, wires, aluminum foil, adhesive tape, 10kΩ resistor)*

Aluminum Foil

Aluminum foil is aluminum pressed into thin sheets (Figure 8-2). The household sheets usually have a thickness of about 0.2 millimeters. In some regions it is still wrongly referred to as tin foil because tin foil was the historical predecessor of aluminum foil. Aluminum foil has the property of being conductive so it can be used as part of an electrical circuit. You could use a simple wire in this chapter's project also, but the foil provides a bigger target area for touch and can be formed however you like. Aluminum foil has one disadvantage if you want to integrate it into your circuit, though. It is not really possible to solder wires onto the foil with normal soldering tin. Aluminum foil has a thin oxide layer that prohibits the soldering tin to form a compound with the aluminum. However, there are some methods to slow down the oxidation of the aluminum when soldering, forcing a compound with the soldering tin. Those methods are tedious and most of the time you will end up with a damaged sheet of aluminum foil, so you will not do that for this project. Instead, you will build a loose connection with the aluminum foil.

Figure 8-2. Aluminum foil

Adhesive Tape

As already mentioned, you will need to build a loose connection between a wire connected to the project circuit and a piece of aluminum foil. To hold the wire tightly on the aluminum foil you will be using adhesive tape (Figure 8-3). You can use any kind of sticky tape, such as duct tape, however, so just go with your preferred tape.

Figure 8-3. Adhesive tape

The Setup

The first thing you'll have to do is build the capacitive touch sensor. You start by cutting a small piece of aluminum foil into form. Keep it fairly small to get the best result; a quarter of the size of the palm of your hand should be sufficient. (See Figure 8-4.)

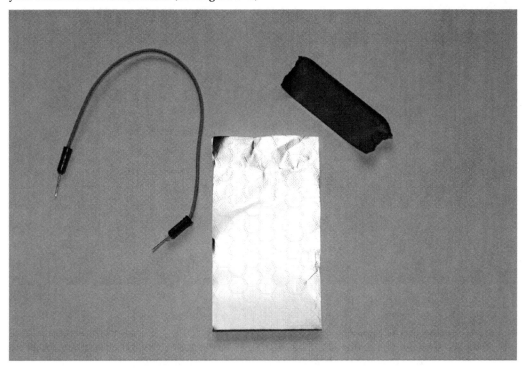

Figure 8-4. Wire, piece of aluminum foil, adhesive tape

Next, place a wire on the foil and affix it with a strip of adhesive tape. You'll want to make sure that the wire touches the foil and is firmly attached to it. An alternative to this approach would be to use alligator clips attached to a wire that can be clipped onto the foil. If you are having problems with your connection you could use those as an alternative. But you might want to try it with adhesive tape first. (See Figure 8-5.)

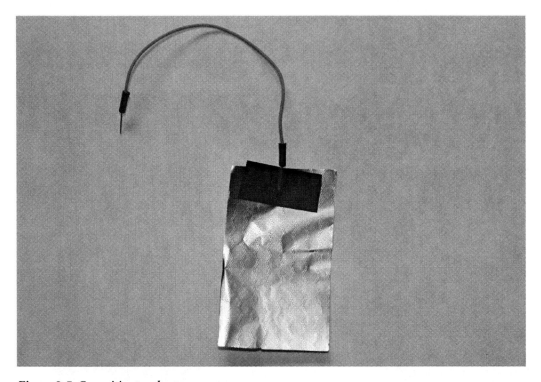

Figure 8-5. *Capacitive touch sensor*

Now that your sensor is ready, you just need to connect it to a circuit. The circuit setup is very simple. You just need to connect one digital pin configured as an output to a digital input pin through a high value resistor. Use a resistance value of about 10kΩ. The resistor is needed so that only very little current is flowing through the circuit, since you don't have an actual consumer in the circuit that draws a lot of current. The touch sensor is just connected to the circuit like a branched-out wire. You can see the complete setup in Figure 8-6.

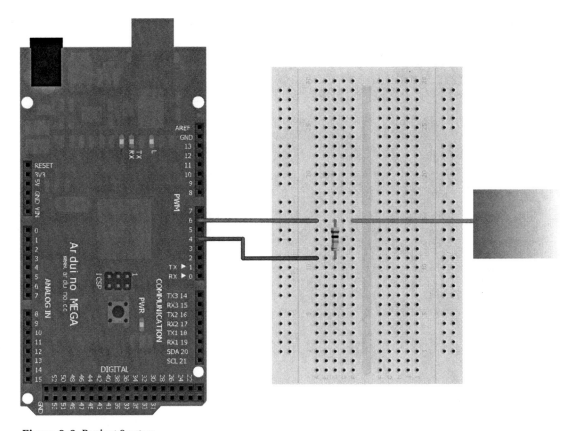

Figure 8-6. *Project 9 setup*

So how does this capacitive sensor actually work? As you can see, you connected an output pin through a resistor to an input pin to read the current state of the output pin. When power is applied to the circuit by the output pin, it takes a moment for the input pin to reach the same voltage level. That's because the input pin has a capacitive property, which means that it charges and discharges energy to a certain degree. The touch sensor is part of the circuit and when power is applied, it generates an electrical field around itself. When a user now touches the sensor or even gets in close proximity to it, the electrical field is disturbed by the water molecules of the human body. This disturbance causes a change of capacity on the input pin and it takes longer for the input pin to reach the same voltage level as the output pin. We will make use of this timing difference to determine if a touch occurred or not.

The Software

This project's software part will show you how to use the CapSense Arduino library to sense a touch with your newly built capacitive touch sensor. You will recognize a touch event when a certain threshold value has been reached and propagate that information to the Android device. The running Android application will play a buzzer sound and vibrate to act like a game show buzzer if a touch has occurred.

The Arduino Sketch

Luckily you don't have to implement the capacitive sensing logic yourself. There is an additional Arduino library, called CapSense, which does the job for you. CapSense was written by Paul Badger to encourage the use of DIY capacitive touch interfaces. You can download it at www.arduino.cc/playground/Main/CapSense and copy it to the libraries folder of your Arduino IDE installation.

What CapSense does is monitor the state change behavior of a digital input pin by changing the state of a connected output pin repeatedly. The principle works as follows. A digital output pin is set to the digital state HIGH, meaning it applies 5V to the circuit. The connected digital input pin needs a certain amount of time to reach the same state. After a certain amount of time, measurements are taken to see if the input pin already reached the same state as the output pin. If it did as expected then no touch has occurred. Afterward, the output pin is set to LOW (0V) again and the process repeats. If a user now touches the attached aluminum foil, the electrical field gets distorted and causes the capacitive value to increase. This slows the process of voltage building up on the input pin. If the output pin now changes its state to HIGH again, it takes the input pin longer to change to the same state. Now the measurements for the state change are taken and the input pin didn't reach its new state as expected. That's the indicator that a touch has occurred.

Take a look at the complete Listing 8-1 first. I will go more into detail about the CapSense library after the listing.

Listing 8-1. *Project 9: Arduino Sketch*

```
#include <Max3421e.h>
#include <Usb.h>
#include <AndroidAccessory.h>
#include <CapSense.h>

#define COMMAND_TOUCH_SENSOR 0x6
#define SENSOR_ID 0x0;
#define THRESHOLD 50

CapSense touchSensor = CapSense(4,6);

AndroidAccessory acc("Manufacturer",
                     "Model",
                     "Description",
                     "Version",
                     "URI",
                     "Serial");

byte sntmsg[3];

void setup() {
  Serial.begin(19200);
  acc.powerOn();
  //disables auto calibration
  touchSensor.set_CS_Autocal_Millis(0xFFFFFFFF);
  sntmsg[0] = COMMAND_TOUCH_SENSOR;
  sntmsg[1] = SENSOR_ID;
}
```

```
void loop() {
  if (acc.isConnected()) {
    //takes 30 measurements to reduce false readings and disturbances
    long value = touchSensor.capSense(30);
    if(value > THRESHOLD) {
      sntmsg[2] = 0x1;
    }
    else {
      sntmsg[2] = 0x0;
    }
    acc.write(sntmsg, 3);
    delay(100);
  }
}
```

In addition to the necessary libraries for the accessory communication, you'll need to include the CapSense library with the following directive:

```
#include <CapSense.h>
```

Since the capacitive touch button is a special kind of button, I used the new command byte 0x6 for the data message. You could use the same command byte used for regular buttons, which was 0x1, but then you'd have to make a distinction between both types further along in your code. The second byte defined here is the id of the touch sensor:

```
#define COMMAND_TOUCH_SENSOR 0x6
#define SENSOR_ID 0x0;
```

Another constant definition is the threshold value. It is needed to specify when a touch occurred. Since electrical disturbances can distort the measured value, you need to define a threshold or a change delta for the measured value to define what is considered a touch and what is simple electrical noise.

```
#define THRESHOLD 50
```

I chose a value of 50 for this project, because the CapSense measurements returned a rather small range of values for this circuit setup. It helps if you monitor the measured value with some Serial.println() method calls to see how the value changes when you touch the capacitive sensor. If you are using another resistor in your setup or you see that 50 is not the best threshold value for your setup then you can simply adjust the THRESHOLD value.

The next thing you see in the sketch is the definition of the CapSense object. The constructor of the CapSense class takes two integer values as input parameters. The first one defines the digital output pin, which alternates between the digital states HIGH and LOW. The second parameter defines the digital input pin, which gets pulled to the same current state as the output pin.

```
CapSense touchSensor = CapSense(4,6);
```

After looking at the variable definitions, let's have a look at the setup method. In addition to the usual initialization steps, which you already know by now, there is a first method call on the CapSense object.

```
touchSensor.set_CS_AutocaL_Millis(0xFFFFFFFF);
```

This method turns off the auto-calibration of the sensing routine which otherwise might occur during the measurements.

The loop method implements the touch detection. First, the capSense method is called where a parameter for the amount of samples must be provided. The value of 30 samples seems to be sufficient. The method returns a value in arbitrary units. If the returned sensed value exceeds the threshold value you defined earlier, a touch has been detected and the corresponding byte is set in the return message.

```
long value =  touchSensor.capSense(30);
if(value > THRESHOLD) {
   sntmsg[2] = 0x1;
}
else {
   sntmsg[2] = 0x0;
}
```

The last thing to do is to send the current data message to the connected Android device.

The Android Application

The Android application uses some of the features you already got to know about, such as using the Vibrator service. A new feature in this application is the audio playback. When receiving the touch sensor data message, the code evaluates the data to determine whether the touch button was pressed or not. If it was pressed, the background color is changed to the color red and a TextView shows which touch button was pressed, just in case you add additional buttons. At the same time, the device's vibrator is turned on and a buzzer sound is played for that final game-show buzzer–like feeling. This project's Android code in Listing 8-2 shows the application logic.

Listing 8-2. Project 9: ProjectNineActivity.java

```
package project.nine.adk;

import …;

public class ProjectNineActivity extends Activity {

    …

    private static final byte COMMAND_TOUCH_SENSOR = 0x6;
    private static final byte SENSOR_ID = 0x0;

    private LinearLayout linearLayout;
    private TextView buzzerIdentifierTextView;

    private Vibrator vibrator;
    private boolean isVibrating;

    private SoundPool soundPool;
    private boolean isSoundPlaying;
    private int soundId;

    private float streamVolumeMax;

    /** Called when the activity is first created. */
```

```java
@Override
public void onCreate(Bundle savedInstanceState) {
    super.onCreate(savedInstanceState);

    …

    setContentView(R.layout.main);
    linearLayout = (LinearLayout) findViewById(R.id.linear_layout);
    buzzerIdentifierTextView = (TextView) findViewById(R.id.buzzer_identifier);

    vibrator = ((Vibrator) getSystemService(VIBRATOR_SERVICE));

    soundPool = new SoundPool(1, AudioManager.STREAM_MUSIC, 0);
    soundId = soundPool.load(this, R.raw.buzzer, 1);

    AudioManager mgr = (AudioManager) getSystemService(Context.AUDIO_SERVICE);
    streamVolumeMax = mgr.getStreamMaxVolume(AudioManager.STREAM_MUSIC);
}

/**
 * Called when the activity is resumed from its paused state and immediately
 * after onCreate().
 */
@Override
public void onResume() {
    super.onResume();
    …
}

/** Called when the activity is paused by the system. */
@Override
public void onPause() {
    super.onPause();
    closeAccessory();
    stopVibrate();
    stopSound();
}

/**
 * Called when the activity is no longer needed prior to being removed from
 * the activity stack.
 */
@Override
public void onDestroy() {
    super.onDestroy();
    unregisterReceiver(mUsbReceiver);
    releaseSoundPool();
}

private final BroadcastReceiver mUsbReceiver = new BroadcastReceiver() {
    @Override
    public void onReceive(Context context, Intent intent) {
```

```
        ...
    }
};

private void openAccessory(UsbAccessory accessory) {
    mFileDescriptor = mUsbManager.openAccessory(accessory);
    if (mFileDescriptor != null) {
        mAccessory = accessory;
        FileDescriptor fd = mFileDescriptor.getFileDescriptor();
        mInputStream = new FileInputStream(fd);
        mOutputStream = new FileOutputStream(fd);
        Thread thread = new Thread(null, commRunnable, TAG);
        thread.start();
        Log.d(TAG, "accessory opened");
    } else {
        Log.d(TAG, "accessory open fail");
    }
}

private void closeAccessory() {
    try {
        if (mFileDescriptor != null) {
            mFileDescriptor.close();
        }
    } catch (IOException e) {
    } finally {
        mFileDescriptor = null;
        mAccessory = null;
    }
}

Runnable commRunnable = new Runnable() {

    @Override
    public void run() {
        int ret = 0;
        byte[] buffer = new byte[3];

        while (ret >= 0) {
            try {
                ret = mInputStream.read(buffer);
            } catch (IOException e) {
                Log.e(TAG, "IOException", e);
                break;
            }

            switch (buffer[0]) {
            case COMMAND_TOUCH_SENSOR:

                if (buffer[1] == SENSOR_ID) {
                    final byte buzzerId = buffer[1];
```

```
                    final boolean buzzerIsPressed = buffer[2] == 0x1;
                    runOnUiThread(new Runnable() {

                        @Override
                        public void run() {
                            if(buzzerIsPressed) {
                                linearLayout.setBackgroundColor(Color.RED);
                                buzzerIdentifierTextView.setText(getString(
                                    R.string.touch_button_identifier, buzzerId));
                                startVibrate();
                                playSound();
                            } else {
                                linearLayout.setBackgroundColor(Color.WHITE);
                                buzzerIdentifierTextView.setText("");
                                stopVibrate();
                                stopSound();
                            }
                        }
                    });
                }
                break;

            default:
                Log.d(TAG, "unknown msg: " + buffer[0]);
                break;
            }
        }
    }
};

private void startVibrate() {
    if(vibrator != null && !isVibrating) {
        isVibrating = true;
        vibrator.vibrate(new long[]{0, 1000, 250}, 0);
    }
}

private void stopVibrate() {
    if(vibrator != null && isVibrating) {
        isVibrating = false;
        vibrator.cancel();
    }
}

private void playSound() {
    if(!isSoundPlaying) {
        soundPool.play(soundId, streamVolumeMax, streamVolumeMax, 1, 0, 1.0F);
        isSoundPlaying = true;
    }
}
```

```
    private void stopSound() {
        if(isSoundPlaying) {
            soundPool.stop(soundId);
            isSoundPlaying = false;
        }
    }

    private void releaseSoundPool() {
        if(soundPool != null) {
            stopSound();
            soundPool.release();
            soundPool = null;
        }
    }
}
```

First off, as always, let's have a look at the variable definitions.

```
private static final byte COMMAND_TOUCH_SENSOR = 0x6;
private static final byte SENSOR_ID = 0x0;

private LinearLayout linearLayout;
private TextView buzzerIdentifierTextView;

private Vibrator vibrator;
private boolean isVibrating;

private SoundPool soundPool;
private boolean isSoundPlaying;
private int soundId;

private float streamVolumeMax;
```

The data message bytes are the same as in the Arduino sketch. The LinearLayout is the container view, which fills the entire screen later on. It is used to indicate the touch button press by changing its background color to red. The TextView shows the current button's identifier. The next two variables are responsible for holding a reference to the Vibrator service of the Android system and for determining if the vibrator is currently vibrating or not. The last variables are responsible for the media playback. Android has several possibilities for media playback. One easy way to play short sound snippets with low latency is to use the SoundPool class, which is even capable of playing multiple streams at once. The SoundPool object is responsible for loading and playing back sounds once it is initialized. In this example, you will need a Boolean flag, the isSoundPlaying flag, so that you don't trigger the buzzer sound again if it is already playing. The soundId will be holding a reference to the sound file once it is loaded. The last variable is needed to set the volume level when playing a sound later on.

Next up is the onCreate method which does the necessary initializations. Besides the View initializations, you can see that a reference to the system's vibrator service is assigned here. Afterward, the SoundPool is initialized. The constructor of the SoundPool class takes three parameters. The first is the number of simultaneous streams that can be played by the SoundPool. The second one defines which kind of stream will be associated with the SoundPool. You can assign streams for music, system sounds, notifications, and so on. The last parameter specifies the source quality, which currently has no effect. The documentation states that you should use 0 as the default value for now. Once it is initialized, you have to load sounds into the SoundPool. In order to do that, you have to call the load method with its parameters being a Context object, the resource id of the sound to be loaded, and a priority id. The load method returns a reference id which you will use to play back the preloaded sound later on. Place your sound file in the res folder under res/raw/buzzer.mp3.

■ **Note** You can use several encoding types for audio files on the Android system. A complete list can be found in the developer pages here at http://developer.android.com/guide/appendix/media-formats.html.

The last thing to do here is to determine the maximum volume possible for the stream type you've used. Later on, when you are playing back the sound, you can define the volume level. Since you want a fairly loud buzzer, it is best to just take the maximum volume.

```
setContentView(R.layout.main);
linearLayout = (LinearLayout) findViewById(R.id.linear_layout);
buzzerIdentifierTextView = (TextView) findViewById(R.id.buzzer_identifier);

vibrator = ((Vibrator) getSystemService(VIBRATOR_SERVICE));

soundPool = new SoundPool(1, AudioManager.STREAM_MUSIC, 0);
soundId = soundPool.load(this, R.raw.buzzer, 1);

AudioManager mgr = (AudioManager) getSystemService(Context.AUDIO_SERVICE);
streamVolumeMax = mgr.getStreamMaxVolume(AudioManager.STREAM_MUSIC);
```

As always when receiving messages, the Runnable object assigned to the receiving worker thread implements the evaluation logic and eventually triggers the buzzer-like behavior.

```
switch (buffer[0]) {
case COMMAND_TOUCH_SENSOR:
    if (buffer[1] == SENSOR_ID) {
        final byte buzzerId = buffer[1];
        final boolean buzzerIsPressed = buffer[2] == 0x1;
        runOnUiThread(new Runnable() {

            @Override
            public void run() {
                if(buzzerIsPressed) {
                    linearLayout.setBackgroundColor(Color.RED);
                    buzzerIdentifierTextView.setText(getString(
                        R.string.touch_button_identifier, buzzerId));
                    startVibrate();
                    playSound();
                } else {
                    linearLayout.setBackgroundColor(Color.WHITE);
                    buzzerIdentifierTextView.setText("");
                    stopVibrate();
                    stopSound();
                }
            }
        }
```

```
            });
        }
        break;

    default:
        Log.d(TAG, "unknown msg: " + buffer[0]);
        break;
}
```

You can see that the background color of the LinearLayout is changed according to the button's state and the TextView is also updated accordingly. The startVibrate and stopVibrate methods are already familiar from project 3 of Chapter 4.

```
private void startVibrate() {
    if(vibrator != null && !isVibrating) {
        isVibrating = true;
        vibrator.vibrate(new long[]{0, 1000, 250}, 0);
    }
}

private void stopVibrate() {
    if(vibrator != null && isVibrating) {
        isVibrating = false;
        vibrator.cancel();
    }
}
```

What the startVibrate and stopVibrate methods do is simply check if the vibrator is already vibrating before they either start vibrating or cancel the current vibrating.

Depending on the touch button's state, the buzzing sound playback is either started or stopped as well. The method implementations can be seen here:

```
private void playSound() {
    if(!isSoundPlaying) {
        soundPool.play(soundId, streamVolumeMax, streamVolumeMax, 1, 0, 1.0F);
        isSoundPlaying = true;
    }
}

private void stopSound() {
    if(isSoundPlaying) {
        soundPool.stop(soundId);
        isSoundPlaying = false;
    }
}
```

To play a sound you have to call the play method on the SoundPool object. Its parameters are the soundId, which you retrieved earlier when loading the sound file, the volume definitions for the left and right audio channels, the sound priority, the loop mode, and the playback rate of the current sound. To stop the sound you simply call the stop method on the SoundPool object and provide the corresponding soundId. You don't need to define any additional permissions in your AndroidManifest.xml for the SoundPool to work.

You should also clean up a bit when the application gets closed. To release the resources that the SoundPool allocated, simply call the release method.

```
private void releaseSoundPool() {
    if(soundPool != null) {
        stopSound();
        soundPool.release();
        soundPool = null;
    }
}
```

Since the screen layout changed a bit from the last project you should have a look at the main.xml layout file for this project, shown in Listing 8-3.

Listing 8-3. Project 9: main.xml

```
<?xml version="1.0" encoding="utf-8"?>
<LinearLayout xmlns:android="http://schemas.android.com/apk/res/android"
    android:id="@+id/linear_layout"
        android:orientation="vertical"
        android:layout_width="fill_parent"
        android:layout_height="fill_parent"
        android:gravity="center"
        android:background="#FFFFFF">
        <TextView android:id="@+id/buzzer_identifier"
                android:layout_width="wrap_content"
                android:layout_height="wrap_content"
                android:textColor="#000000"/>
</LinearLayout>
```

You can see that the layout only defines a TextView embedded into a LinearLayout container.

That's all there is to the coding of this chapter's project. If you like, you can extend this project with additional buzzers so that you can use your own custom buzzers when playing a trivia game with your friends and family. Deploy your applications and give the project a test run. Your final result should look like Figure 8-7.

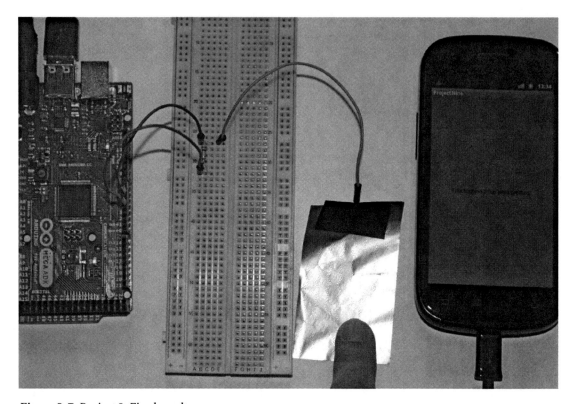

Figure 8-7. Project 9: Final result

Bonus Practical Example: The ADK Paper Piano

You have seen that building a simple DIY capacitive touch sensor is neither hard nor expensive. As you can easily imagine, this technique is used a lot in the hobby community to build projects with beautiful and cool interactive user interfaces. To get your own creative juices flowing, I want to take this opportunity to show you one of my projects that I realized for the Google Developer Day 2011 in Berlin as just one example of what can be achieved.

In July 2011, Google announced the Open Call for Google Developer Day. Google Developer Day is Google's biggest developer conference outside of the US. It is hosted in several big cities across the globe. The venues for 2011 were Argentina, Australia, Brazil, Czech Republic, Germany, Israel, Japan, and Russia. The Open Call gives developers the opportunity to showcase their skills and projects to an audience of about 2000 developers. Two challenges were part of the Open Call: the HTML5 Challenge and the ADK Challenge. Participants first had to answer some basic questions about the corresponding technology of their challenge. When they successfully answered the questions, they were eligible for round 2 of the challenge. Now, I don't know how the process for the HTML5 Challenge worked exactly, but the ADK Challenge's second round required coming up with a reasonable project plan. The project plan should incorporate the ADK technology in conjunction with an Android device to create something fun such as robots, musical instruments, or even devices to solve everyday problems. My project plan was to build a piano made out of paper with capacitive touch keys, the ADK paper piano. When a user touches a key, the connected ADK board should recognize it and play back the corresponding note of that key, with the help of a connected Android device.

I started with a small prototype with just four capacitive touch keys. I wanted to see if the capacitive touch sensor, which I made out of aluminum foil, would be responsive enough when I insulated it with a top and bottom layer of paper. I used the CapSense library to recognize the different keys when touched and I used the SoundPool class to play back the corresponding note of each key. A schematic for the design is shown in Figure 8-8.

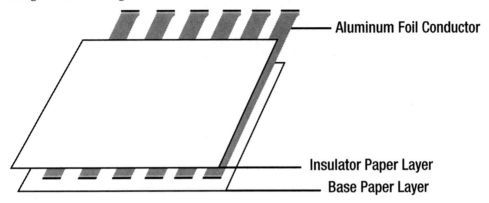

Figure 8-8. Piano key construction schematic

The prototype worked really well and my project plan was considered among the top ten submissions, so I landed a spot for the exposition area of the Google Developer Day. Google provided the Google ADK board and the Demo Shield to realize the project for the event.

I had about three months to complete the project before November 19, 2011. Let me tell you, three months sounds like a lot of time, but when you are working at a full-time job and writing a book at the same time, you tend to have very little time left for such a project. Nevertheless, I finished the project just in time and everything worked out great in the end. The building process itself was challenging, though.

As I did with the prototype, I decided to build the capacitive touch piano keys with strips of aluminum foil covered with paper. Each key has its own aluminum foil strip underneath. I had to make sure that the strips cover a large area of the key without touching the other strips nearby.

Figure 8-9. Piano key layout sheet

This tedious task of cutting the strips in form and glueing those beneath the paper keys had to be done for 61 keys in total (see Figure 8-10.).

Figure 8-10. Complete piano key layout

Now if you remember, the Google ADK board is based on the Arduino Mega design and has only 54 digital pins. With the board alone I couldn't recognize the targeted 61 keys. That's why I built my own extension boards which were able to provide more inputs. The boards hosted so-called 8-bit input shift-registers. Those ICs provide eight input channels that can be read by using only three pins of the ADK board. With eight of those ICs I was able to have 64 inputs by only using about half of the ADK digital pins. (See Figure 8-11.)

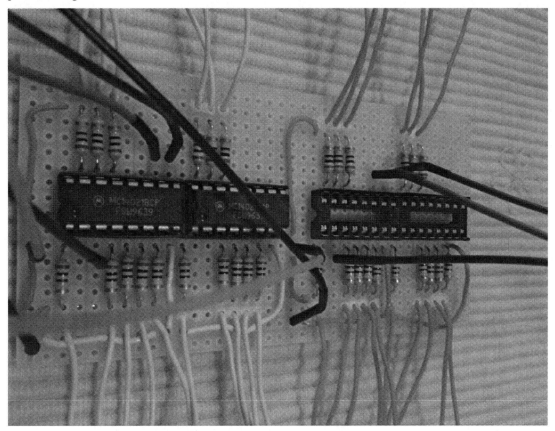

Figure 8-11. Custom input shift-register boards

Since I could not solder the input connections to the aluminum foil strips directly, I used alligator clips to build the connections (Figure 8-12).

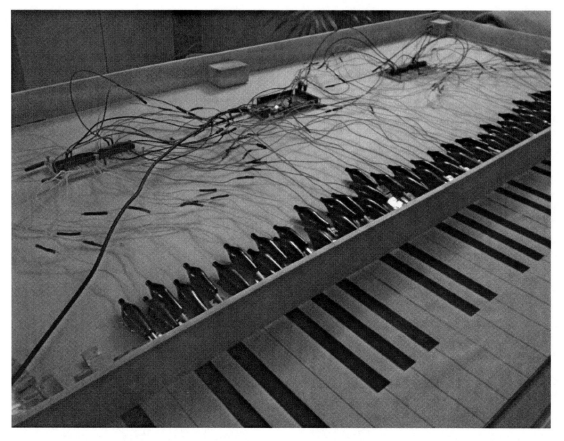

Figure 8-12. *Finished paper piano construction*

The construction phase was finished and I had to write software to recognize the touch events and play the corresponding notes. I couldn't use the CapSense library anymore because I was using the digital pins of the ADK board now to address the input shift-registers. So I implemented my own routine similar to the CapSense library, which also depended on timing of the inputs for reaching a certain state. For the Android part I also used the SoundPool class to play preloaded mp3s of musical notes when the corresponding keys were touched. The waveform of the current note was also visualized on the device's screen.

After finishing the project (shown in Figure 8-13) just before the deadline, I had to transport the piano all the way through Berlin to the venue (Figure 8-14). The exposition area for the ADK projects was well visited and the ADK paper piano made an audible impression. It was even picked up for a story in the local newspaper. The ADK projects presented at the event raised a lot of interest in the community and gave a good overview of what can be done with the ADK and, hopefully, inspired some people to give it a try themselves.

Figure 8-13. The ADK Paper Piano at Google Developer Day 2011 in Berlin

Figure 8-14. Google Developer Day 2011 in Berlin at the ICC Berlin

▓ **Note** You can find more information about the project and the event in my blog at
`http://marioboehmer.blogspot.com/2011/11/adk-paper-piano-at-google-developer-day.html`.

You should also check out this web site, which gives an overview of all ADK projects shown at the different venues of the Google Developer Day tour: `www.open-accessories.com`.

Summary

For the first time since you started this book you have built your own sensor out of household objects. You have learned how easy it is to build your own capacitive touch sensor. For the Arduino part, you learned how to use the Arduino CapSense library for sensing touch events. By combining some previously learned Android capabilities, such as using the Vibrator service and adding the ability to play back sounds via the SoundPool class, you created your own game-show buzzer. You also read about a personal practical example using the DIY capacitive touch sensor in a bigger project.

CHAPTER 9

Making Things Move

Probably one of the most interesting aspects of hobby electronics is building robots or making your projects move. There are many ways of achieving general movement depending on the use case. One common way to make a project move is through *motors*. Motors are referred to as *actuators* because they act on something rather than sense something, as sensors do. Different kinds of motors provide different levels of freedom of movement and power. The three most common motors are DC motors, servos, and stepper motors (see Figure 9-1).

DC motors are electrical motors that run on direct current (DC) and are mostly used in toys such as remote-controlled cars and such. They provide a continuous rotation of an axis that can be connected to gears to achieve different power transmissions. They have no positional feedback, meaning you can't determine how many degrees the motor has turned.

Servos are commonly used in robots to move joints of an arm or a leg, for example. Their rotation is mostly restricted to a certain range of degrees. Most servos provide no continuous rotation and only support movement in the range of 180 degrees. However, there are special servos capable of rotating a full 360 degrees and there are even hacks of restricted servos to suppress their 180-degree restriction. Servos have positional feedback, which makes it possible to set them to a certain position by sending a specific signal.

Stepper motors are mainly used for precise machine movement as in scanners or printers. They provide full rotation with precise positional feedback. That allows gears or conveyer belts to move to exact positions when they are attached to a stepper motor.

Since stepper motor projects aren't as popular as DC motor projects and servo projects, I will only describe the latter in this chapter. However, if you want to give stepper motors a try, you can find some tutorials on the Arduino website at `http://arduino.cc/hu/Tutorial/StepperUnipolar` and `http://arduino.cc/en/Tutorial/MotorKnob`.

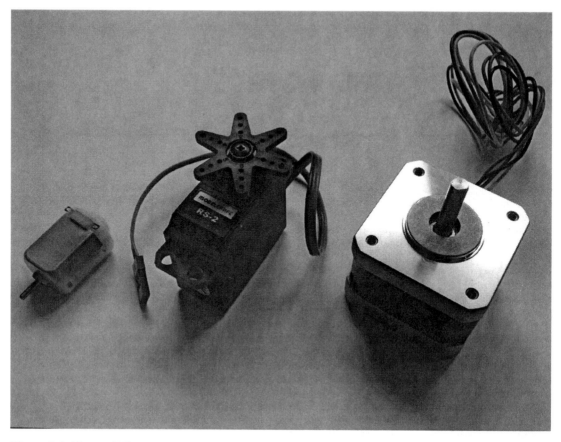

Figure 9-1. Motors (DC motor, servo, stepper motor)

Project 10: Controlling Servos

Servos are perfect for controlling limited movement. In order to control a servo you will need to send different waveforms to the servo via a digital pin of your ADK board. To define in which direction your servo should move, you will write an Android application that utilizes your device's accelerometer sensor. So when you tilt your device in a certain direction along the x-axis, your servo will reflect the relative movement as well.

What the device's *accelerometer* actually does is to measure the acceleration applied to the device. The acceleration is the rate of change of velocity relative to a set of axes. The force of gravity influences the measured acceleration. When the Android device is resting on a table, no acceleration will be measured. When tilting the device along one of its axes, the acceleration along that axis changes. (See Figure 9-2).

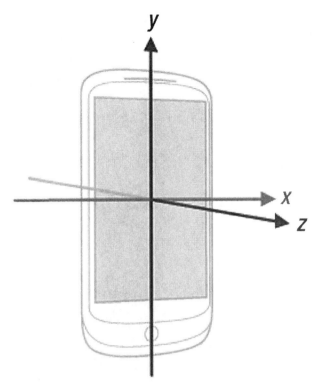

Figure 9-2. *Device axes overview (image property of Google Inc., under Creative Commons 2.5, http://developer.android.com/reference/android/hardware/SensorEvent.html)*

The Parts

Luckily servos don't need fancy circuits or additional parts. They just have one data line that receives waveform pulses to set the servo in the correct position. So in addition to a servo you'll only need your ADK board and some wires (shown in Figure 9-3).

- ADK board
- Servo
- Some wires

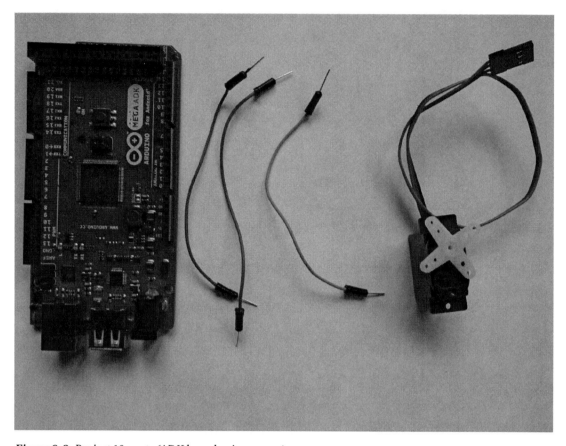

Figure 9-3. Project 10 parts (ADK board, wires, servo)

ADK Board

As in previous projects in which you had to generate waveforms, you will use one of the digital pins of your ADK board. The ADK board will send electrical pulses to the servo. The widths of these pulses are responsible for setting the servo to a specific position. To produce the necessary waveforms you can either implement the logic on your own by setting a digital pin to an alternating HIGH/LOW signal in a defined period of time or you can use the Arduino Servo library, but more on that later.

Servo

As already described, a servo is a kind of motor limited for the most part to turning its axis within a predefined range. The range for hobby servos is usually 180 degrees. The restriction is achieved mechanically by blocking an internal gear when it reaches the predefined position. You can find hacks on the Web to get rid of that block but you have to open up your servo to break the blocking and do some soldering afterwards. Another possibility to get more rotational freedom is to use a special 360-degree servo. Those tend to be a bit more expensive, which is why the hacking of low-budget 180-degree servos seems to be a good alternative for some people. Anyway, in most cases you won't need a full rotational servo for most projects. You would be better off using a DC motor or a stepper motor in those use cases.

So how does a servo work? Basically, a servo is just an electric motor that transfers its power to a set of gears that can turn an axis in a predefined range of degrees. The range for turning the axis is mechanically limited. An integrated circuit, combined with a potentiometer, receives waveform pulses sent to the servo and determines to which angle the servo has to be set. The usual hobby servos operate with pulses in the frequency of 50Hz, which describes a signal-period of about 20ms. The amount of time in which the signal is set to HIGH specifies the servo angle. According to the servo industry standard, the signal has to be set to HIGH for 1ms and afterward set to LOW for the remaining time to move the servo to its outmost left position. To move the servo to its outmost right position the signal has to be set to HIGH for 2ms and afterward set to LOW for the remaining time. (See Figure 9-4.) Note that those signal times are defaults and they may differ in practice from servo to servo, so the values could be even lower for the left position or higher for the right position. In some cases you won't even have to adhere to the 20ms period, so even that could be defined as even shorter. In general, you should stick to the defaults first and only change those values if you run into trouble.

Figure 9-4. *Servo control signal waveforms (top : full left position, bottom: full right position)*

Servos come in many different form factors for different use cases (Figure 9-5). In hobby electronics, you'll find small servos for model planes or robots. Those servos can differentiate in size and speed but they are generally small and are easily mountable.

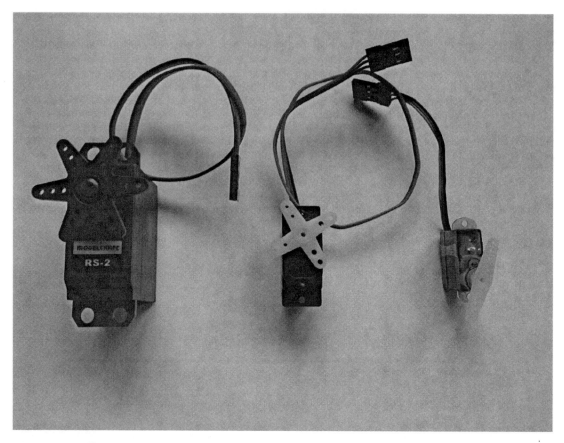

Figure 9-5. *Different servo form factors*

Most servos come with different attachments for their drive shaft or axis, so that you can use them as joints for robots or to control a rudder on a model plane or ship. (See Figure 9-6).

Figure 9-6. Servo drive shaft attachments

Since you don't need a special circuit to control a servo, connecting a servo is very straightforward if you have a microcontroller capable of producing the required waveforms. A servo has three wires attached to it. Usually they are colored in a certain way. You have a red wire, which is Vin, and it connects to +5V. However, you should read the datasheet to see if your servo has a different input voltage rating. The black wire has to be connected to ground (GND). The last wire, which is usually orange, yellow, or white, is the data line. That's where you connect the digital output pin of your microcontroller. It is used to transmit the pulses to the servo, which in turn moves to the desired position.

The Setup

Since you won't have to build a special circuit for this project, you can connect your servo directly to your ADK board. As described before, connect the red wire to +5V, the black wire to GND, and the orange, yellow, or white wire to digital pin 2. Servos usually come with female connectors, so you either connect wires directly to the connector or use a male-to-male connector in between. (See Figure 9-7).

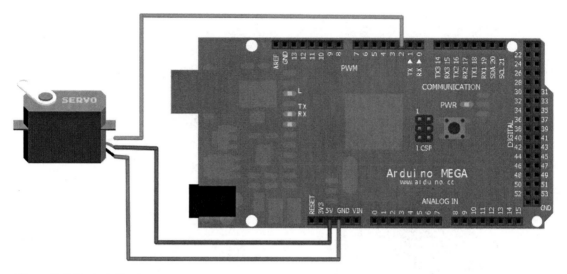

Figure 9-7. Project 10 setup

The Software

To control the servo you will write an Android application that requests updates of its accelerometer sensor's current tilt on the x-axis. When you tilt your device left or right, you will send the resulting orientation update to the ADK board. The Arduino sketch receives the new tilt value and sends the corresponding positioning pulse to the servo.

The Arduino Sketch

The Arduino sketch is responsible for receiving the accelerometer data and setting the servo to the correct position. You have two possibilities for doing that. You can either implement your own method for creating the desired waveform to send to the servo, or you can use the Servo library that comes with the Arduino IDE. Personally, I prefer to use the library because it is more precise, but I will show you both approaches here. You can decide which solution fits better to your needs.

Manual Waveform Generation

The first approach is to implement the waveform generation on your own. Have a look at the complete Listing 9-1 first.

Listing 9-1. Project 10: Arduino Sketch (Custom Waveform Implementation)

```
#include <Max3421e.h>
#include <Usb.h>
#include <AndroidAccessory.h>

#define COMMAND_SERVO 0x7
#define SERVO_ID_1 0x1
```

```
#define SERVO_ID_1_PIN 2

int highSignalTime;
float microSecondsPerDegree;
// default boundaries, change them for your specific servo
int leftBoundaryInMicroSeconds = 1000;
int rightBoundaryInMicroSeconds = 2000;

AndroidAccessory acc("Manufacturer", "Model", "Description",
                     "Version", "URI", "Serial");

byte rcvmsg[6];

void setup() {
  Serial.begin(19200);
  pinMode(SERVO_ID_1_PIN, OUTPUT);
  acc.powerOn();
  microSecondsPerDegree = (rightBoundaryInMicroSeconds - leftBoundaryInMicrosSeconds) / 180.0;
}

void loop() {
  if (acc.isConnected()) {
    int len = acc.read(rcvmsg, sizeof(rcvmsg), 1);
    if (len > 0) {
      if (rcvmsg[0] == COMMAND_SERVO) {
        if(rcvmsg[1] == SERVO_ID_1) {
          int posInDegrees = ((rcvmsg[2] & 0xFF) << 24)
                  + ((rcvmsg[3] & 0xFF) << 16)
                  + ((rcvmsg[4] & 0xFF) << 8)
                  + (rcvmsg[5] & 0xFF);
          posInDegrees = map(posInDegrees, -100, 100, 0, 180);
          moveServo(SERVO_ID_1_PIN, posInDegrees);
        }
      }
    }
  }
}

void moveServo(int servoPulsePin, int pos){
  // calculate time for high signal
  highSignalTime = leftBoundaryInMicroSeconds + (pos * microSecondsPerDegree);
  // set Servo to HIGH
  digitalWrite(servoPulsePin, HIGH);
  // wait for calculated amount of microseconds
  delayMicroseconds(highSignalTime);
  // set Servo to LOW
  digitalWrite(servoPulsePin, LOW);
  // delay to complete waveform
  delayMicroseconds(20000 - highSignalTime);
}
```

As always, let's begin by having a look at the variables of the sketch.

```
#define COMMAND_SERVO 0x7
#define SERVO_ID_1 0x1
#define SERVO_ID_1_PIN 2
```

You can see that a new command-type constant is defined for the servo control messages. The second constant is the ID of the servo, which should be controlled, in case that you want to attach more than one to your ADK board. The third constant is the corresponding pin on the ADK board where your servo is connected. Next, you have some variables to specify the waveform later on.

```
int highSignalTime;
float microSecondsPerDegree;
int leftBoundaryInMicroSeconds = 1000;
int rightBoundaryInMicroSeconds = 2000;
```

The variable highSignalTime is calculated later on and it describes the amount of time in microseconds for which the signal is set to HIGH. As you remember, setting the signal to HIGH for about 1ms means turning the servo left, and setting it to HIGH for about 2ms results in the servo turning right. The microSecondsPerDegree variable is used for conversion purposes and it describes, as the name already implies, the necessary microseconds that have to be added to the HIGH signal time per degree. The last two variables are the servo boundaries in microseconds. As already stated, a HIGH signal of about 1ms should result in full servo movement to the left, and 2ms should result in full movement to the right. In practice, however, that's usually not the case. If you work with those default values you might see that your servo won't turn to its full potential. You should experiment with the boundary values to adjust the code to your servo as each servo is different. I even had to change the defaults for one of my servos to the boundaries from 600 to 2100, which means that the servo fully moved to the left if I applied a HIGH signal for 0.6ms and it moved fully to the right if I applied a HIGH signal for about 2.1ms. As you can see, you can work with the defaults but, if you experiencing problems, you should experiment with the servo's boundaries.

In the setup method you will have to set the pinMode for the servo's signal pin as an output.

```
pinMode(SERVO_ID_1_PIN, OUTPUT);
```

You should also calculate here the microseconds per degree so that you can use the value later on in your positioning calculations.

```
microSecondsPerDegree = (rightBoundaryInMicroSeconds - leftBoundaryInMicroSeconds) / 180.0;
```

The calculation is easy. Since your servo most likely only has a range of up to 180 degrees, you just need to divide the difference between the right boundary value and the left boundary value by 180.

Next up is the loop method. After reading the received data message from the Android application, you need to decode the transmitted value by using the bit-shifting technique.

```
int posInDegrees = ((rcvmsg[2] & 0xFF) << 24)
                 + ((rcvmsg[3] & 0xFF) << 16)
                 + ((rcvmsg[4] & 0xFF) << 8)
                 + (rcvmsg[5] & 0xFF);
```

The Android application you will write afterward will transmit values from -100 for the left position and 100 for the right position. Since you need to provide the corresponding degrees for the servo position, you'll need to use the map function first.

```
posInDegrees = map(posInDegrees, -100, 100, 0, 180);
```

The position value can now be given to your custom moveServo method along with the signal pin of the corresponding servo.

```
moveServo(SERVO_ID_1_PIN, posInDegrees);
```

The implementation of the moveServo method describes the construction of the necessary waveform to control the servo.

```
void moveServo(int servoPulsePin, int pos){
  // calculate time for high signal
  highSignalTime = leftBoundaryInMicroSeconds + (pos * microSecondsPerDegree);
  // set Servo to HIGH
  digitalWrite(servoPulsePin, HIGH);
  // wait for calculated amount of microseconds
  delayMicroseconds(highSignalTime);
  // set Servo to LOW
  digitalWrite(servoPulsePin, LOW);
  // delay to complete waveform
  delayMicroseconds(20000 - highSignalTime);
}
```

Let's work through this with an example. Consider that you received a desired position of 90 degrees. To determine the time of the HIGH signal you would multiply 90 with microSecondsPerDegree and add the left boundary value. If you are using the default boundary values, then your calculation looks like this:

```
highSignalTime = 1000 + (90 * 5.55556);
```

This results in a HIGH signal time of about 1500 microseconds, so it should be the middle position of the servo. What you have to do now is set the signal pin of your servo to digital HIGH wait for the calculated amount of time and afterward set it to LOW again. The remaining delay for one signal-period of 20ms can now be calculated to complete a full pulse. That's all there is to it.

Waveform Generation with Servo Library

As you can see, implementing the waveform generation is not particularly hard, but it can be made even easier if you use the Servo library that comes with the Arduino IDE. Listing 9-2 shows the sketch rewritten using the Servo library.

Listing 9-2. Project 10: Arduino Sketch (Using the Servo Library)

```
#include <Max3421e.h>
#include <Usb.h>
#include <AndroidAccessory.h>
#include <Servo.h>

#define COMMAND_SERVO 0x7
#define SERVO_ID_1 0x1
#define SERVO_ID_1_PIN 2

Servo servo;

AndroidAccessory acc("Manufacturer", "Model", "Description",
```

```
                            "Version", "URI", "Serial");

    byte rcvmsg[6];

    void setup() {
      Serial.begin(19200);
      servo.attach(SERVO_ID_1_PIN);
      acc.powerOn();
    }

    void loop() {
      if (acc.isConnected()) {
        int len = acc.read(rcvmsg, sizeof(rcvmsg), 1);
        if (len > 0) {
          if (rcvmsg[0] == COMMAND_SERVO) {
            if(rcvmsg[1] == SERVO_ID_1) {
              int posInDegrees = ((rcvmsg[2] & 0xFF) << 24)
                        + ((rcvmsg[3] & 0xFF) << 16)
                        + ((rcvmsg[4] & 0xFF) << 8)
                        + (rcvmsg[5] & 0xFF);
              posInDegrees = map(posInDegrees, -100, 100, 0, 180);
              servo.write(posInDegrees);
              // give the servo time to reach its position
              delay(20);
            }
          }
        }
      }
    }
```

At first glance, you can see that the code got a lot shorter. You won't need any calculations or custom methods anymore. To use the Servo library, you first have to include it in your sketch.

```
#include <Servo.h>
```

By including it in your sketch, you can work with a Servo object that does all the heavy lifting for you.

```
Servo servo;
```

To initialize the Servo object you have to call the attach method and provide the digital pin to which the servo's signal wire is connected.

```
servo.attach(SERVO_ID_1_PIN);
```

To actually control the servo you just have to call its write method along with your desired position value in degrees.

```
servo.write(posInDegrees);
delay(20);
```

Note that you have to call the delay method here to give the servo some time to reach its position and to complete a full pulse. If you did not provide a delay the servo would just jitter, as the positional updates would come in too fast. The waveform generation is handled within the Servo library in the background so you don't have to worry about that anymore. It's a lot easier, isn't it?

That's it for the Arduino part. Remember, you can choose which approach best fits your needs as you implement your Arduino sketch.

The Android Application

Most Android devices have means to identify their orientation in three-dimensional space. Usually they achieve this by requesting sensor updates from their accelerometer sensors and their magnetic field sensors. For the Android part you will also request orientation updates from the accelerometer, which will directly relate to the servo's movement later on. Listing 9-3 shows the activity implementation, which I'll discuss in detail after.

Listing 9-3. Project 10: ProjectTenActivity.java

```java
package project.ten.adk;

import …;

public class ProjectTenActivity extends Activity {

    …

    private static final byte COMMAND_SERVO = 0x7;
    private static final byte SERVO_ID_1 = 0x1;

    private TextView servoDirectionTextView;

    private SensorManager sensorManager;
    private Sensor accelerometer;

    /** Called when the activity is first created. */
    @Override
    public void onCreate(Bundle savedInstanceState) {
        super.onCreate(savedInstanceState);

        …

        setContentView(R.layout.main);
        servoDirectionTextView = (TextView) findViewById(R.id.x_axis_tilt_text_view);

        sensorManager = (SensorManager) getSystemService(SENSOR_SERVICE);
        accelerometer = sensorManager.getDefaultSensor(Sensor.TYPE_ACCELEROMETER);
    }

    /**
     * Called when the activity is resumed from its paused state and immediately
     * after onCreate().
     */
    @Override
    public void onResume() {
        super.onResume();
```

```
        sensorManager.registerListener(sensorEventListener, accelerometer,
            SensorManager.SENSOR_DELAY_GAME);

        …

    }

    /** Called when the activity is paused by the system. */
    @Override
    public void onPause() {
        super.onPause();
        closeAccessory();
        sensorManager.unregisterListener(sensorEventListener);
    }

    /**
     * Called when the activity is no longer needed prior to being removed from
     * the activity stack.
     */
    @Override
    public void onDestroy() {
        super.onDestroy();
        unregisterReceiver(mUsbReceiver);
    }

    private final SensorEventListener sensorEventListener = new SensorEventListener() {

        int x_acceleration;

        @Override
        public void onAccuracyChanged(Sensor sensor, int accuracy) {
            // not implemented
        }

        @Override
        public void onSensorChanged(SensorEvent event) {
            x_acceleration = (int)(-event.values[0] * 10);
            moveServoCommand(SERVO_ID_1, x_acceleration);
            runOnUiThread(new Runnable() {

                @Override
                public void run() {
                    servoDirectionTextView.setText(getString(
                        R.string.x_axis_tilt_text_placeholder, x_acceleration));
                }
            });
        }
    };

    private final BroadcastReceiver mUsbReceiver = new BroadcastReceiver() {
```

```
    @Override
    public void onReceive(Context context, Intent intent) {
        …
    }
};

private void openAccessory(UsbAccessory accessory) {
    …
}

private void closeAccessory() {
    …
}

public void moveServoCommand(byte target, int value) {
    byte[] buffer = new byte[6];
    buffer[0] = COMMAND_SERVO;
    buffer[1] = target;
    buffer[2] = (byte) (value >> 24);
    buffer[3] = (byte) (value >> 16);
    buffer[4] = (byte) (value >> 8);
    buffer[5] = (byte) value;
    if (mOutputStream != null) {
        try {
            mOutputStream.write(buffer);
        } catch (IOException e) {
            Log.e(TAG, "write failed", e);
        }
    }
}
}
```

As was done in the Arduino sketch, you'll first have to define the same command and target IDs for your control message you intend to send later on.

```
private static final byte COMMAND_SERVO = 0x7;
private static final byte SERVO_ID_1 = 0x1;
```

The only visual component you will use is a simple TextView element for debugging purposes and to give you an overview on how the orientation value of the x-axis changes when you tilt your device.

```
private TextView servoDirectionTextView;
```

In order to request updates from any sensor of your Android device you will first need to acquire references to the SensorManager and the Sensor itself. There are other ways to fetch data from certain sensors, but the SensorManager is a general registry for most of them.

```
private SensorManager sensorManager;
private Sensor accelerometer;
```

After doing the usual setup of your content view elements in the onCreate() method, you acquire the aforementioned reference to the SensorManager by calling the context method getSystemService and providing the SENSOR_SERVICE constant as a parameter. This method provides access to all kinds of system services such as connectivity services, audio services, and so on.

```
sensorManager = (SensorManager) getSystemService(SENSOR_SERVICE);
```

With the SensorManager ready to be used you have access to the Android device's sensors. You want the accelerometer sensor in particular, so that's what you have to specify as a parameter when you call the getDefaultSensor method on the SensorManager.

```
accelerometer = sensorManager.getDefaultSensor(Sensor.TYPE_ACCELEROMETER);
```

The Android system provides a mechanism to register for sensor changes so that you don't have to worry about that. Since you can't get sensor readings directly from the Sensor object you will have to register for those SensorEvents.

In the onResume() method you call the registerListener method on the SensorManager object and pass along three parameters. The first is a SensorEventListener, which implements methods to react on sensor changes. (I will come to that in a moment.) The second parameter is the actual Sensor reference, which should be listened to. The last parameter is the update rate.

There are different rate constants defined in the SensorManager class. I had the best experience with the SENSOR_DELAY_GAME constant. It gives a very fast update rate. The normal delay caused somewhat laggy behavior in the servo movement. I would not recommend using the SENSOR_DELAY_FASTEST constant, either, as this usually makes the servo jitter a lot; the updates come in too quickly.

```
sensorManager.registerListener(sensorEventListener, accelerometer,
    SensorManager.SENSOR_DELAY_GAME);
```

Since you registered the listener in the onResume() method you should also make sure that the application frees up resources and cancels the listening process in the onPause() method accordingly.

```
sensorManager.unregisterListener(sensorEventListener);
```

Now let's have a look at the listener itself since it is responsible for handling the sensor updates.

```
private final SensorEventListener sensorEventListener = new SensorEventListener() {

    int x_acceleration;

    @Override
    public void onAccuracyChanged(Sensor sensor, int accuracy) {
        // not implemented
    }

    @Override
    public void onSensorChanged(SensorEvent event) {
        x_acceleration = (int)(-event.values[0] * 10);
        moveServoCommand(SERVO_ID_1, x_acceleration);
        runOnUiThread(new Runnable() {

            @Override
            public void run() {
                servoDirectionTextView.setText(getString(
                    R.string.x_axis_tilt_text_placeholder, x_acceleration));
            }
        });
    }
};
```

When you implement a `SensorEventListener` you will have to write two methods, the `onAccuracyChanged` method and the `onSensorChanged` method. The first is not really of interest to you in this project; you don't care about accuracy right now. The second, however, provides a parameter called `SensorEvent` that is provided by the system and holds the sensor values you are interested in. The `SensorEvent` values for the accelerometer contain three values, the acceleration on the x-axis, the acceleration on the y-axis and the acceleration on the z-axis. You are only interested in the acceleration on the x-axis so you only need to worry about the first value. The values returned are in the range from 10.0, for complete left tilt, to -10.0, for complete right tilt. This seems a bit counter-intuitive for the user seeing those values later on. That's why the values have been negated in this example project. For easier transmission of the values it is also best to multiply the values by the factor of ten so that you can transmit integer numbers rather than floats later on. By doing so, the transmittable numbers will be in the range from -100 to 100.

```
x_acceleration = (int)(-event.values[0] * 10);
```

Now that you have the acceleration data on the x-axis, you can update the `TextView` element to give visual feedback.

```
runOnUiThread(new Runnable() {

    @Override
    public void run() {
        servoDirectionTextView.setText(getString(
            R.string.x_axis_tilt_text_placeholder, x_acceleration));
    }
});
```

The last thing to do is to send the control message to the ADK board. For that purpose you'll use the custom method `moveServoCommand` by providing the ID of the servo to be controlled and the actual acceleration data.

```
moveServoCommand(SERVO_ID_1, x_acceleration);
```

The method's implementation is straightforward. You'll just set up the basic data structure, bit-shift the integer acceleration value to four single bytes, and send the complete message via the outputstream to the ADK board.

```
public void moveServoCommand(byte target, int value) {
    byte[] buffer = new byte[6];
    buffer[0] = COMMAND_SERVO;
    buffer[1] = target;
    buffer[2] = (byte) (value >> 24);
    buffer[3] = (byte) (value >> 16);
    buffer[4] = (byte) (value >> 8);
    buffer[5] = (byte) value;
    if (mOutputStream != null) {
        try {
            mOutputStream.write(buffer);
        } catch (IOException e) {
            Log.e(TAG, "write failed", e);
        }
    }
}
```

That's it for the Android part, the final result of which is shown in Figure 9-8. When you're ready, deploy both applications and see how your servo turns whenever you tilt your Android device sideways.

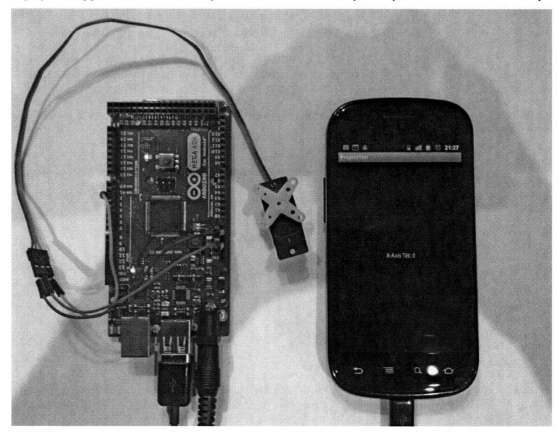

Figure 9-8. Project 10: Final result

Project 11: Controlling DC Motors

The next project shows you how to control another kind of motor, a so-called DC motor. As I already explained at the beginning of this chapter, DC motors provide continuous rotation and are not artificially limited the way servos are. You will again use your device's accelerometer to control the DC motor, only this time you will work with the acceleration changes along the y-axis of your device. So when you tilt your device forward, the motor will begin to spin. You will also be able to control its speed while doing that. Note that I don't cover spin direction changes, which require a bit more hardware. Before you begin, you'll need to learn about the parts you will need to control a DC motor and how the motor operates.

The Parts

You won't need many parts to get the motor running. In fact, the only new component for the circuit you are about to build is a so-called NPN transistor. I will explain its purpose in a moment.

■ **Note** If you are using an Arduino design–based ADK board and you happen to use a DC motor that operates at a voltage higher than 5V, or if it consumes more than 40mA, you might need an additional external power supply as the output pins of the board are limited to those values.

The part list looks like this (Figure 9-9):

- ADK board
- Breadboard
- NPN transistor (BC547B)
- DC motor
- Some wires
- Optional: 1-10kΩ resistor, external battery

Figure 9-9. Project 11 parts (ADK board, breadboard, wires, NPN transistor, DC motor)

ADK Board

You will be using the pulse-width modulation (PWM) capability of an output pin to produce the different voltages that influence the motor's speed later on.

DC Motor

DC motors run on direct current, hence their name. There are two types of DC motors: brushed DC motors and brushless DC motors.

Brushed DC motors work on the principle that stationary magnets interfere with an electromagnetic field. A mounted coil on the driveshaft generates an electromagnetic field around its armature, which constantly gets attracted and rejected by the surrounding stationary magnets, causing the drive shaft to spin. Brushed DC motors are usually cheaper than brushless DC motors, which is why they are more widely used in hobby electronics.

Brushless DC motors are built just like the opposite of brushed DC motors. They have stationary magnets mounted on their drive shaft that are set in motion when an electromagnetic field is applied to them. What's also different about them is that a motor controller converts the direct current (DC) to alternating current (AC). Brushless DC motors are a bit more expensive than their counterparts. Different DC motor form factors are shown in Figure 9-10.

Figure 9-10. DC motors in different form factors

Most of the hobby DC motors have a two-wire connection, Vin and GND. To change the direction of the spin, you usually just change the polarity of the connections. When you want to switch the spin direction of the motor on the fly, you need a more sophisticated circuit than the one you are about to build here. For those purposes you would need a special circuit setup called H-bridge or a special motor driver IC. For further details about those just search the Web, where you will find plenty of tutorials and information. To avoid complicating the project, I will stick to only one motor direction. The speed of the motor can be influenced by the voltage level applied. The more you supply the faster it generally gets, but be careful not to supply more than it can handle. A quick look at the datasheet of the motor will give you an overview of the operating voltage range.

DC motors are usually used in conjunction with gears and transmissions, so that their torque can be projected onto those gears to turn, for example, wheels or other mechanical constructions. (See Figure 9-11.)

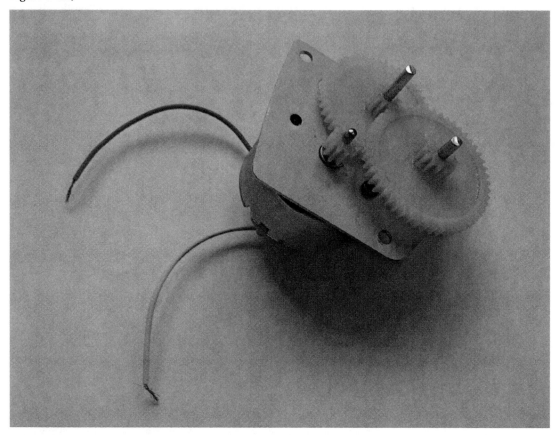

Figure 9-11. DC motor with gear attachment

Note that most DC motors don't come with preattached wires, so you might have to solder on wires first.

NPN Transistor (BC547B)

Transistors are semiconductors capable of switching and amplifying power in a circuit. They usually have three connectors called base, collector, and emitter (see Figure 9-12).

Figure 9-12. Transistor (flat side facing toward: emitter, base, collector)

A transistor is able to influence the current flow between one pair of the connections by applying a smaller voltage or current to the other pair. So, for example, when current is flowing from the collector to the emitter, you can apply a smaller fraction of that current to the base flowing through the emitter to control the higher current. So basically a transistor can be used as a switch or amplifier for the power in a circuit.

There are several different types of transistors for different tasks. In this project you will need an NPN transistor. An *NPN transistor* operates with the base connector pulled high, meaning that it is set "on" when a high voltage or current is applied to the base. So when the voltage on the base increases, the connection from collector to emitter will let more current pass through. The electrical symbol for an NPN transistor is shown in Figure 9-13.

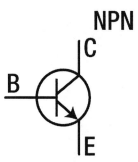

Figure 9-13. Electrical symbol for NPN transistor

The opposite of the NPN transistor is the PNP transistor, which operates in the exact opposite way. To switch the current flow between the collector and emitter, you need to pull the base low. So with a decreasing voltage you let more current pass through the collector-emitter connection. The electrical symbol for PNP transistors is shown in Figure 9-14.

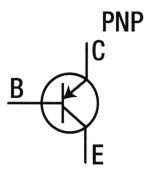

Figure 9-14. Electrical symbol for PNP transistor

You will be using a NPN transistor to control the power applied to the motor later on so that you can control its speed.

The Setup

The connection setup for this chapter's second project is fairly easy as well (Figure 9-15). Depending on the DC motor you use, you connect one wire of the motor determined by your motor's voltage rating to either +3.3V or 5V. If you happen to use a motor that works with even higher voltage ratings, you might want to connect an external battery. In that case you'll have to make sure to connect the battery and the ADK board to a common ground (GND). The second wire of the motor needs to be connected to the collector of the transistor. The emitter of the transistor is connected to GND and the base of the transistor is connected to the digital pin 2. If you are having trouble finding the correct connection on the transistor just hold the transistor facing the flat side toward you. The right pin is the collector, the middle pin is the base, and the left pin is the emitter.

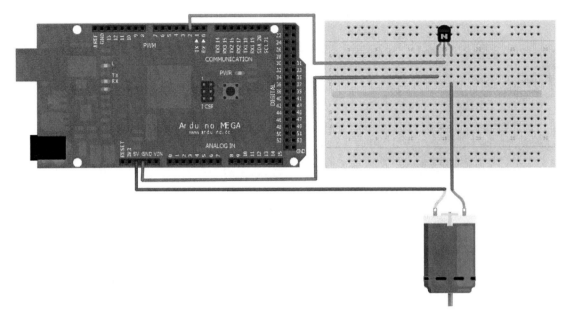

Figure 9-15. Project 11 setup

The NPN transistor has been added to the circuit in case your motor needs more power than the ADK board can supply. So if you are experiencing a really slow running motor or no movement at all you can easily attach an external battery to the circuit. If you do that you should make sure to also add a high valued resistor in the range from 1kΩ to 10kΩ to the digital pin 2 to keep the ADK board safe from power anomalies that might come from the higher-powered circuit. If you need an external battery your circuit would look like Figure 9-16.

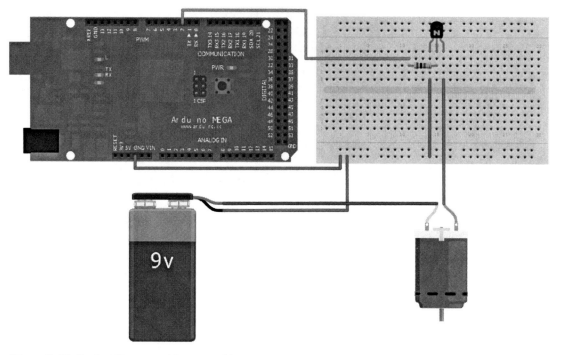

Figure 9-16. Project 11 setup with external battery

You should try using the first circuit setup first, but if your motor needs more power it is easy to just switch to the second circuit setup.

The Software

The software component of this little project is fairly easy. You will use the Android device's accelerometer again to acquire the change of the tilt value when the device is tilted, only this time you are interested in the tilt value of the y-axis instead of the x-axis. The y-axis tilt describes the tilt motion when your device's screen is facing upward and its top edge gets pushed down and its bottom edge gets pulled up. It's as though you were to push a throttle lever in an airplane forward. The tilt value will be transmitted to the ADK board and the running Arduino sketch will map the received value, which will be only in the range from 0 to 100, since you are not interested in the other tilt direction, to a value between 0 and 255 to feed into the analogWrite method. This causes the digital pin 2 to act in its PWM mode and the output voltage of the pin will change accordingly. Remember that the transistor's base connector is connected to pin 2, so with the changing voltage you will influence the overall power provided for the motor and the speed will vary according to your tilt.

The Arduino Sketch

The Arduino sketch will be a bit shorter than the one you wrote for controlling the servo (shown in Listing 9-4). There are no official DC motor libraries that come with the Arduino IDE, but for this example you won't need a library because the code is really simple. There are custom libraries on the

Web written by the community, for the case in which you use an H-bridge to also control the spin direction, but this is out of scope for the example here. You will only need to use the analogWrite method to change the voltage output on the digital pin 2 according to the tilt value you will receive from the connected Android device.

Listing 9-4. Project 11: Arduino Sketch

```
#include <Max3421e.h>
#include <Usb.h>
#include <AndroidAccessory.h>

#define COMMAND_DC_MOTOR 0x8
#define DC_MOTOR_ID_1 0x1
#define DC_MOTOR_ID_1_PIN 2

AndroidAccessory acc("Manufacturer", "Model", "Description",
                     "Version", "URI", "Serial");

byte rcvmsg[3];

void setup() {
  Serial.begin(19200);
  pinMode(DC_MOTOR_ID_1_PIN, OUTPUT);
  acc.powerOn();
}

void loop() {
  if (acc.isConnected()) {
    int len = acc.read(rcvmsg, sizeof(rcvmsg), 1);
    if (len > 0) {
      if (rcvmsg[0] == COMMAND_DC_MOTOR) {
        if(rcvmsg[1] == DC_MOTOR_ID_1) {
          int motorSpeed = rcvmsg[2] & 0xFF;
          motorSpeed = map(motorSpeed, 0, 100, 0, 255);
          analogWrite(DC_MOTOR_ID_1_PIN, motorSpeed);
        }
      }
    }
  }
}
```

The first thing to do here is to change the command and target bytes as usual.

```
#define COMMAND_DC_MOTOR 0x8
#define DC_MOTOR_ID_1 0x1
#define DC_MOTOR_ID_1_PIN 2
```

Next you configure the digital pin 2 as an output pin.

```
pinMode(DC_MOTOR_ID_1_PIN, OUTPUT);
```

Once you have received a valid message from the connected Android device you'll have to convert the original tilt value from a byte to an int.

```
int motorSpeed = rcvmsg[2] & OxFF;
```

Since the analogWrite method works with values from 0 to 255 rather than with values from 0 to 100, you'll have to map them to the appropriate range first before feeding them to the analogWrite method.

```
motorSpeed = map(motorSpeed, 0, 100, 0, 255);
```

Finally you can do the call to the analogWrite method by providing the target pin 2 and the converted value for the motor's speed.

```
analogWrite(DC_MOTOR_ID_1_PIN, motorSpeed);
```

This short snippet of code is all there is to do to control a simple DC motor's speed in one direction.

The Android Application

The Android application is almost the same as in the previous servo project. The only things that need changing are the message bytes and the value you get when a SensorEvent is received by the SensorEventListener. Let's have a look what needs to be done (Listing 9-5).

Listing 9-5. Project 11: ProjectElevenActivity.java

```
package project.eleven.adk;

import …;

public class ProjectElevenActivity extends Activity {

    …

    private static final byte COMMAND_DC_MOTOR = 0x8;
    private static final byte DC_MOTOR_ID_1 = 0x1;

    private TextView motorSpeedTextView;

    private SensorManager sensorManager;
    private Sensor accelerometer;

    /** Called when the activity is first created. */
    @Override
    public void onCreate(Bundle savedInstanceState) {
        super.onCreate(savedInstanceState);

        …

        setContentView(R.layout.main);
        motorSpeedTextView = (TextView) findViewById(R.id.y_axis_tilt_text_view);

        sensorManager = (SensorManager) getSystemService(SENSOR_SERVICE);
        accelerometer = sensorManager.getDefaultSensor(Sensor.TYPE_ACCELEROMETER);
    }
```

```java
/**
 * Called when the activity is resumed from its paused state and immediately
 * after onCreate().
 */
@Override
public void onResume() {
    super.onResume();

    sensorManager.registerListener(sensorEventListener, accelerometer,
        SensorManager.SENSOR_DELAY_GAME);

    …

}

/** Called when the activity is paused by the system. */
@Override
public void onPause() {
    super.onPause();
    closeAccessory();
    sensorManager.unregisterListener(sensorEventListener);
}

/**
 * Called when the activity is no longer needed prior to being removed from
 * the activity stack.
 */
@Override
public void onDestroy() {
    super.onDestroy();
    unregisterReceiver(mUsbReceiver);
}

private final SensorEventListener sensorEventListener = new SensorEventListener() {

    int y_acceleration;

    @Override
    public void onAccuracyChanged(Sensor sensor, int accuracy) {
        // not implemented
    }

    @Override
    public void onSensorChanged(SensorEvent event) {
        y_acceleration = (int)(-event.values[1] * 10);
        if(y_acceleration < 0) {
            y_acceleration = 0;
        } else if(y_acceleration > 100) {
            y_acceleration = 100;
        }
        moveMotorCommand(DC_MOTOR_ID_1, y_acceleration);
        runOnUiThread(new Runnable() {
```

```
            @Override
            public void run() {
                motorSpeedTextView.setText(getString(
                    R.string.y_axis_tilt_text_placeholder, y_acceleration));
            }
        });
    }
};

private final BroadcastReceiver mUsbReceiver = new BroadcastReceiver() {
    @Override
    public void onReceive(Context context, Intent intent) {
        ...
    }
};

private void openAccessory(UsbAccessory accessory) {
    ...
}

private void closeAccessory() {
    ...
}

public void moveMotorCommand(byte target, int value) {
    byte[] buffer = new byte[3];
    buffer[0] = COMMAND_DC_MOTOR;
    buffer[1] = target;
    buffer[2] = (byte) value;
    if (mOutputStream != null) {
        try {
            mOutputStream.write(buffer);
        } catch (IOException e) {
            Log.e(TAG, "write failed", e);
        }
    }
}
}
```

The command and target message bytes have been changed here to match the ones in the Arduino sketch.

```
private static final byte COMMAND_DC_MOTOR = 0x8;
private static final byte DC_MOTOR_ID_1 = 0x1;
```

As in the servo example, you will provide visual feedback for the user with a simple TextView element that displays the current tilt value of the device along the y-axis.

```
private TextView motorSpeedTextView;
```

Really, the only interesting new part here is the implementation of the SensorEventListener.

```
private final SensorEventListener sensorEventListener = new SensorEventListener() {
```

```
    int y_acceleration;

    @Override
    public void onAccuracyChanged(Sensor sensor, int accuracy) {
        // not implemented
    }

    @Override
    public void onSensorChanged(SensorEvent event) {
        y_acceleration = (int)(-event.values[1] * 10);
        if(y_acceleration < 0) {
            y_acceleration = 0;
        } else if(y_acceleration > 100) {
            y_acceleration = 100;
        }
        moveMotorCommand(DC_MOTOR_ID_1, y_acceleration);
        runOnUiThread(new Runnable() {

            @Override
            public void run() {
                motorSpeedTextView.setText(getString(
                    R.string.y_axis_tilt_text_placeholder, y_acceleration));
            }
        });
    }
};
```

Again, you don't need to implement the onAccuracyChanged method, as you only want to know the current tilt value and not its accuracy. In the onSensorChanged method you can see that you access the second element of the event's values. As you may remember, the SensorEvent provides three values for this sensor type: the values for the x-axis, y-axis, and z-axis. Since you need the value change on the y-axis, you'll have to access the second element.

```
y_acceleration = (int)(-event.values[1] * 10);
```

As was done in the servo example, you'll need to adjust the value for better user readability and easier transmission later on. Normally you would receive values from -10.0 to 0.0 if you tilt your device in the forward direction. To avoid confusing the user you will negate the value first so that an increasing tilt forward will visualize with an increasing number rather than a decreasing number. For easier transmission, just multiply the value by ten and cast it to an integer data-type as in the previous project.

You could still receive sensor values when tilting backward which you wouldn't want to transmit to the ADK board later on, so just define the boundaries and adjust the received value.

```
if(y_acceleration < 0) {
    y_acceleration = 0;
} else if(y_acceleration > 100) {
    y_acceleration = 100;
}
```

Now that you have your final tilt value, you can update the TextView and send the data message to the ADK board. The transmission is done in a separate method called moveMotorCommand.

```
public void moveMotorCommand(byte target, int value) {
```

```
byte[] buffer = new byte[3];
buffer[0] = COMMAND_DC_MOTOR;
buffer[1] = target;
buffer[2] = (byte) value;
if (mOutputStream != null) {
    try {
        mOutputStream.write(buffer);
    } catch (IOException e) {
        Log.e(TAG, "write failed", e);
    }
}
}
```

The Android code wasn't much trouble this time as you only had to adjust some lines of code from the last example. However, you completed the Android part and now you are ready to see your DC motor in action (Figure 9-17). Deploy the Arduino sketch and the Android application and see your motor spinning as you tilt your device forward.

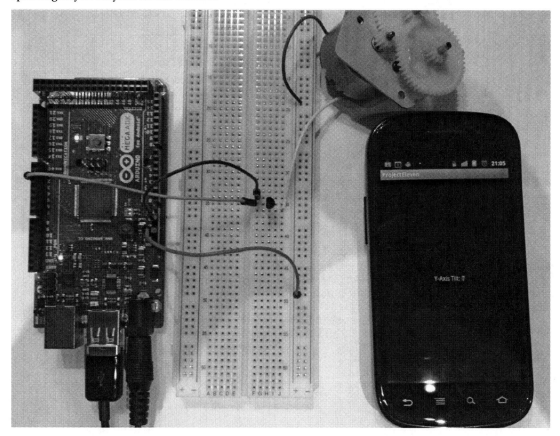

Figure 9-17. Project 11: Final result

Summary

This chapter gave you a brief overview about some possibilities to make your project move in any way. That overview is far from complete. There are plenty of ways to bring movement into the game, but using a servo or a DC motor is the most common way and it gives you a perfect start for further experiments. You learned how those actuators operate and how to drive them with your ADK board. You also learned how to address the accelerometer sensor of your Android device and how you can use it to read the current acceleration or tilt value of any of its three axes. Finally, you used the accelerometer sensor of your device to control your actuators.

Alarm System

Now that you are comfortable with your ADK board and the different sensors and components you have used so far, it is time for something bigger. In the final chapter you will be combining some of the components you used in the previous chapters to build two versions of an alarm system. You will get to know new components—the tilt-switch and the IR light barrier, consisting of an IR LED and an IR detector—widely used in the real world for numerous applications. In two separate projects you will learn how to integrate these components into a small alarm system so that they trigger an alarm. On the hardware side, the alarm will be expressed by a blinking red LED and a piezo buzzer that generates a high-pitched sound. Your Android device will persist the alarm event in a log file and, depending on the current project, it will additionally either send a notification SMS or take a picture of the intruder and save it to your filesystem.

Project 12: SMS Alarm System with Tilt-Switch

In this project you will be using a so-called tilt-switch to trigger an alarm if the switch is tilted to its closing position. The trigger will cause a red LED to pulse and a piezo buzzer to produce an alarm sound. Additionally, the Android device will be notified of the alarm and it will write a log file on its filesystem. If your Android device has telephony capabilities, it will also send an SMS to a specified telephone number showing the time of the alarm and an alarm message.

The Parts

You will need several parts for your first alarm system. You will use a red LED to visually signal that an alarm has occurred. For audible feedback you will be using a piezo buzzer that produces an alarm sound. A tilt-switch will trigger the alarm if it is tilted to its closing position. To reset the alarm system so that it can report the next alarm you will be using a simple button. The following is a complete list of the parts needed for your alarm system (see Figure 10-1):

- ADK board
- Breadboard
- 220Ω resistor
- 2 × 10kΩ resistor
- Some wires
- Button

- Tilt-switch
- LED operating at 5V
- Piezo buzzer

Figure 10-1. Project 12 parts (ADK board, breadboard, wires, resistors, button, tilt-switch, piezo buzzer, red LED)

ADK Board

The ADK board will be used in this project to provide two possibilities for inputs, the tilt-switch and the button, and two possibilities for outputs, the LED and the piezo buzzer. Since you don't have any analog input requirements you will only use the digital pins of the ADK board. You will use the digital input capabilities to sense a button press or the closing of the tilt-switch. The digital output capabilities, especially the PWM functionality, will be used to pulse the LED and to produce sound with the piezo buzzer.

LED

As you learned in Chapter 3, you can dim a LED by using the PWM capabilities of the ADK board. The LED will be used to give visual feedback when an alarm has occurred. This will be done by letting the LED pulse, meaning that it will continuously dim between its brightest maximum level and its darkest minimum level until the alarm is reset.

Piezo Buzzer

Chapter 5 showed you that you can produce sounds when applying power to a piezo buzzer's piezo element, which is described as the reverse piezoelectric effect. The oscillation of the piezo element produces pressure waves which are perceived as sound by the human ear. The oscillation is achieved by using the PWM capabilities of the ADK board to modulate the voltage output to the piezo buzzer.

Button

In Chapter 4 you learned how buttons or switches can be used as inputs for your project. The principle is simple. When the button or switch is pressed or closed, it closes the circuit.

Tilt-Switch

The tilt-switch is very similar to a normal switch. The difference is that the user has no real switch to press or flip to close the connected circuit. The most common tilt-switches are usually constructed in a way that the connector leads within the component are separated from each other. Additionally there is a ball made out of conductive material within the component as well. (See Figure 10-2).

Figure 10-2. Open tilt-switch (inside view)

When the switch is tilted in a certain way, the conductive ball moves and touches the open connections. The ball closes the connections and current can flow from one end to the other. Since the ball is affected by gravity you just have to tilt the tilt-switch so that the connections point toward the ground. (See Figure 10-3).

Figure 10-3. Closed tilt-switch (inside view)

It's as simple as that. When you shake the tilt-switch you can hear the ball moving inside the component.

Tilt-switches are also referred to as mercury-switches because, in the past, most tilt-switches had a mercury blob inside them to close the connections. The advantage of mercury was that it didn't bounce as easily as other materials so it wasn't affected that much by vibrations. The disadvantage, however, was that mercury is highly toxic, so if a tilt-switch got damaged it caused a danger to the environment. Nowadays, other conductive materials are generally used for tilt switches.

Tilt-switches are used in numerous real-world applications. The automotive industry makes wide use of them. A car's trunk light is just one example: if you open the trunk to a specific angle, the light will turn on. Another example is a classic pinball machine that registers if a user excessively tilts the machine to gain an advantage. You could also easily imagine a use case for an alarm system, such as sensing when a door handle has been pushed down.

Some tilt-switches may come with soldering pins, which you can't just plug into a breadboard, so you might need to solder some wires on these pins to connect the tilt-switch to the circuit later on. (See Figure 10-4). Sometimes tilt-switches can have more than two connectors so that you can connect them to more than one circuit. You just need to make sure that you always connect the correct pin pair. Have a look at the datasheet or build a simple circuit to test which connections relate to one another.

Figure 10-4. *Tilt-switch with soldered connector pins and stock tilt-switch*

The Setup

The setup will be made by connecting one component at a time so that you don't get confused and end up damaging something later on when you power up your project. I will show you each separate circuit setup first and then the complete circuit setup with all the components.

LED Circuit

Let's start with the LED. As you know, LEDs usually operate with a current of about 20mA to 30mA. To limit the current to a value of at least 20mA, you will need to connect a resistor to the LED. The output pins of the ADK board provide 5V, so you need to apply Ohm's law to calculate the resistor value.

R = 5V / 0.02A
R = 250Ω

The nearest most common resistor would be a 220Ω resistor. With this resistor you'll end up with a current of about 23mA which is just fine. Now connect one end of the resistor to digital pin 2 and the other end to the anode of the LED (the long lead). The cathode of the LED is connected to ground (GND). The LED circuit setup looks like that shown in Figure 10-5.

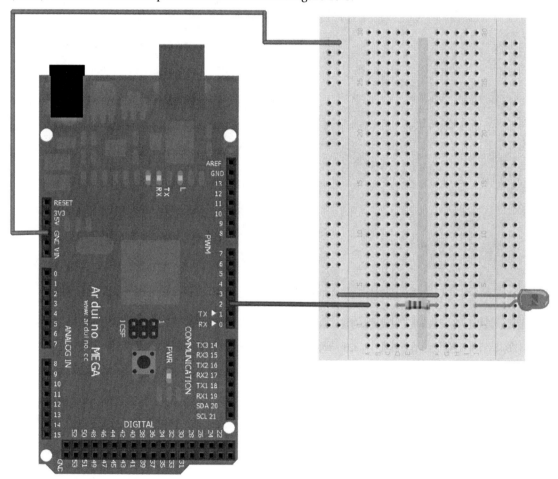

Figure 10-5. Project 12: LED circuit setup

Piezo Buzzer Circuit

Next, you will connect the piezo buzzer to the ADK board. This is very simple because you don't need additional components. If you happen to have a piezo buzzer that is directional, make sure to connect the positive and negative leads correctly as marked. Otherwise, just connect one lead to digital pin 3 and the other to ground (GND). The piezo buzzer circuit setup is shown in Figure 10-6.

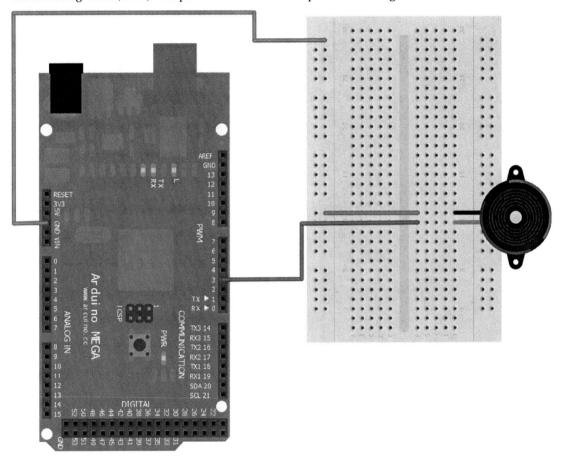

Figure 10-6. *Project 12: Piezo buzzer circuit setup*

Button Circuit

As you may remember from Chapter 4, it is best to pull the circuit up to the operating voltage when working with buttons to eliminate electrical disturbances. To pull up the button circuit without damaging the input pin with a high current flow, you use a 10kΩ pull-up resistor in conjunction with the button. In order to do that, you connect the +5V Vcc pin of the ADK board to one lead of the 10kΩ resistor. The other lead is connected to the digital pin 4. The digital pin 4 also connects to one lead of the button. The opposite lead is connected to ground (GND). The button circuit is shown in Figure 10-7.

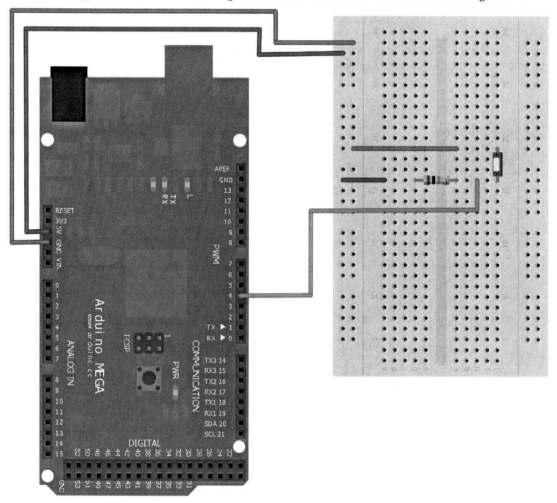

Figure 10-7. Project 12: Button circuit setup

Tilt-Switch Circuit

Since the tilt-switch works similarly to the button, you can connect it just like you connected the button. You connect the +5V Vcc pin of the ADK board to one lead of a 10kΩ resistor. The other lead is connected to the digital pin 5. The digital pin 5 also connects to one lead of the tilt-switch. The opposite lead is connected to ground (GND). The tilt-switch circuit setup is shown in Figure 10-8.

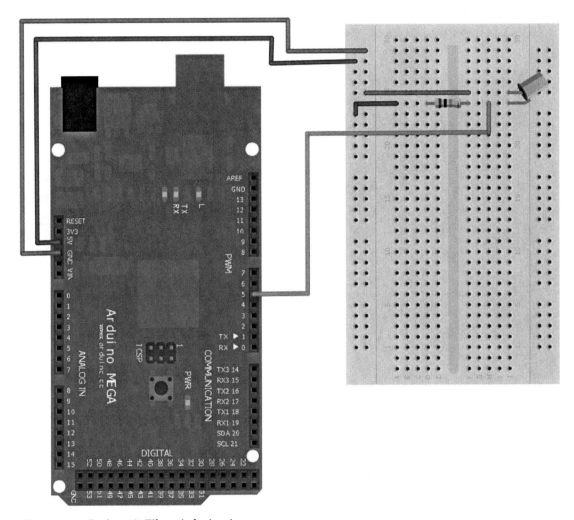

Figure 10-8. *Project 12: Tilt-switch circuit setup*

Complete Circuit Setup

Now that you know how to connect each component, have a look at the complete circuit setup shown in Figure 10-9.

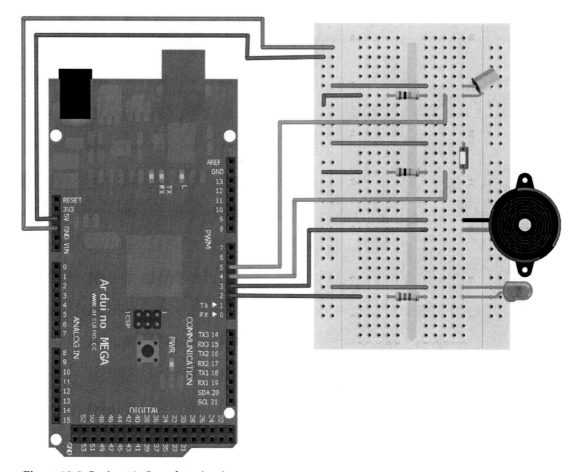

Figure 10-9. *Project 12: Complete circuit setup*

So how does this alarm system work? Imagine that the tilt-switch is attached to a door handle or a trap window. When the handle is pushed down or the trap window is opened, the tilt-switch will tilt to the position where the conductive ball touches the internal leads, which causes the switch to close. Now an alarm is registered and the piezo buzzer and the LED start to give audible and visual alarm feedback. To reset the alarm so that it can be triggered again, the button must be pressed.

The Software

Now that you have set up everything, it is time to write the necessary software to get the alarm system up and running. The Arduino sketch will monitor if the tilt-switch has been tilted to its contact closing position. If the tilt-switch triggered the alarm, the Arduino tone method will be used to get the piezo buzzer to oscillate so that a high-pitched sound is produced. Additionally, the red LED will be pulsed by using the analogWrite method, which modulates the voltage output and causes the LED to light up at different lighting intensities. To reset the alarm so that it can be triggered again, the state of a simple button is read. Once it is pressed, all necessary variables are reset and the alarm system can register an alarm once again.

If the alarm was triggered, a message is sent to the Android device if it is connected. Once the Android device has received the alarm message, it will give visual feedback in form of a red-screen background and an alarm message. The alarm message along with a timestamp will be persisted on the device's external storage system. Don't be misled by the term *external*, though. *External* in the context of Android doesn't necessarily mean *storage*, as in removable SD cards. The term *external* can also describe internal, nonremovable storage. It is an expression to describe that files stored there can be read and modified by a user, and that the storage can be mounted by another operating system as mass storage for file browsing.

If the connected Android device supports telephony features, an SMS containing the alarm message is sent to a preconfigured telephone number. Keep in mind that most Android tablets don't have a telephony function because their main use case is browsing the Internet rather than calling people. You can imagine that nobody looks cool holding a 10-inch tablet against their cheek in public to make a phone call.

The Arduino Sketch

As described in the software section, you will be using some of the well-known methods you used in prior examples. The only difference now is that you will be working with multiple components. Have a look at the complete Listing 10-1 before I describe it in detail.

Listing 10-1. Project 12: Arduino Sketch

```
#include <Max3421e.h>
#include <Usb.h>
#include <AndroidAccessory.h>

#define LED_OUTPUT_PIN 2
#define PIEZO_OUTPUT_PIN 3
#define BUTTON_INPUT_PIN 4
#define TILT_SWITCH_INPUT_PIN 5

#define NOTE_C7 2100

#define COMMAND_ALARM 0x9
#define ALARM_TYPE_TILT_SWITCH 0x1
#define ALARM_OFF 0x0
#define ALARM_ON 0x1

int tiltSwitchValue;
int buttonValue;
int ledBrightness;
int fadeSteps = 5;

boolean alarm = false;

AndroidAccessory acc("Manufacturer", "Model", "Description",
                     "Version", "URI", "Serial");
```

```
byte sntmsg[3];

void setup() {
  Serial.begin(19200);
  acc.powerOn();
  sntmsg[0] = COMMAND_ALARM;
  sntmsg[1] = ALARM_TYPE_TILT_SWITCH;
}

void loop() {
  acc.isConnected();
  tiltSwitchValue = digitalRead(TILT_SWITCH_INPUT_PIN);
  if((tiltSwitchValue == LOW) && !alarm) {
    startAlarm();
  }
  buttonValue = digitalRead(BUTTON_INPUT_PIN);
  if((buttonValue == LOW) && alarm) {
    stopAlarm();
  }
  if(alarm) {
    fadeLED();
  }
  delay(10);
}

void startAlarm() {
  alarm = true;
  tone(PIEZO_OUTPUT_PIN, NOTE_C7);
  ledBrightness = 0;
  //inform Android device
  sntmsg[2] = ALARM_ON;
  sendAlarmStateMessage();
}

void stopAlarm() {
  alarm = false;
  //turn off piezo buzzer
  noTone(PIEZO_OUTPUT_PIN);
  //turn off LED
  digitalWrite(LED_OUTPUT_PIN, LOW);
   //inform Android device
  sntmsg[2] = ALARM_OFF;
  sendAlarmStateMessage();
}

void sendAlarmStateMessage() {
  if (acc.isConnected()) {
    acc.write(sntmsg, 3);
  }
}
```

```
void fadeLED() {
  analogWrite(LED_OUTPUT_PIN, ledBrightness);
  //increase or decrease brightness
  ledBrightness = ledBrightness + fadeSteps;
  //change fade direction when reaching max or min of analog values
  if (ledBrightness < 0 || ledBrightness > 255) {
    fadeSteps = -fadeSteps ;
  }
}
```

First let's look at the variable definitions and declarations. If you connected all input and output components like I described in the project hardware setup section, then your pin definitions should look like shown here.

```
#define LED_OUTPUT_PIN 2
#define PIEZO_OUTPUT_PIN 3
#define BUTTON_INPUT_PIN 4
#define TILT_SWITCH_INPUT_PIN 5
```

The next definition you see is the frequency of the high-pitched sound that should be generated by the piezo buzzer when an alarm occurs. The frequency of 2100 Hz defines the musical note *C7*, which is the highest note on most musical keyboards, except for the classical 88-key piano. The note provides a perfect high-pitched sound which can be heard better by the human ear than any lower-pitched sound. That's the reason why systems like fire alarms use high-pitched alarm sounds.

```
#define NOTE_C7 2100
```

Next, you see the usual data message byte definition. A new byte value has been chosen for the alarm command and a type byte defines the tilt-switch used in this project to trigger the alarm. The type byte is defined in case you intend to add additional switches or sensors to your alarm system later on. The last two byte definitions just define if the alarm has been triggered or if it has been turned off.

```
#define COMMAND_ALARM 0x9
#define ALARM_TYPE_TILT_SWITCH 0x1
#define ALARM_OFF 0x0
#define ALARM_ON 0x1
```

When you use the digitalRead method to read the digital state of the button or the tilt-switch, the return value will be an int value which can be compared with the constants HIGH and LOW later on. So you will need two variables to store the button and the tilt-switch readings.

```
int tiltSwitchValue;
int buttonValue;
```

Remember that you want to pulse a LED when an alarm occurs. In order to do that you need to use the analogWrite method to modulate the voltage supply for the LED. The analogWrite method accepts values in the range from 0 to 255. That's why you will store the current brightness value as an int value. When you increase or decrease the brightness of the LED you can define a step value for the fade process. The lower the step value, the smoother and slower the LED will fade, because it takes more loop cycles to reach the maximum or minimum value of the analogWrite range.

```
int ledBrightness;
int fadeSteps = 5;
```

The last new variable is a boolean flag which just stores the current state of the alarm system to determine if the alarm is currently active or off. It is initialized in an off state at the beginning.

```
boolean alarm = false;
```

That's it for the variables. The setup method does nothing new apart from filling the first two bytes of the data message with the new command byte and the type byte. The interesting part is the loop method.

```
void loop() {
  acc.isConnected();
  tiltSwitchValue = digitalRead(TILT_SWITCH_INPUT_PIN);
  if((tiltSwitchValue == LOW) && !alarm) {
    startAlarm();
  }
  buttonValue = digitalRead(BUTTON_INPUT_PIN);
  if((buttonValue == LOW) && alarm) {
    stopAlarm();
  }
  if(alarm) {
    fadeLED();
  }
  delay(10);
}
```

In the previous projects the code within the loop method was enclosed by an if-clause which checked if the Android device was connected and only then executed the program logic. Since this is an alarm system, I thought it would be best to let it work at least on the Arduino side even if no Android device is connected. The reason why the isConnected method call is done at all in the beginning of the loop is that the logic within this method determines if a device is connected, and it sends a message to the Android device so that its corresponding application can be started. The rest of the loop logic is pretty straightforward. First you read the state of the tilt-switch.

```
tiltSwitchValue = digitalRead(TILT_SWITCH_INPUT_PIN);
```

If the tilt-switch closed its circuit, the digital state will be LOW because it is connected to ground if closed. Only then, and if the alarm is not already turned on, you'll want the alarm to start. The implementation of the startAlarm method will be explained later.

```
if((tiltSwitchValue == LOW) && !alarm) {
  startAlarm();
}
```

The code for the case in which the button is pressed does the exact opposite. It should stop the alarm and reset the alarm system to be able to be activated once again. The implementation of the stopAlarm method is also described later in the chapter.

```
buttonValue = digitalRead(BUTTON_INPUT_PIN);
if((buttonValue == LOW) && alarm) {
  stopAlarm();
}
```

If the system is currently in the alarm state you'll need to fade the LED to visualize the alarm. The fadeLED method implementation will follow shortly.

```
if(alarm) {
  fadeLED();
}
```

Now let's have a look at the other method implementations starting with the startAlarm method.

```
void startAlarm() {
  alarm = true;
  tone(PIEZO_OUTPUT_PIN, NOTE_C7);
  ledBrightness = 0;
  //inform Android device
  sntmsg[2] = ALARM_ON;
  sendAlarmStateMessage();
}
```

As you can see, the alarm flag has been set to true so that the method will not accidentally be called in the next loop cycle. The tone method was already used before in Chapter 5. Here it is used to generate the note C7 on the piezo buzzer. When the alarm is started, the ledBrightness variable needs to be reset to start the LED fading with a fade-in from dark to bright. At last the message byte for describing that the alarm was triggered is set on the data message and the message is sent to the Android device if it is connected.

Next up is the opposing method stopAlarm.

```
void stopAlarm() {
  alarm = false;
  //turn off piezo buzzer
  noTone(PIEZO_OUTPUT_PIN);
  //turn off LED
  digitalWrite(LED_OUTPUT_PIN, LOW);
  //inform Android device
  sntmsg[2] = ALARM_OFF;
  sendAlarmStateMessage();
}
```

First you set the alarm flag to false to allow the alarm to be triggered once again. Then you need to turn off the piezo buzzer by calling the noTone method. It stops the voltage output to the piezo buzzer so that it no longer can oscillate. The LED is turned off by calling the digitalWrite method and setting it to LOW (0V). The last step here is also to set the corresponding message byte and send the stop message to the Android device if it is connected.

The sendAlarmStateMessage method just checks if an Android device is connected, and if that's the case, the three-byte message is transmitted by using the write method of the Accessory object.

```
void sendAlarmStateMessage() {
  if (acc.isConnected()) {
    acc.write(sntmsg, 3);
  }
}
```

The last method implementation is the logic for fading the LED in and out.

```
void fadeLED() {
  analogWrite(LED_OUTPUT_PIN, ledBrightness);
  //increase or decrease brightness
  ledBrightness = ledBrightness + fadeSteps;
```

```
    //change fade direction when reaching max or min of analog values
    if (ledBrightness < 0 || ledBrightness > 255) {
      fadeSteps = -fadeSteps ;
    }
}
```

To provide different voltage levels for the LED, the analogWrite method must be used here along with the current brightness value. In each loop cycle the fadeLED method is called when the system is set into alarm mode. To change the brightness level of the LED you have to add the fadeSteps value to the current ledBrightness value. If you happen to exceed the possible analogWrite limits of 0 to 255, you need to negate the sign of the fadeSteps value. A value of 5 would become -5 and instead of increasing the brightness value in the next loop you would decrease it now, to dim the LED to a darker brightness level.

That's it for the Arduino part of the software. If you were to run your sketch now you would actually already have a functional alarm system. You'll want to implement the Android application, though, so that your alarm system becomes even more powerful by using the Android device as a gateway for text messaging and for storing information.

The Android Application

The Android software part will show you how to use the storage capabilities of your Android device to write a log file to the device's filesystem. When an alarm occurs and the connected Android device receives the trigger message, it will write the message and a timestamp to your application's storage folder for later inspection. Additionally, if you are using a device that supports the telephony feature, such as an Android phone, the device will send an SMS to a predefined number to notify about the alarm remotely. To visualize that an alarm has occurred, the screen's background color will be changed to red and an alarm message will be displayed. If the alarm is reset on the ADK board, a corresponding message is sent to the Android device and the application will be reset as well to enable the alarm system once again.

Project 12 Activity Java File

Have a look at the complete Listing 10-2 before I go into detail.

Listing 10-2. Project 12: ProjectTwelveActivity.java

```
package project.twelve.adk;

import …;

public class ProjectTwelveActivity extends Activity {

    …

    private PendingIntent smsSentIntent;
    private PendingIntent logFileWrittenIntent;

    private static final byte COMMAND_ALARM = 0x9;
    private static final byte ALARM_TYPE_TILT_SWITCH = 0x1;
    private static final byte ALARM_OFF = 0x0;
```

```java
    private static final byte ALARM_ON = 0x1;

    private static final String SMS_DESTINATION = "put_telephone_number_here";
    private static final String SMS_SENT_ACTION = "SMS_SENT";
    private static final String LOG_FILE_WRITTEN_ACTION = "LOG_FILE_WRITTEN";

    private PackageManager packageManager;
    boolean hasTelephony;

    private TextView alarmTextView;
    private TextView smsTextView;
    private TextView logTextView;
    private LinearLayout linearLayout;

    /** Called when the activity is first created. */
    @Override
    public void onCreate(Bundle savedInstanceState) {
        super.onCreate(savedInstanceState);

        mUsbManager = UsbManager.getInstance(this);
        mPermissionIntent = PendingIntent.getBroadcast(this, 0, new Intent(
                        ACTION_USB_PERMISSION), 0);
        smsSentIntent = PendingIntent.getBroadcast(this, 0, new Intent(
                        SMS_SENT_ACTION), 0);
        logFileWrittenIntent = PendingIntent.getBroadcast(this, 0, new Intent(
                        LOG_FILE_WRITTEN_ACTION), 0);
        IntentFilter filter = new IntentFilter(ACTION_USB_PERMISSION);
        filter.addAction(UsbManager.ACTION_USB_ACCESSORY_DETACHED);
        filter.addAction(SMS_SENT_ACTION);
        filter.addAction(LOG_FILE_WRITTEN_ACTION);
        registerReceiver(broadcastReceiver, filter);

        packageManager = getPackageManager();
        hasTelephony = packageManager.hasSystemFeature(PackageManager.FEATURE_TELEPHONY);

        setContentView(R.layout.main);
        linearLayout = (LinearLayout) findViewById(R.id.linear_layout);
        alarmTextView = (TextView) findViewById(R.id.alarm_text);
        smsTextView = (TextView) findViewById(R.id.sms_text);
        logTextView = (TextView) findViewById(R.id.log_text);
    }

    /**
     * Called when the activity is resumed from its paused state and immediately
     * after onCreate().
     */
    @Override
    public void onResume() {
        super.onResume();
        ...
    }
```

```java
/** Called when the activity is paused by the system. */
@Override
public void onPause() {
    super.onPause();
    closeAccessory();
}

/**
 * Called when the activity is no longer needed prior to being removed from
 * the activity stack.
 */
@Override
public void onDestroy() {
    super.onDestroy();
    unregisterReceiver(broadcastReceiver);
}

private final BroadcastReceiver broadcastReceiver = new BroadcastReceiver() {
    @Override
    public void onReceive(Context context, Intent intent) {
        String action = intent.getAction();
        if (ACTION_USB_PERMISSION.equals(action)) {
            synchronized (this) {
                UsbAccessory accessory = UsbManager.getAccessory(intent);
                if (intent.getBooleanExtra(UsbManager.EXTRA_PERMISSION_GRANTED, false)) {
                    openAccessory(accessory);
                } else {
                    Log.d(TAG, "permission denied for accessory " + accessory);
                }
                mPermissionRequestPending = false;
            }
        } else if (UsbManager.ACTION_USB_ACCESSORY_DETACHED.equals(action)) {
            UsbAccessory accessory = UsbManager.getAccessory(intent);
            if (accessory != null && accessory.equals(mAccessory)) {
                closeAccessory();
            }
        } else if (SMS_SENT_ACTION.equals(action)) {
            smsTextView.setText(R.string.sms_sent_message);
        } else if (LOG_FILE_WRITTEN_ACTION.equals(action)) {
            logTextView.setText(R.string.log_written_message);
        }
    }
};

private void openAccessory(UsbAccessory accessory) {
    ...
}

private void closeAccessory() {
    ...
}
```

```java
Runnable commRunnable = new Runnable() {

    @Override
    public void run() {
        int ret = 0;
        byte[] buffer = new byte[3];

        while (ret >= 0) {
            try {
                ret = mInputStream.read(buffer);
            } catch (IOException e) {
                Log.e(TAG, "IOException", e);
                break;
            }

            switch (buffer[0]) {
            case COMMAND_ALARM:

                if (buffer[1] == ALARM_TYPE_TILT_SWITCH) {
                    final byte alarmState = buffer[2];
                    final String alarmMessage = getString(R.string.alarm_message,
                                    getString(R.string.alarm_type_tilt_switch));
                    runOnUiThread(new Runnable() {

                        @Override
                        public void run() {
                            if(alarmState == ALARM_ON) {
                                linearLayout.setBackgroundColor(Color.RED);
                                alarmTextView.setText(alarmMessage);
                            } else if(alarmState == ALARM_OFF) {
                                linearLayout.setBackgroundColor(Color.WHITE);
                                alarmTextView.setText(R.string.alarm_reset_message);
                                smsTextView.setText("");
                                logTextView.setText("");
                            }
                        }
                    });
                    if(alarmState == ALARM_ON) {
                        sendSMS(alarmMessage);
                        writeToLogFile(new StringBuilder(alarmMessage).append(" - ")
                                            .append(new Date()).toString());
                    }
                }
                break;

            default:
                Log.d(TAG, "unknown msg: " + buffer[0]);
                break;
            }
        }
```

```
        }
    };

    private void sendSMS(String smsText) {
        if(hasTelephony) {
            SmsManager smsManager = SmsManager.getDefault();
            smsManager.sendTextMessage(SMS_DESTINATION, null, smsText, smsSentIntent, null);
        }
    }

    private void writeToLogFile(String logMessage) {
        File logDirectory = getExternalLogFilesDir();
        if(logDirectory != null) {
            File logFile = new File(logDirectory, "ProjectTwelveLog.txt");
            if(!logFile.exists()) {
                try {
                    logFile.createNewFile();
                } catch (IOException e) {
                    Log.d(TAG, "Log File could not be created.", e);
                }
            }
            BufferedWriter bufferedWriter = null;
            try {
                bufferedWriter = new BufferedWriter(new FileWriter(logFile, true));
                bufferedWriter.write(logMessage);
                bufferedWriter.newLine();
                Log.d(TAG, "Written message to file: " + logFile.toURI());
                logFileWrittenIntent.send();
            } catch (IOException e) {
                Log.d(TAG, "Could not write to Log File.", e);
            } catch (CanceledException e) {
                Log.d(TAG, "LogFileWrittenIntent was cancelled.", e);
            } finally {
                if(bufferedWriter != null) {
                    try {
                        bufferedWriter.close();
                    } catch (IOException e) {
                        Log.d(TAG, "Could not close Log File.", e);
                    }
                }
            }
        }
    }

    private File getExternalLogFilesDir() {
        String state = Environment.getExternalStorageState();
        if (Environment.MEDIA_MOUNTED.equals(state)) {
            return getExternalFilesDir(null);
        } else {
            return null;
        }
```

```
        }
}
```

As you may have seen while browsing through the code, you have multiple UI elements for displaying some texts. So before you start looking into the code, see how the layout and the texts are defined.

XML Resource Definitions

The main.xml layout file contains three TextViews wrapped in a LinearLayout. The TextViews just display the notifications messages later on. The LinearLayout is responsible for changing the background color. You can also see that the SMS and file notification TextViews have a green color definition (#00FF00) so that they have a better contrast when the background turns red.

Listing 10-3. Project 12: main.xml

```xml
<?xml version="1.0" encoding="utf-8"?>
<LinearLayout xmlns:android="http://schemas.android.com/apk/res/android"
    android:id="@+id/linear_layout"
        android:orientation="vertical"
        android:layout_width="fill_parent"
        android:layout_height="fill_parent"
        android:gravity="center"
        android:background="#FFFFFF">
        <TextView android:id="@+id/alarm_text"
                android:layout_width="wrap_content"
                android:layout_height="wrap_content"
                android:textColor="#000000"
                android:text="@string/alarm_reset_message"/>
        <TextView android:id="@+id/sms_text"
                android:layout_width="wrap_content"
                android:layout_height="wrap_content"
                android:textColor="#00FF00"/>
        <TextView android:id="@+id/log_text"
                android:layout_width="wrap_content"
                android:layout_height="wrap_content"
                android:textColor="#00FF00"/>
</LinearLayout>
```

The texts that are referenced in the layout, along with the alarm message text, which should be displayed once an alarm is triggered, are defined in the strings.xml file as shown in Listing 10-4.

Listing 10-4. Project 12: strings.xml

```xml
<?xml version="1.0" encoding="utf-8"?>
<resources>
    <string name="app_name">ProjectTwelve</string>
    <string name="alarm_message">%1$s triggered an alarm!</string>
    <string name="alarm_reset_message">Alarm system is reset and active!</string>
    <string name="alarm_type_tilt_switch">Tilt switch</string>
    <string name="sms_sent_message">SMS has been sent.</string>
    <string name="log_written_message">Log has been written.</string>
```

```
</resources>
```

Variable Declarations and Definitions

Now let's talk about the actual code from Listing 10-2 in detail. First up are the variables. You can see two additional PendingIntents. Those will be necessary to notify the activity later on that the corresponding event has taken place to update the corresponding TextView.

```
private PendingIntent smsSentIntent;
private PendingIntent logFileWrittenIntent;
```

Then you have the usual message data bytes, which are defined as in the Arduino sketch.

```
private static final byte COMMAND_ALARM = 0x9;
private static final byte ALARM_TYPE_TILT_SWITCH = 0x1;
private static final byte ALARM_OFF = 0x0;
private static final byte ALARM_ON = 0x1;
```

Next, you see some string definitions. The SMS_DESTINATION is the destination phone number to which you want to send the notification SMS. You have to change this to a real phone number. Then you have two action strings which are used to identify the PendingIntents later on when they are broadcasting that their corresponding event has happened.

```
private static final String SMS_DESTINATION = "put_telephone_number_here";
private static final String SMS_SENT_ACTION = "SMS_SENT";
private static final String LOG_FILE_WRITTEN_ACTION = "LOG_FILE_WRITTEN";
```

In order to determine whether your Android device supports the telephony feature you'll need access to the PackageManager. The boolean flag hasTelephony is used to store the information if telephony is supported so that you don't have to do the lookup every time.

```
private PackageManager packageManager;
private boolean hasTelephony;
```

At the end of the global variable section you can see the LinearLayout and the TextView declarations for the UI elements which are used to give visual alarm feedback.

```
private TextView alarmTextView;
private TextView smsTextView;
private TextView logTextView;
private LinearLayout linearLayout;
```

Lifecycle Methods

That's it for the variables. Now let's have a look at the onCreate method. In addition to the PendingIntent for granting the USB permission, you define two new PendingIntents. They will be used to broadcast that their specific events, writing a log file to the filesystem or sending an SMS, have happened so that the UI can be updated accordingly.

```
smsSentIntent = PendingIntent.getBroadcast(this, 0, new Intent(SMS_SENT_ACTION), 0);
logFileWrittenIntent = PendingIntent.getBroadcast(
                    this, 0, new Intent(LOG_FILE_WRITTEN_ACTION), 0);
```

You can see that they define a broadcast, where the action string-constants for their specific events are used to initialize their Intent. In order to filter these intents later on when the BroadcastReceiver handles the broadcasts, you'll need to add the corresponding actions to the IntentFilter which is registered at the system along with the BroadcastReceiver itself.

```
IntentFilter filter = new IntentFilter(ACTION_USB_PERMISSION);
filter.addAction(UsbManager.ACTION_USB_ACCESSORY_DETACHED);
filter.addAction(SMS_SENT_ACTION);
filter.addAction(LOG_FILE_WRITTEN_ACTION);
registerReceiver(broadcastReceiver, filter);
```

The next important thing in the onCreate method is getting a reference to the PackageManager to determine if the telephony feature is supported on your Android device.

```
packageManager = getPackageManager();
hasTelephony = packageManager.hasSystemFeature(PackageManager.FEATURE_TELEPHONY);
```

The PackageManager is a system utility class used to resolve global package information. You can check if your device supports certain features or if certain applications are installed on the device, or you can get access to your own application information. In this project, we are only interested in the telephony support so you call the hasSystemFeature method with the constant FEATURE_TELEPHONY.

The last part of the onCreate method defines the usual UI initializations.

```
setContentView(R.layout.main);
linearLayout = (LinearLayout) findViewById(R.id.linear_layout);
alarmTextView = (TextView) findViewById(R.id.alarm_text);
smsTextView = (TextView) findViewById(R.id.sms_text);
logTextView = (TextView) findViewById(R.id.log_text);
```

BroadcastReceiver

The other lifecycle methods haven't changed, so you can just continue with the BroadcastReceiver's onReceive method. As you can see, two new else-if-clauses have been added to evaluate the action that has triggered the broadcast.

```
else if (SMS_SENT_ACTION.equals(action)) {
    smsTextView.setText(R.string.sms_sent_message);
} else if (LOG_FILE_WRITTEN_ACTION.equals(action)) {
    logTextView.setText(R.string.log_written_message);
}
```

According to the action that has triggered the broadcast, the corresponding TextView is updated. The onReceive method of the BroadcastReceiver runs on the UI thread, so it is safe to make the UI updates here.

Runnable Implementation

The next interesting part is the alarm message evaluation in the Runnable implementation.

```
final byte alarmState = buffer[2];
final String alarmMessage = getString(R.string.alarm_message,
                getString(R.string.alarm_type_tilt_switch));
runOnUiThread(new Runnable() {
```

```
    @Override
    public void run() {
        if(alarmState == ALARM_ON) {
            linearLayout.setBackgroundColor(Color.RED);
            alarmTextView.setText(alarmMessage);
        } else if(alarmState == ALARM_OFF) {
            linearLayout.setBackgroundColor(Color.WHITE);
            alarmTextView.setText(R.string.alarm_reset_message);
            smsTextView.setText("");
            logTextView.setText("");
        }
    }
});
if(alarmState == ALARM_ON) {
    sendSMS(alarmMessage);
    writeToLogFile(new StringBuilder(alarmMessage).append(" - ")
                            .append(new Date()).toString());
}
```

After checking the current state of the alarm system, you can update the corresponding TextViews in the runOnUiThread method. If the alarm has been triggered, you set the background color of the LinearLayout to red and set the alarm text on the alarmTextView. If the alarm got cancelled and reset, you set the background color of the LinearLayout back to white, update the alarmTextView with a text that tells the user that the system is reset again, and clear the TextViews that notify about the SMS and the log file event. After you have updated the UI according to the current condition of the alarm, you can continue with sending the SMS and writing of the log file, if the alarm has been triggered. The implementation is encapsulated in separate methods, which we will look at next.

Sending a Text Message (SMS)

First let's see how to send an SMS in Android.

```
private void sendSMS(String smsText) {
    if(hasTelephony) {
        SmsManager smsManager = SmsManager.getDefault();
        smsManager.sendTextMessage(SMS_DESTINATION, null, smsText, smsSentIntent, null);
    }
}
```

Here the boolean flag you set in the beginning is used to check if the connected Android device is capable of sending an SMS. If it isn't, there will be no point in calling the code at all. In order to be able to send an SMS, you need to get a reference to the system's SmsManager first. The SmsManager class provides a convenient static method to get the default SmsManager implementation of the system. Once you have a reference to the SmsManager, you can call the sendTextMessage method, which takes several parameters. First you have to provide the SMS destination number. Then you can provide a service center address. Usually you can just use null so that the default service center is used. The third parameter is the actual message you want to send via SMS. The last two parameters are PendingIntents you can provide to be notified when the SMS was sent and when the SMS was received. You already defined the PendingIntent to notify that the SMS was sent, so you will use it here to be notified once it is sent out. Once that happens, the BroadcastReceiver will be notified to update the UI accordingly.

Writing a Log File to the Filesystem

The writeToLogFile method, as the name already implies, is responsible for writing a log file to the application's storage directory on the device's filesystem.

```
private void writeToLogFile(String logMessage) {
    File logDirectory = getExternalLogFilesDir();
    if(logDirectory != null) {
        File logFile = new File(logDirectory, "ProjectTwelveLog.txt");
        if(!logFile.exists()) {
            try {
                logFile.createNewFile();
            } catch (IOException e) {
                Log.d(TAG, "Log File could not be created.", e);
            }
        }
        BufferedWriter bufferedWriter = null;
        try {
            bufferedWriter = new BufferedWriter(new FileWriter(logFile, true));
            bufferedWriter.write(logMessage);
            bufferedWriter.newLine();
            Log.d(TAG, "Written message to file: " + logFile.toURI());
            logFileWrittenIntent.send();
        } catch (IOException e) {
            Log.d(TAG, "Could not write to Log File.", e);
        } catch (CanceledException e) {
            Log.d(TAG, "LogFileWrittenIntent was cancelled.", e);
        } finally {
            if(bufferedWriter != null) {
                try {
                    bufferedWriter.close();
                } catch (IOException e) {
                    Log.d(TAG, "Could not close Log File.", e);
                }
            }
        }
    }
}
```

Before you can write to the external storage of the Android device you need to check if the storage is mounted in the Android system and not currently used by another system, for example, when connected to a computer for transferring files. For that purpose you use another method that checks the current state of the external storage and returns the path to the application's file storage directory.

```
private File getExternalLogFilesDir() {
    String state = Environment.getExternalStorageState();
    if (Environment.MEDIA_MOUNTED.equals(state)) {
        return getExternalFilesDir(null);
    } else {
        return null;
    }
}
```

If the method returns a valid directory path you can create a `File` object by providing the directory and the filename.

```
File logFile = new File(logDirectory, "ProjectTwelveLog.txt");
```

If the file doesn't already exist in the directory, you should create it first.

```
if(!logFile.exists()) {
    try {
        logFile.createNewFile();
    } catch (IOException e) {
        Log.d(TAG, "Log File could not be created.", e);
    }
}
```

To write to the file itself you will create a `BufferedWriter` object which takes a `FileWriter` object as a parameter. The `FileWriter` is created by providing the reference to the `File` object and a boolean flag. The boolean flag defines if the text to be written should be appended to the file or if the file should be overwritten. If you want to append the text you should use the boolean flag true.

```
bufferedWriter = new BufferedWriter(new FileWriter(logFile, true));
bufferedWriter.write(logMessage);
bufferedWriter.newLine();
```

If you are done writing to the file you can fire the corresponding broadcast by calling the send method on the `logFileWrittenIntent` object.

```
logFileWrittenIntent.send();
```

It is important to always close open connections to free up memory and release file handles, so don't forget to call the `close` method on the `BufferedWriter` object in the finally block. This closes all underlying open connections.

```
bufferedWriter.close();
```

Permissions

That's it for the java coding part. However, if you were to run the application now it would crash when trying to send an SMS or writing to the filesystem. That's because you require special permissions for these tasks. You need to add the `android.permission.SEND_SMS` permission and the `android.permission.WRITE_EXTERNAL_STORAGE` permission to your `AndroidManifest.xml`. Have a look at how it is done in Listing 10-5.

Listing 10-5. Project 12: AndroidManifest.xml

```
<?xml version="1.0" encoding="utf-8"?>
<manifest xmlns:android="http://schemas.android.com/apk/res/android"
    package="project.twelve.adk"
    android:versionCode="1"
    android:versionName="1.0">
    <uses-sdk android:minSdkVersion="10" />
    <uses-feature android:name="android.hardware.usb.accessory" />
    <uses-permission android:name="android.permission.SEND_SMS" />
    <uses-permission android:name="android.permission.WRITE_EXTERNAL_STORAGE" />
```

```
<application android:icon="@drawable/icon" android:label="@string/app_name" >
    <uses-library android:name="com.android.future.usb.accessory" />
    <activity android:name=".ProjectTwelveActivity"
        android:label="@string/app_name" android:screenOrientation="portrait">
        <intent-filter>
            <action android:name="android.intent.action.MAIN" />
            <category android:name="android.intent.category.LAUNCHER" />
        </intent-filter>
        <intent-filter>
            <action android:name="android.hardware.usb.action.USB_ACCESSORY_ATTACHED" />
        </intent-filter>

        <meta-data android:name="android.hardware.usb.action.USB_ACCESSORY_ATTACHED"
            android:resource="@xml/accessory_filter" />
    </activity>
</application>
</manifest>
```

Final Result

The Android application is now ready to be deployed on the device. Upload the Arduino sketch as well, connect both devices, and see your alarm system in action. If you set up everything correctly and tilt your tilt-switch to an upright position you should have a result that looks like Figure 10-10.

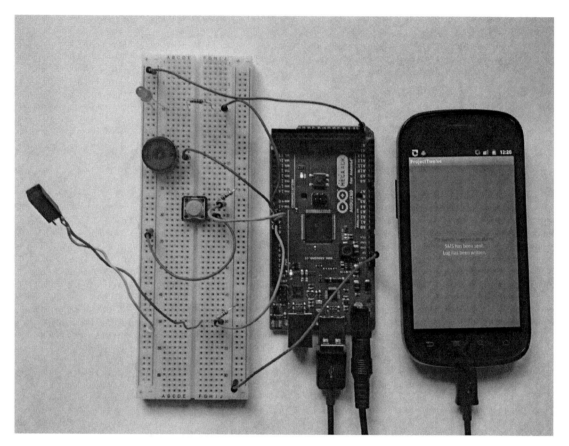

Figure 10-10. *Project 12: Final result*

Project 13: Camera Alarm System with IR Light Barrier

The final project will be a camera alarm system that is able to take a quick photo of an intruder when the alarm is triggered. The hardware will be more or less the same as in the previous project. The only difference is that you will use an IR light barrier for triggering the alarm instead of the tilt-switch. After the photo is taken, it will be persisted in the application's external storage along with a log file that logs the alarm event.

The Parts

In order to integrate the IR light barrier into your hardware setup from the previous project you'll need a few additional parts. In addition to the parts you have already used, you will need an additional 220Ω resistor, an IR emitter or an IR LED, and an IR detector. The complete part list is shown here (See Figure 10-11):

- ADK board

- Breadboard
- 2 × 220Ω resistor
- 2 × 10kΩ resistor
- Some wires
- Button
- IR light barrier (IR emitter, IR detector)
- LED operating at 5V
- Piezo buzzer

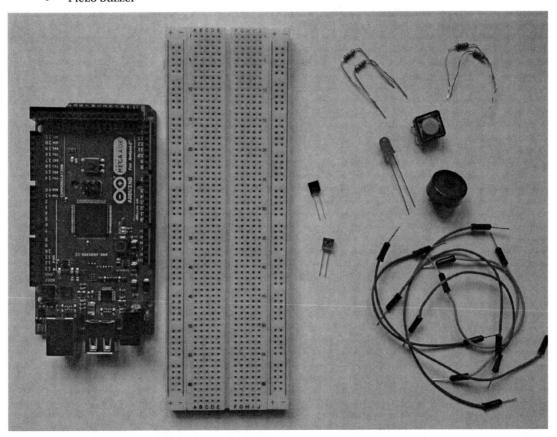

Figure 10-11. Project 13 parts (ADK board, breadboard, wires, resistors, button, IR emitter (clear), IR detector (black), piezo buzzer, red LED)

ADK Board

The IR light barrier circuit will be connected to an analog input of the ADK board. The analog input pin will be used to detect sudden changes in the measured voltage level. When the IR detector is exposed to light in the infrared light wavelength, the measured input voltage on the connected analog input pin will be very low. If the IR light exposure is interrupted, the measured voltage will increase significantly.

IR Light Barrier

The IR light barrier you will build in this project will consist of two components, an IR emitter and an IR detector. The emitter is usually a normal IR LED, which emits infrared light in the wavelength of about 940nm. You will find IR LEDs in different forms. The usual form of a single IR LED is the standard bulb-shaped LED, but LEDs can also be found in a transistor-like shape. Both are shown in Figure 10-12.

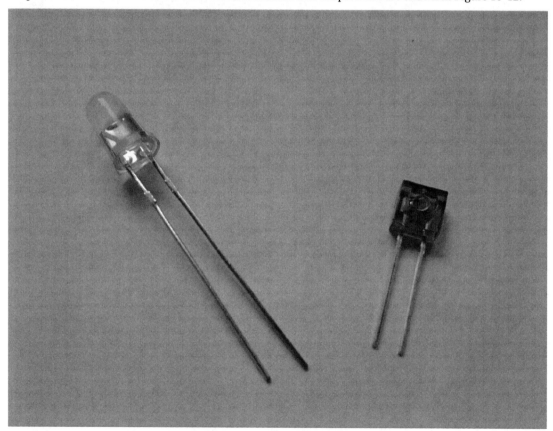

Figure 10-12. Bulb-shaped IR LED (left), transistor-shaped IR LED (right)

The IR detector is usually a two-legged phototransistor having only a collector and an emitter connector. Often both components are sold as a matching pair to create IR light barrier circuits. This matching set is most commonly sold in the transistor-shaped form. (See Figure 10-13.)

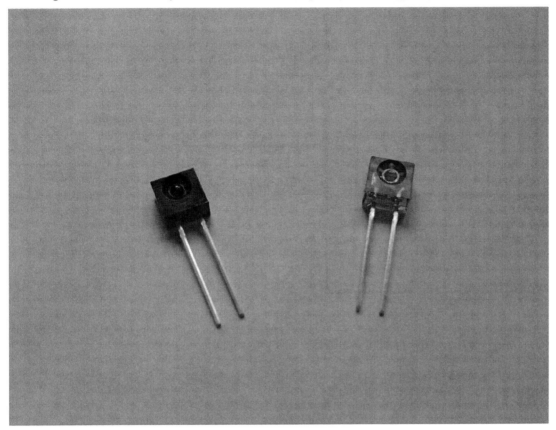

Figure 10-13. Matching IR detector (left) and emitter (right) in set TEMIC K153P

The advantage of the matching-pair sets is that both components are optically and electrically matched to provide the best compatibility. The IR emitter and detector set I used in this project is called TEMIC K153P. You don't have to use the exact same set. All you need is an IR LED and a phototransistor and you will achieve the same final result. You might only have to adjust the resistors in the IR light barrier circuit or the alarm-triggering threshold value in the code later on. The typical circuit for an IR light barrier is shown in Figure 10-14.

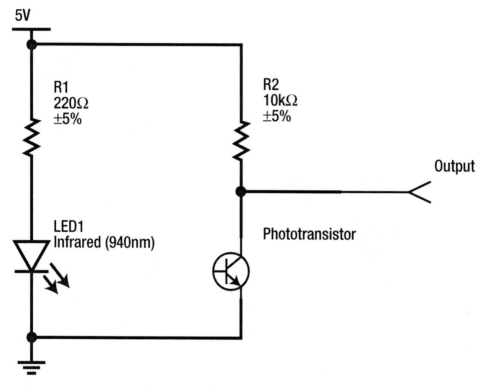

5V

R1
220Ω
±5%

R2
10kΩ
±5%

Output

LED1
Infrared (940nm)

Phototransistor

Figure 10-14. Common IR light barrier circuit

As described before, the principle of operation is that output voltage decreases if the detector (phototransistor) is exposed to IR light. So if you place your finger or any other object between the emitter and the detector the exposure to IR light at the detector is interrupted and the output voltage increases. Once a self-defined threshold value is reached, you can trigger an alarm.

The Setup

For this project's setup you basically only have to disconnect your tilt-switch circuit from the previous project and replace it with the IR circuit shown in Figure 10-15.

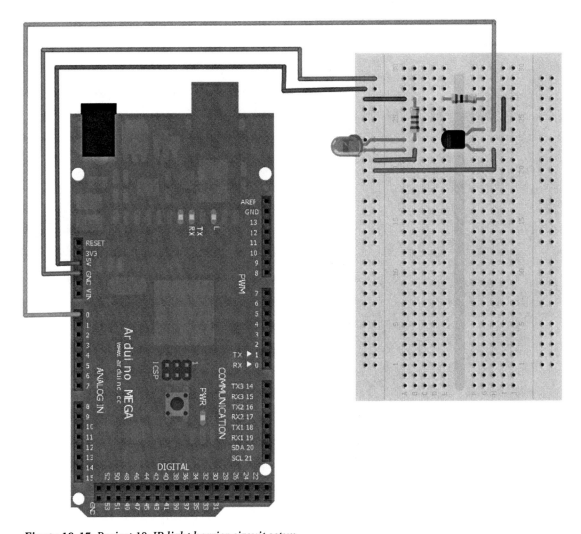

Figure 10-15. Project 13: IR light barrier circuit setup

As you can see, the IR LED (emitter) is connected like a normal LED. Just connect +5V to one lead of a 220Ω resistor and the other lead of the resistor to the positive lead of the IR LED. The negative lead of the IR LED is connected to ground (GND). The IR phototransistor's emitter lead is connected to ground (GND). The collector lead has to be connected through a 10kΩ resistor to +5V and additionally to analog input A0. Have a look into your component's datasheet if you are not sure which lead is which.

The complete circuit setup, combined with the other alarm system components from the previous project, looks like Figure 10-16.

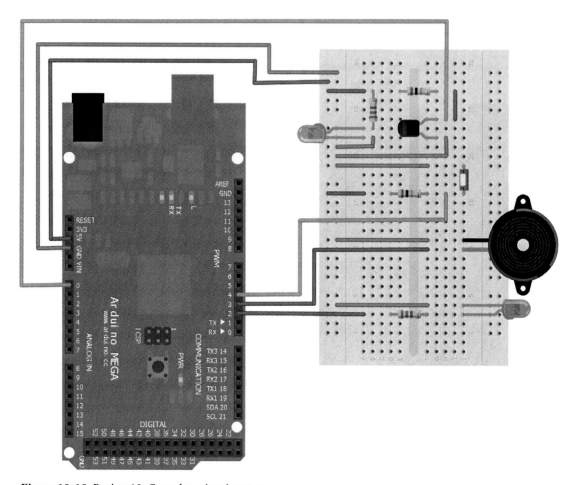

Figure 10-16. Project 13: Complete circuit setup

The Software

The Arduino software part will only change slightly. Instead of reading the state of a digital input pin where the tilt-switch was connected previously, you will be reading the input values of an analog input pin connected to the IR light barrier's IR detector. If the measured input value reaches a predefined threshold an alarm is triggered and, as in the previous project, the alarm sound should be generated and the red LED should fade in and out. Once the alarm is sent to the connected Android device, a log file will be stored in the application's external storage directory. Instead of sending an SMS to notify about a possible intruder, the device will now take a picture if it has a camera. Once the picture is taken, it will also be saved in the application's external storage directory along with the log file.

The Arduino Sketch

As I just described, the Arduino sketch for this project is very similar to the one used in project 12. It only needs some minor changes to comply with the IR light barrier circuit. Have a look at the complete Listing 10-6 first; I will explain the necessary changes after.

Listing 10-6. Project 13: Arduino Sketch

```
#include <Max3421e.h>
#include <Usb.h>
#include <AndroidAccessory.h>

#define LED_OUTPUT_PIN 2
#define PIEZO_OUTPUT_PIN 3
#define BUTTON_INPUT_PIN 4
#define IR_LIGHT_BARRIER_INPUT_PIN A0

#define IR_LIGHT_BARRIER_THRESHOLD 511
#define NOTE_C7 2100

#define COMMAND_ALARM 0x9
#define ALARM_TYPE_IR_LIGHT_BARRIER 0x2
#define ALARM_OFF 0x0
#define ALARM_ON 0x1

int irLightBarrierValue;
int buttonValue;
int ledBrightness = 0;
int fadeSteps = 5;

boolean alarm = false;

AndroidAccessory acc("Manufacturer", "Model", "Description",
                     "Version", "URI", "Serial");

byte sntmsg[3];

void setup() {
  Serial.begin(19200);
  acc.powerOn();
  sntmsg[0] = COMMAND_ALARM;
  sntmsg[1] = ALARM_TYPE_IR_LIGHT_BARRIER;
}

void loop() {
  acc.isConnected();
  irLightBarrierValue = analogRead(IR_LIGHT_BARRIER_INPUT_PIN);
  if((irLightBarrierValue > IR_LIGHT_BARRIER_THRESHOLD) && !alarm) {
    startAlarm();
  }
  buttonValue = digitalRead(BUTTON_INPUT_PIN);
```

```
    if((buttonValue == LOW) && alarm) {
      stopAlarm();
    }
    if(alarm) {
      fadeLED();
    }
    delay(10);
}

void startAlarm() {
  alarm = true;
  tone(PIEZO_OUTPUT_PIN, NOTE_C7);
  ledBrightness = 0;
  //inform Android device
  sntmsg[2] = ALARM_ON;
  sendAlarmStateMessage();
}

void stopAlarm() {
  alarm = false;
  //turn off piezo buzzer
  noTone(PIEZO_OUTPUT_PIN);
  //turn off LED
  digitalWrite(LED_OUTPUT_PIN, LOW);
  //inform Android device
  sntmsg[2] = ALARM_OFF;
  sendAlarmStateMessage();
}

void sendAlarmStateMessage() {
  if (acc.isConnected()) {
    acc.write(sntmsg, 3);
  }
}

void fadeLED() {
  analogWrite(LED_OUTPUT_PIN, ledBrightness);
  //increase or decrease brightness
  ledBrightness = ledBrightness + fadeSteps;
  //change fade direction when reaching max or min of analog values
  if (ledBrightness < 0 || ledBrightness > 255) {
    fadeSteps = -fadeSteps ;
  }
}
```

You can see that the tilt-switch pin definition has been replaced by the analog pin definition for the IR light barrier.

```
#define IR_LIGHT_BARRIER_INPUT_PIN A0
```

The next new definition is the threshold value for the voltage change on the IR light barrier. When the IR detector is exposed to the IR emitter, the voltage output measured is very low. The read ADC value is usually in the lower two-digit range. Once the IR exposure is interrupted, the voltage output is noticeably increasing. Now the read ADC value will usually be in the range close to the maximum ADC value of 1023. A value in between of 0 and 1023 makes a good threshold value to trigger an alarm. If you want your alarm trigger to be more responsive to only slight changes in IR lighting, you should reduce the threshold value. A value of 511 is a good start, though.

```
#define IR_LIGHT_BARRIER_THRESHOLD 511
```

To store the read ADC value of the IR light barrier on pin A0, you just use an integer variable.

```
int irLightBarrierValue;
```

The rest of the code is pretty straightforward and already familiar from project 12. The only new thing you need to do in the loop method is read the ADC value on the analog input pin of the IR light barrier and check if it exceeded the predefined threshold value. If it did and the alarm was not triggered before, you can start the alarm routine.

```
irLightBarrierValue = analogRead(IR_LIGHT_BARRIER_INPUT_PIN);
if((irLightBarrierValue > IR_LIGHT_BARRIER_THRESHOLD) && !alarm) {
  startAlarm();
}
```

That wasn't hard, was it? Let's see what you have to do on the Android software side of your alarm system.

The Android Application

Once the Android application received the data message expressing that an alarm has occurred, it will notify the user visually about the alarm and additionally write a log file in the application's external storage directory. To be able to identify an intruder that may have triggered the alarm, the Android application will utilize the Android camera API to take a photo if the device has a built-in camera. The front-facing camera will be the preferred camera if it is present. If the device has only a back camera, this will be used instead.

To provide a better overview in this last project, I have split up the listings to talk about them individually.

Variables and Lifecycle Methods

Have a look at Listing 10-7 before I go into detail.

Listing 10-7. Project 13: ProjectThirteenActivity.java (Part 1)

```
package project.thirteen.adk;

import …;

public class ProjectThirteenActivity extends Activity {

    …

    private PendingIntent photoTakenIntent;
    private PendingIntent logFileWrittenIntent;
```

```java
    private static final byte COMMAND_ALARM = 0x9;
    private static final byte ALARM_TYPE_IR_LIGHT_BARRIER = 0x2;
    private static final byte ALARM_OFF = 0x0;
    private static final byte ALARM_ON = 0x1;

    private static final String PHOTO_TAKEN_ACTION = "PHOTO_TAKEN";
    private static final String LOG_FILE_WRITTEN_ACTION = "LOG_FILE_WRITTEN";

    private PackageManager packageManager;
    private boolean hasFrontCamera;
    private boolean hasBackCamera;

    private Camera camera;
    private SurfaceView surfaceView;

    private TextView alarmTextView;
    private TextView photoTakenTextView;
    private TextView logTextView;
    private LinearLayout linearLayout;
    private FrameLayout frameLayout;

    /** Called when the activity is first created. */
    @Override
    public void onCreate(Bundle savedInstanceState) {
        super.onCreate(savedInstanceState);

        mUsbManager = UsbManager.getInstance(this);
        mPermissionIntent = PendingIntent.getBroadcast(this, 0, new Intent(
                            ACTION_USB_PERMISSION), 0);
        photoTakenIntent = PendingIntent.getBroadcast(this, 0, new Intent(
                            PHOTO_TAKEN_ACTION), 0);
        logFileWrittenIntent = PendingIntent.getBroadcast(this, 0, new Intent(
                            LOG_FILE_WRITTEN_ACTION), 0);
        IntentFilter filter = new IntentFilter(ACTION_USB_PERMISSION);
        filter.addAction(UsbManager.ACTION_USB_ACCESSORY_DETACHED);
        filter.addAction(PHOTO_TAKEN_ACTION);
        filter.addAction(LOG_FILE_WRITTEN_ACTION);
        registerReceiver(broadcastReceiver, filter);

        packageManager = getPackageManager();
        hasFrontCamera = packageManager.hasSystemFeature(PackageManager.FEATURE_CAMERA_FRONT);
        hasBackCamera = packageManager.hasSystemFeature(PackageManager.FEATURE_CAMERA);

        setContentView(R.layout.main);
        linearLayout = (LinearLayout) findViewById(R.id.linear_layout);
        frameLayout = (FrameLayout) findViewById(R.id.camera_preview);
        alarmTextView = (TextView) findViewById(R.id.alarm_text);
        photoTakenTextView = (TextView) findViewById(R.id.photo_taken_text);
        logTextView = (TextView) findViewById(R.id.log_text);
    }
```

```
/**
 * Called when the activity is resumed from its paused state and immediately
 * after onCreate().
 */
@Override
public void onResume() {
    super.onResume();

    camera = getCamera();
    dummySurfaceView = new CameraPreview(this, camera);
    frameLayout.addView(dummySurfaceView);

    ...
}

/** Called when the activity is paused by the system. */
@Override
public void onPause() {
    super.onPause();
    closeAccessory();
    if(camera != null) {
        camera.release();
        camera = null;
        frameLayout.removeAllViews();
    }
}

/**
 * Called when the activity is no longer needed prior to being removed from
 * the activity stack.
 */
@Override
public void onDestroy() {
    super.onDestroy();
    unregisterReceiver(broadcastReceiver);
}

...
```

The first part of the ProjectThirteenActivity shows the initializations and lifecycle methods that have to be adjusted for the final project. Let's go through the variable declarations and definitions really quickly. You can see that you use PendingIntents again for notification purposes. You will be using them for the log file–writing event and for the event when a photo has been taken by the camera.

```
private PendingIntent photoTakenIntent;
private PendingIntent logFileWrittenIntent;
```

Next, you see the same alarm type byte identifier as was used in the Arduino sketch to identify the IR light barrier as the trigger source for the alarm.

```
private static final byte ALARM_TYPE_IR_LIGHT_BARRIER = 0x2;
```

You also have to define a new action constant to identify the broadcast of the photo event later on.

```
private static final String PHOTO_TAKEN_ACTION = "PHOTO_TAKEN";
```

The PackageManager is used once again in this project to determine if the device has a front camera and a back camera.

```
private PackageManager packageManager;
private boolean hasFrontCamera;
private boolean hasBackCamera;
```

You will also hold a reference to the device's camera because you need to call certain lifecycle methods on the Camera object itself in order to take photos. The SurfaceView is a special View element that will display the current camera preview before you take a photo.

```
private Camera camera;
private SurfaceView surfaceView;
```

You might also have noticed that you have two new UI elements. One is a TextView to display a text indicating that a photo has been taken. The second is a FrameLayout View container. This kind of container is used to render multiple Views on top of each other to achieve an overlay effect.

```
private TextView photoTakenTextView;
private FrameLayout frameLayout;
```

Now let's see what you have to do in the lifecycle methods of the ProjectThirteenActivity. In the onCreate method you do your usual initializations. Again, you have to define the new PendingIntent for the photo event and register the broadcast action at the IntentFilter.

```
photoTakenIntent = PendingIntent.getBroadcast(this, 0, new Intent(PHOTO_TAKEN_ACTION), 0);
filter.addAction(PHOTO_TAKEN_ACTION);
```

You use the PackageManager again to check for device features. Only this time you check for a front-facing camera and a back-facing camera on the device.

```
hasFrontCamera = packageManager.hasSystemFeature(PackageManager.FEATURE_CAMERA_FRONT);
hasBackCamera = packageManager.hasSystemFeature(PackageManager.FEATURE_CAMERA);
```

The last step is the usual UI initialization.

```
setContentView(R.layout.main);
linearLayout = (LinearLayout) findViewById(R.id.linear_layout);
frameLayout = (FrameLayout) findViewById(R.id.camera_preview);
alarmTextView = (TextView) findViewById(R.id.alarm_text);
photoTakenTextView = (TextView) findViewById(R.id.photo_taken_text);
logTextView = (TextView) findViewById(R.id.log_text);
```

Those were the steps that are necessary at creation time of the Activity. You also have to take care about certain things when the application pauses and when it resumes. When the application is resumed, you'll have to get a reference to the device's camera. You also need to prepare a preview View element of the type SurfaceView so that the device can render the current camera preview and show it to the user. This preview SurfaceView is then added to your FrameLayout container to be displayed. The details about the implementation of the SurfaceView, and how to get the actual camera reference, are shown later on.

```
camera = getCamera();
dummySurfaceView = new CameraPreview(this, camera);
frameLayout.addView(dummySurfaceView);
```

Respectively, you need to free up resources when the application is paused. The documentation states that you should release the handle to the camera itself so that other applications are able to use the camera. Additionally you should remove the SurfaceView from the FrameLayout so that only one newly created SurfaceView is present in the container when the application is resumed again.

```
if(camera != null) {
    camera.release();
    camera = null;
    frameLayout.removeAllViews();
}
```

That's it for the lifecycle methods.

XML Resource Definitions

You saw that you need to define a new layout and some new texts again, as shown in Listing 10-8.

Listing 10-8. Project 13: main.xml

```xml
<?xml version="1.0" encoding="utf-8"?>
<LinearLayout xmlns:android="http://schemas.android.com/apk/res/android"
    android:id="@+id/linear_layout"
    android:orientation="vertical"
    android:layout_width="fill_parent"
    android:layout_height="fill_parent"
    android:gravity="center"
    android:background="#FFFFFF">
    <FrameLayout android:id="@+id/camera_preview"
        android:layout_width="fill_parent"
        android:layout_height="fill_parent"
        android:layout_weight="1"/>
    <TextView android:id="@+id/alarm_text"
        android:layout_width="wrap_content"
        android:layout_height="wrap_content"
        android:textColor="#000000"
        android:text="@string/alarm_reset_message"/>
    <TextView android:id="@+id/photo_taken_text"
        android:layout_width="wrap_content"
        android:layout_height="wrap_content"
        android:textColor="#00FF00"/>
    <TextView android:id="@+id/log_text"
        android:layout_width="wrap_content"
        android:layout_height="wrap_content"
        android:textColor="#00FF00"/>
</LinearLayout>
```

The referenced texts are defined in the strings.xml file as shown in Listing 10-9.

Listing 10-9. Project 13: strings.xml

```xml
<?xml version="1.0" encoding="utf-8"?>
<resources>
    <string name="app_name">ProjectThirteen</string>
    <string name="alarm_message">%1$s triggered an alarm!</string>
    <string name="alarm_reset_message">Alarm system is reset and active!</string>
    <string name="alarm_type_ir_light_barrier">IR Light Barrier</string>
    <string name="photo_taken_message">Photo has been taken.</string>
    <string name="log_written_message">Log has been written.</string>
</resources>
```

BroadcastReceiver and Runnable Implementation

Now let's have a look at the BroadcastReceiver and the Runnable implementation that handles the communication part (Listing 10-10).

Listing 10-10. Project 13: ProjectThirteenActivity.java (Part 2)

```java
    ...

    private final BroadcastReceiver broadcastReceiver = new BroadcastReceiver() {
        @Override
        public void onReceive(Context context, Intent intent) {
            String action = intent.getAction();
            if (ACTION_USB_PERMISSION.equals(action)) {
                synchronized (this) {
                    UsbAccessory accessory = UsbManager.getAccessory(intent);
                    if (intent.getBooleanExtra(UsbManager.EXTRA_PERMISSION_GRANTED, false)) {
                        openAccessory(accessory);
                    } else {
                        Log.d(TAG, "permission denied for accessory " + accessory);
                    }
                    mPermissionRequestPending = false;
                }
            } else if (UsbManager.ACTION_USB_ACCESSORY_DETACHED.equals(action)) {
                UsbAccessory accessory = UsbManager.getAccessory(intent);
                if (accessory != null && accessory.equals(mAccessory)) {
                    closeAccessory();
                }
            } else if (PHOTO_TAKEN_ACTION.equals(action)) {
                photoTakenTextView.setText(R.string.photo_taken_message);
            } else if (LOG_FILE_WRITTEN_ACTION.equals(action)) {
                logTextView.setText(R.string.log_written_message);
            }
        }
    };

    private void openAccessory(UsbAccessory accessory) {
        ...
```

```
}

private void closeAccessory() {
    …
}

Runnable commRunnable = new Runnable() {

    @Override
    public void run() {
        int ret = 0;
        byte[] buffer = new byte[3];

        while (ret >= 0) {
            try {
                ret = mInputStream.read(buffer);
            } catch (IOException e) {
                Log.e(TAG, "IOException", e);
                break;
            }

            switch (buffer[0]) {
            case COMMAND_ALARM:

                if (buffer[1] == ALARM_TYPE_IR_LIGHT_BARRIER) {
                    final byte alarmState = buffer[2];
                    final String alarmMessage = getString(R.string.alarm_message,
                                getString(R.string.alarm_type_ir_light_barrier));
                    runOnUiThread(new Runnable() {

                        @Override
                        public void run() {
                            if(alarmState == ALARM_ON) {
                                linearLayout.setBackgroundColor(Color.RED);
                                alarmTextView.setText(alarmMessage);
                            } else if(alarmState == ALARM_OFF) {
                                linearLayout.setBackgroundColor(Color.WHITE);
                                alarmTextView.setText(R.string.alarm_reset_message);
                                photoTakenTextView.setText("");
                                logTextView.setText("");
                            }
                        }
                    });
                    if(alarmState == ALARM_ON) {
                        takePhoto();
                        writeToLogFile(new StringBuilder(alarmMessage).append(" - ")
                                            .append(new Date()).toString());
                    } else if(alarmState == ALARM_OFF){
                        camera.startPreview();
                    }
                }
```

```
                    break;

            default:
                Log.d(TAG, "unknown msg: " + buffer[0]);
                break;
            }
        }
    }
};
```

...

The BroadcastReceiver has only to be enhanced to also react on the photo event once the corresponding broadcast is received. You will be updating the photoTakenTextView to display to the user that a photo has been taken.

```
else if (PHOTO_TAKEN_ACTION.equals(action)) {
    photoTakenTextView.setText(R.string.photo_taken_message);
}
```

The Runnable implementation evaluates the received message. After the current alarm state is determined and the alarm message is set, you can update the UI elements accordingly in the runOnUiThread method.

```
if(alarmState == ALARM_ON) {
    linearLayout.setBackgroundColor(Color.RED);
    alarmTextView.setText(alarmMessage);
} else if(alarmState == ALARM_OFF) {
    linearLayout.setBackgroundColor(Color.WHITE);
    alarmTextView.setText(R.string.alarm_reset_message);
    photoTakenTextView.setText("");
    logTextView.setText("");
}
```

Outside of the UI thread you continue with the additional tasks of taking a photo and writing to the filesystem.

```
if(alarmState == ALARM_ON) {
    takePhoto();
    writeToLogFile(new StringBuilder(alarmMessage).append(" - ")
                            .append(new Date()).toString());
} else if(alarmState == ALARM_OFF){
    camera.startPreview();
}
```

These method calls should not be made on the UI thread as they deal with IO operations that could block the UI itself. The implementation for taking a photo and writing the log file, in case of an alarm, will be shown in the next listings. When the alarm is reset you must also reset the lifecycle of the camera and start a new preview of the camera picture. Note that the startPreview method must always be called before taking a picture. Otherwise, your application would crash.

Using the Camera

Now let's see the really interesting part of the new Android application: how to take a picture with the device's integrated camera (Listing 10-11).

Listing 10-11. Project 13: ProjectThirteenActivity.java (Part 3)

```
...

private Camera getCamera(){
    Camera camera = null;
    try {
        if(hasFrontCamera) {
            int frontCameraId = getFrontCameraId();
            if(frontCameraId != -1) {
                camera = Camera.open(frontCameraId);
            }
        }
        if((camera == null) && hasBackCamera) {
            camera = Camera.open();
        }
    } catch (Exception e){
        Log.d(TAG, "Camera could not be initialized.", e);
    }
    return camera;
}

private int getFrontCameraId() {
    int cameraId = -1;
    int numberOfCameras = Camera.getNumberOfCameras();
    for (int i = 0; i < numberOfCameras; i++) {
        CameraInfo cameraInfo = new CameraInfo();
        Camera.getCameraInfo(i, cameraInfo);
        if (CameraInfo.CAMERA_FACING_FRONT == cameraInfo.facing) {
            cameraId = i;
            break;
        }
    }
    return cameraId;
}

private void takePhoto() {
    if(camera != null) {
        camera.takePicture(null, null, pictureTakenHandler);
    }
}

private PictureCallback pictureTakenHandler = new PictureCallback() {

    @Override
    public void onPictureTaken(byte[] data, Camera camera) {
```

```
        writePictureDataToFile(data);
    }
};
```

...

The getCamera method shows two ways of getting a reference to the device's camera. The Camera class provides two static methods to get the reference. The first shown here is the open method which takes an int parameter to get a specific camera by its id.

```
camera = Camera.open(frontCameraId)
```

The second open method takes no parameter and returns the device's default camera reference. This is usually the back-facing camera.

```
camera = Camera.open();
```

Unfortunately, to determine the id of the front-facing camera, you have to go through each camera the device has to offer and check its orientation to find the correct one, as shown in the getFrontCameraId method.

The takePhoto method shows how to instruct the camera to take a picture. To do that, you call the takePicture method on the camera object. The takePicture method takes three parameters. The parameters are callback interfaces that provide hooks into the lifecycle of the picture-taking process. The first is an interface of the type ShutterCallback, which is called at the moment the picture is captured by the camera. The second parameter is a PictureCallback interface which is called once the camera has prepared the uncompressed raw picture data. I am only providing the last parameter, also a PictureCallback, which is called once the jpeg data of the current picture is processed and ready.

```
camera.takePicture(null, null, pictureTakenHandler);
```

The implementation of the PictureCallback interface is fairly easy. You just have to implement the onPictureTaken method.

```
private PictureCallback pictureTakenHandler = new PictureCallback() {

    @Override
    public void onPictureTaken(byte[] data, Camera camera) {
        writePictureDataToFile(data);
    }
};
```

The callback method provides the processed jpeg data in a byte array which can be written to a picture file on the filesystem.

Filesystem Operations

The filesystem operations are shown in Listing 10-12.

Listing 10-12. Project 13: ProjectThirteenActivity.java (Part 4)

```
    ...

    private void writeToLogFile(String logMessage) {
        File logFile = getFile("ProjectThirteenLog.txt");
```

```java
    if(logFile != null) {
        BufferedWriter bufferedWriter = null;
        try {
            bufferedWriter = new BufferedWriter(new FileWriter(logFile, true));
            bufferedWriter.write(logMessage);
            bufferedWriter.newLine();
            Log.d(TAG, "Written message to file: " + logFile.toURI());
            logFileWrittenIntent.send();
        } catch (IOException e) {
            Log.d(TAG, "Could not write to Log File.", e);
        } catch (CanceledException e) {
            Log.d(TAG, "LogFileWrittenIntent was cancelled.", e);
        } finally {
            if(bufferedWriter != null) {
                try {
                    bufferedWriter.close();
                } catch (IOException e) {
                    Log.d(TAG, "Could not close Log File.", e);
                }
            }
        }
    }
}

private void writePictureDataToFile(byte[] data) {
    SimpleDateFormat dateFormat = new SimpleDateFormat("yyyy-MM-dd-HH-mm-ss");
    String currentDateAndTime = dateFormat.format(new Date());
    File pictureFile = getFile(currentDateAndTime + ".jpg");
    if(pictureFile != null) {
        BufferedOutputStream bufferedOutputStream = null;
        try {
            bufferedOutputStream = new BufferedOutputStream(
                        new FileOutputStream(pictureFile));
            bufferedOutputStream.write(data);
            Log.d(TAG, "Written picture data to file: " + pictureFile.toURI());
            photoTakenIntent.send();
        } catch (IOException e) {
            Log.d(TAG, "Could not write to Picture File.", e);
        } catch (CanceledException e) {
            Log.d(TAG, "photoTakenIntent was cancelled.", e);
        } finally {
            if(bufferedOutputStream != null) {
                try {
                    bufferedOutputStream.close();
                } catch (IOException e) {
                    Log.d(TAG, "Could not close Picture File.", e);
                }
            }
        }
    }
}
```

```
    private File getFile(String fileName) {
        File file = new File(getExternalDir(), fileName);
        if(!file.exists()) {
            try {
                file.createNewFile();
            } catch (IOException e) {
                Log.d(TAG, "File could not be created.", e);
            }
        }
        return file;
    }

    private File getExternalDir() {
        String state = Environment.getExternalStorageState();
        if (Environment.MEDIA_MOUNTED.equals(state)) {
            return getExternalFilesDir(null);
        } else  {
            return null;
        }
    }
}
```

The task of getting or creating the specified File object has been extracted to its own method, called getFile, so that it can be reused when writing the log file or picture file. Writing the log file has already been described in the previous project so I will just concentrate on the writePictureDataToFile method, which handles writing the picture data to a file in the application's external storage directory.

The first step is to create a file to write the data to. It is a good idea to use the current date and time as the file name so that you can quickly see later on when the photo was taken.

```
SimpleDateFormat dateFormat = new SimpleDateFormat("yyyy-MM-dd-HH-mm-ss");
String currentDateAndTime = dateFormat.format(new Date());
File pictureFile = getFile(currentDateAndTime + ".jpg");
```

The SimpleDateFormat class is a utility class used to format date representations into a specific form. Let's say your current date is December 23rd, 2012 and your time is 1 a.m. The formatted String representation would be 2012-12-23-01-00-00. Now you just have to append the file ending for the file type jpeg and create your File object.

The created File is provided to a FileOutputStream, which is wrapped by a BufferedOutputStream, to write the picture data to the File. If everything worked out fine, the broadcast describing that the photo has been taken and saved can be sent.

```
bufferedOutputStream = new BufferedOutputStream(new FileOutputStream(pictureFile));
bufferedOutputStream.write(data);
Log.d(TAG, "Written picture data to file: " + pictureFile.toURI());
photoTakenIntent.send();
```

That's it for the coding of the Activity.

SurfaceView Implementation

Remember that you still have to implement a class of the type SurfaceView so that the camera preview can be rendered in your application. Have a look at Listing 10-13, which shows the CameraPreview class extending the SurfaceView class.

Listing 10-13. Project 13: CameraPreview.java

```
package project.thirteen.adk;

import java.io.IOException;

import android.content.Context;
import android.hardware.Camera;
import android.util.Log;
import android.view.SurfaceHolder;
import android.view.SurfaceView;

public class CameraPreview extends SurfaceView implements SurfaceHolder.Callback {
    private static final String TAG = CameraPreview.class.getSimpleName();
    private SurfaceHolder mHolder;
    private Camera mCamera;

    public CameraPreview(Context context, Camera camera) {
        super(context);
        mCamera = camera;

        // Add a SurfaceHolder.Callback so we get notified when the
        // underlying surface is created.
        mHolder = getHolder();
        mHolder.addCallback(this);
        // deprecated setting, but required on Android versions prior to 3.0
        mHolder.setType(SurfaceHolder.SURFACE_TYPE_PUSH_BUFFERS);
    }

    public void surfaceCreated(SurfaceHolder holder) {
        try {
            mCamera.setPreviewDisplay(holder);
            mCamera.setDisplayOrientation(90);
            mCamera.startPreview();
        } catch (IOException e) {
            Log.d(TAG, "Error setting camera preview: " + e.getMessage());
        }
    }

    @Override
    public void surfaceChanged(SurfaceHolder holder, int format, int width, int height) {
        // not implemented
    }

    @Override
    public void surfaceDestroyed(SurfaceHolder holder) {
```

```
        // not implemented
    }
}
```

The `CameraPreview` class has only two fields: the reference to the device's camera and a so-called `SurfaceHolder`. The `SurfaceHolder` is an interface to a `SurfaceView`'s display surface that will display the preview pictures captured by the camera.

```
private SurfaceHolder mHolder;
private Camera mCamera;
```

In the `CameraPreview`'s constructor you initialize the `SurfaceHolder` by calling the `SurfaceView`'s `getHolder` method and assign a callback interface to have a hook into its lifecycle.

```
mHolder = getHolder();
mHolder.addCallback(this);
```

The callback is needed because you need to set up the `Camera` object properly with your fully initialized `SurfaceHolder` as the preview display. The `CameraPreview` class itself implements the `SurfaceHolder.Callback` interface. You have to address all three of its methods, but you only need to fully implement the `surfaceCreated` method. When the `surfaceCreated` callback method is called, the `SurfaceHolder` is fully initialized and you can set it as the preview display. Additionally, the orientation of the camera is set to 90 degrees here, so that Android phones in portrait mode will display the preview pictures in the usual orientation. Note that tablets have another natural orientation so you might have to adjust this orientation value to address your needs. If you are having trouble with the orientation, you should use another rotation value. The rotation values are expressed in degrees and possible values are 0, 90, 180 and 270. Here you can also start the first preview of the camera picture. Remember, before you can take a picture, you must call the `startPreview` method to comply with the `Camera` lifecycle.

```
mCamera.setPreviewDisplay(holder);
mCamera.setDisplayOrientation(90);
mCamera.startPreview();
```

That's it for the Java coding part, but as you learned from the previous project, you might need additional permission definitions in your `AndroidManifest.xml` file.

Permissions

You already know that you need the `android.permission.WRITE_EXTERNAL_STORAGE` permission. In order to take pictures with the device's camera, you also need the `android.permission.CAMERA` permission. The complete `AndroidManifest.xml` file is shown in Listing 10-14.

Listing 10-14. Project 13: AndroidManifest.xml

```
<?xml version="1.0" encoding="utf-8"?>
<manifest xmlns:android="http://schemas.android.com/apk/res/android"
    package="project.thirteen.adk"
    android:versionCode="1"
    android:versionName="1.0">
    <uses-sdk android:minSdkVersion="10" />
    <uses-feature android:name="android.hardware.usb.accessory" />
    <uses-permission android:name="android.permission.WRITE_EXTERNAL_STORAGE" />
    <uses-permission android:name="android.permission.CAMERA" />
```

```
    <application android:icon="@drawable/icon" android:label="@string/app_name" >
        <uses-library android:name="com.android.future.usb.accessory" />
        <activity android:name=".ProjectThirteenActivity"
                    android:label="@string/app_name" android:screenOrientation="portrait">
            <intent-filter>
                <action android:name="android.intent.action.MAIN" />
                <category android:name="android.intent.category.LAUNCHER" />
            </intent-filter>
            <intent-filter>
                <action android:name="android.hardware.usb.action.USB_ACCESSORY_ATTACHED" />
            </intent-filter>

            <meta-data android:name="android.hardware.usb.action.USB_ACCESSORY_ATTACHED"
                    android:resource="@xml/accessory_filter" />
        </activity>
    </application>
</manifest>
```

Final Result

Now you are all set and ready for your final project test run. Upload the Arduino sketch to the ADK board and deploy your Android application on your Android device and have a look at your new camera-supported alarm system (Figure 10-17).

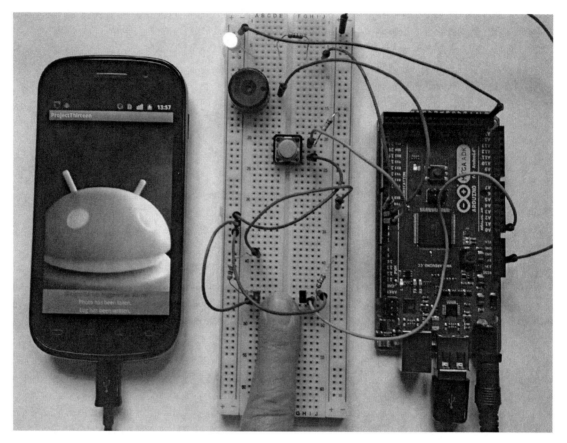

Figure 10-17. Project 13: Final result

Summary

In this final chapter you built your very own alarm system by composing a setup of some of the parts you got to know throughout the book. You built two versions of the alarm system, one that was triggered by a tilt-switch and another triggered by a self-built IR light barrier. The alarm system gave audible and visual feedback with the help of a piezo buzzer and a red LED. A connected Android device enhanced the alarm system by providing the possibility of sending a notification SMS or taking a picture of a possible intruder. You learned how to programmatically send these SMS message and how to use the camera API to instruct the camera to take pictures. By saving the alarm event to a log file you also learned about one of the ways to persist data in Android.

Index

CPSIA information can be obtained at www.ICGtesting.com
Printed in the USA
LVOW051905180512

282351LV00001B/8/P